1991

POCKETBOOK OF INFECTIOUS DISEASE THERAPY

John G. Bartlett, M.D.

Chief, Division of Infectious Diseases
The Johns Hopkins University School of Medicine
and The Johns Hopkins Hospital
Baltimore, Maryland

WILLIAMS & WILKINS
BALTIMORE · HONG KONG · LONDON · MUNICH
SAN FRANCISCO · SYDNEY · TOKYO

Editor: Timothy S. Satterfield
Associate Editor: Marjorie Kidd Keating
Copy Editor: Bill Cady
Designer: Wilma Rosenberger
Illustration Planner: Lorraine Wrzosek
Production Coordinator: Ady Boyd

Copyright © 1991
Williams & Wilkins
428 East Preston Street
Baltimore, Maryland 21202, USA

Accurate indications, adverse reactions, and dosage schedules for drugs are provided in this book, but it is possible that they may change. The reader is urged to review the package information data of the manufacturers of the medications mentioned.

Printed in the United States of America

First Edition 1990
ISBN 0-683-00441-7

91 92 93
1 2 3 4 5 6 7 8 9 10

PREFACE

The <u>1991 Pocketbook of Infectious Disease Therapy</u> is intended for physicians and other care providers who manage adult patients with infectious diseases. These include internists, generalists, surgeons, obstetricians, gynecologists and subspecialists within internal medicine and the various surgical specialties.

This, the second edition, has the same lofty goals as the first edition: to provide standards of care with particular emphasis on antimicrobial agent selection and dosing regimens for infections resulting from heterogeneous microbes at diverse anatomical sites. As with the first edition, there is extensive use of recommendations from various authoritative sources such as the Centers for Disease Control (CDC), the <u>Medical Letter on Drugs and Therapeutics</u>, the American Hospital Formulary Service, and learned societies, such as official statements of the American Heart Association (AHA), the American Thoracic Society (ATS), and the Infectious Disease Society of America (IDSA).

There have been substantive changes from the first edition in terms of revisions and additions. Nearly all tabular material has been updated to account for new drugs (cefixime, cefmetazole, fluconazole, ganciclovir, interferon-alpha, etc.) and new recommendations.

There are several new sections accounting for an additional 46 pages including: dosing guidelines for dialysis patients, drug interactions, treatment guidelines for viral hepatitis, management guidelines for HIV infection, Lyme disease, skin and soft tissue infections, bone and joint infections, ocular infections, <u>Helicobacter</u> <u>pylori</u>, and duration of treatment. Extensive revisions have been made in guidelines for vaccines, reflecting new recommendations of the Advisory Committee on Immunization Practices of the CDC; in guidelines for managing tuberculosis, reflecting new recommendations of the ATS and CDC, guidelines for treating endocarditis, reflecting new recommendations of the AHA; in new guidelines for treating sexually transmitted diseases, reflecting new recommendations of the CDC; and in a completely revised section on HIV infection, reflecting rapidly changing recommendations in this field.

The reader is encouraged to notify the author of any errors or differences of opinion; several such comments have led to subsequent revisions.

The author thanks Colleen Townsley for her tireless devotion to this work.

CONTENTS

PREPARATIONS AND RECOMMENDED DOSING REGIMENS FOR ANTIMICROBIAL AGENTS (ADAPTED FROM DRUG INFORMATION 88, AMERICAN HOSPITAL FORMULARY SERVICE, 1990 pp 31-466

Agent	Trade Names	Dosage Form	Usual Adult Regimen: Daily Dose, Route & Dose Interval
Acyclovir	Zovirax	5% ointment 3 & 15 gm tubes 200 mg caps 200 mg/5 ml susp 500 mg vials (IV)	Topical q3h 200 mg po; x2-5/day 15-36 mg/kg/day IV over 1-3 hr q8h
Amantadine	Symmetrel	100 mg cap & tabs 50 mg/5 ml syrup	100-200 mg/day po q12-24h
Amdinocillin	Coactin	0.5; 1 gm vial	40-60 mg/kg/day IM or IV q4-6h
Amikacin	Amikin	0.1;0.5;1 gm vials	15 mg/kg/day IV q8-12h
Aminosalicylic acid	PAS	0.5 gm tab	150 mg/kg/day po q6-12h
Amoxicillin	Amoxil, Polymox, Trimox, Utimox, Wymox	250;500 mg caps 125;250 mg/5 ml syrup	.75-2 gm/day po q6-8h
Amoxicillin + K clavulanate	Augmentin	125/31 mg/5 ml susp 250/62 mg/5 ml susp 250/125 mg tab 500/125 mg tab	.75-1.5 gm/day (amoxicillin) po q8h
Amphotericin B	Fungizone	50 mg vial	0.3-1 mg/kg/day IV over 4-8 hr q 1-2 days
Ampicillin	Omnipen, Amcill, Penamp, Polycillin, Principen, Totacillin	250;500 mg cap 125;250;500 mg/5 ml susp	1-2 gm/day po q6h
Ampicillin sodium	Omnipen-N, Polycillin-N, Totacillin-N	0.125;0.25;0.5; 1; 2; 10 gm vials	2-8 gm/day IV q4-6h
Ampicillin + sulbactam	Unasyn	1:0.5 gm + 2:1.0 gm vials (Amp:sulbactam)	4-8 gm ampicillin/ day IV or IM q6h (continued)

1

Agent	Trade Names	Dosage Form	Usual Adult Regimen: Daily Dose, Route & Dose Interval
Azlocillin	Azlin	2; 3; 4 gm vials	8-24 gm/day IV q6-8h
Aztreonam	Azactam	0.5; 1; 2 gm vials	1.5-6 gm/day IV or IM q6-8h
Bacampicillin	Spectrobid	400 mg tabs (equivalent to 280 mg ampicillin) 125 mg/ 5 ml syrup (equiv to 87 mg amp)	.8-1.6 gm/day po q12h
Bacitracin		10,000; 50,000 unit vials	10,000-25,000 units IM q6h; 25,000 units po q6h
Capreomycin	Capastat	1 gm vial	1 gm/day IM
Carbenicillin disodium	Geopen, Pyopen	1;2;5;10;30 gm vials	8-40 gm/day IV q4-6h
Carbenicillin indanyl sodium	Geocillin	382 mg tabs	382-764 mg po q6h
Cefaclor	Ceclor	250;500 mg caps 125;187;250 & 375 mg/5 ml susp	1-2 gm/day po q8h
Cefadroxil	Duricef, Ultracef	500 mg caps; 1 gm tab; 125; 250; 500 mg/5 ml susp	1-2 gm/day po 1-2 x/day
Cefamandole nafate	Mandol	0.5;1;2;10 gm vials	2-18 gm/day IM or IV q4-6h
Cefazolin	Ancef, Kefzol Zolicef	0.25;0.5;1;5;10;20 gm vials	2-6 gm/day IV or IM q8h
Cefixime	Suprex	200;400 mg tabs; 100 mg/5 ml susp	400 mg/day po, 1-2 x/day
Cefmetazole	Zefazone	1;2 gm vials	4-8 gm/day IV q6-12h
Cefonicid	Monocid	0.5;1;10 gm vials	1-2 gm/day IV or IM in 1 dose/day
Cefoperazone	Cefobid	1;2 gm vials	2-8 gm/day IM or IV q8-12h

(continued)

2

Agent	Trade Names	Dosage Form	Usual Adult Regimen: Daily Dose, Route & Dose Interval
Ceforanide lysine	Precef	0.5;1;10 gm vials	1-3 gm/day IV or IM q12h
Cefotaxime sodium	Claforan	1;2;10 gm vials	2-12 gm/day IV or IM q6h
Cefotetan	Cefotan	1;2;10 gm vials	2-4 gm/day IV or IM q12h
Cefoxitin sodium	Mefoxin	1;2;10 gm vials	2-18 gm/day IV or IM q4-6h
Ceftazidime	Fortaz, Tazidime, Tazicef	0.5;1;2;6 gm vials	3-6 gm/day IV or IM q8-12h
Ceftizoxime sodium	Cefizox	1;2;10 gm vials	2-12 gm/day IV or IM q6-8h
Ceftriaxone	Rocephin	0.25;0.5;1;2;10 gm vial	1-4 gm IV or IM 1-2 doses/day
Cefuroxime	Zinacef	0.75;1.5 gm vial	2.25-4.5 gm/day IV or IM q6-8h
Cefuroxime axetil	Ceftin	0.125;0.25 gm cap	0.5-1.0 gm/day po q12h
Cephalexin monohydrate	Keflex Keftab	0.25;0.5 gm cap 0.25;0.5;1 gm tab 125;250 mg/5 ml susp	1-2 gm/day po q6h
Cephalothin sodium	Keflin	1;2;4; 10 gm vials	2-12 gm/day IV q4-6h
Cephapirin sodium	Cefadyl	1;2;4 gm vials	2-4 gm/day q6h
Cephradine	Anspor	250;500 mg caps 125;250 mg/5 ml susp	1-2 gm/day po q6h
	Velosef	0.25;0.5;1 gm vials	2-8 gm/day IV or IM q6h
Chloramphenicol	Chloromycetin	250 mg cap	1-2 gm/day po q6h
Chloramphenicol palmitate	Chloromycetin	150 mg/5 ml syrup	1-2 gm/day po q6h

(continued)

3

Agent	Trade Names	Dosage Form	Usual Adult Regimen: Daily Dose, Route & Dose Interval
Chloramphenicol Na succinate	Chloromycetin sodium succinate	1 gm vial	2-4 gm/day IV q6h
Chloroquine HCl	Aralen HCl	250 mg amp (200 mg base)	5 mg base/kg IM
Chloroquine PO4	Aralen PO4	500 mg tab (300 mg base) 250 mg tab (150 mg base)	300-600 mg (base) qd - q week
Chloroquine hydroxy	Plaquenil	200 mg tab (155 mg base)	10 mg/kg/day po q24h
Cinoxacin	Cinobac	250;500 mg cap	1 gm/day po q6-12h
Ciprofloxacin	Cipro	250;500;750 mg tabs	0.5-1.5 gm/day po q12h
Clindamycin HCl	Cleocin HCl	75;150 mg cap	0.6-1.8 gm/day po q6-8h
Clindamycin PO4	Cleocin PO4	150 mg/ml in vials (2,4,6 ml)	1.8-2.7 gm/day IV q6-8h
Clindamycin palmitate HCl	Cleocin pediatric	75 mg/5 ml solution	0.6-1.8 gm/day po q6-8h
Clofazimine	Lamprene	50;100 mg caps	50-300 mg/day po q8-24h
Cloxacillin Na	Tegopen Cloxapen	250;500 mg cap 125 mg/5 ml solution	1-2 gm/day po q6h
Colistimethate Na	Coly-Mycin	150 mg (IM or IV) vial	2.5-5.0 mg/kg IV or IM q6-12h
Colistin SO4	Coly-Mycin S	25 mg/5 ml susp 150 mg vial (IV)	2.5-5.0 mg/kg/day q6-12h
Cyclacillin	Cyclapen-W	250;500 mg cap 125;250 mg/5 ml susp	1-2 gm/day po q6h
Cycloserine	Seromycin	250 mg cap	0.5-1 gm/day po in 2 doses
Dapsone		25;100 mg tab	1-2 mg/kg/day po q24h **(continued)**

Agent	Trade Names	Dosage Form	Usual Adult Regimen: Daily Dose, Route & Dose Interval
Demeclocycline	Declomycin	125 mg cap 150;300 mg cap	600 mg/day po q6-12h
Dicloxacillin	Dycill, Dynapen Pathocil	125;250;500 mg cap 62.5 mg/5 ml susp	1-2 gm/day po q6h
Dideoxyinosine (ddI)	Videx	167;250;375 mg packets	167-375 mg po bid
Diethylcarba- mazine	Hetrazan	50 mg tab	6-13 mg/kg/day, 1-3 doses
Doxycycline	Vibramycin Doxy caps Doxychel, etc.	50 mg/5 ml susp 100 mg tabs 50;100 mg caps 100;200 mg vial	100-200 mg/day po q12-24h 200 mg/day IV q12h
Emetine HCl		65 mg/ml	1 mg/kg/day up to 65 mg/day; IM or deep SC injection
Erythromycin	E-mycin;ERYC; Ery-Tab Erythromycin Base Ilotycin, RP-Mycin, Robimycin	125;250 mg caps 250;333;500 mg tabs 2% topical	1-2 gm/day po q6h (topical for acne)
Erythromycin estolate	Ilosone	250 mg caps, 125;250;500 mg tabs 125;250;500 mg/5 ml susp	1-2 gm/day po q6h
Erythromycin ethylsuccinate	E.E.S.; E-Mycin EryPed, Pediamycin, Wyamycin	200;400 mg tabs 100;200;400 mg/ 5 ml susp	1.6-3.2 gm/day po q6h
Erythromycin gluceptate	Ilotycin gluceptate	0.25;0.5; 1 gm vial	2-4 gm/day IV q6h
Erythromycin lactobionate	Erythrocin lactobionate	0.5;1 gm vial	1-4 gm/day IV q6h

(continued)

Agent	Trade Names	Dosage Form	Usual Adult Regimen: Daily Dose, Route & Dose Interval
Erythromycin stearate	Eramycin Erypar; Erythrocin stearate; Ethril; Wyamycin S SK-erythromycin	250;500 mg tab	102 gm/day po q6h
Ethambutol hydrochloride	Myambutol	400 mg tab	15 mg/kg/day po q24h
Ethionamide	Trecator-SC	250 mg tab	0.5-1 gm/day po in 1-3 daily doses
Fluconazole	Diflucan	50;100;200 mg tabs 100;200 mg vials	100-200 mg/day po or IV in 1 daily dose
Flucytosine	Ancobon	250;500 mg cap	50-150 mg/kg/day po q6h
Foscarnet	(Investigational)	24 mg/ml, 500 ml	90-180 mg/kg/day IV qd or tid
Furazolidone	Furoxone	100 mg tab 50 mg/15 ml susp	100 mg po q6h
Ganciclovir sodium	Cytovene	0.5 gm vial	5 mg/kg IV in 2 daily doses (induction) or 1 daily dose (maintenance)
Gentamicin SO4	Garamycin Gentamicin SO4 Injection Isotonic (NaCl) Gentamicin SO4 ADD-Vantage Gentamicin SO4 in 5% dextrose piggyback	0.4-2.4 mg/ml in 40-120 mg vials 10 mg & 40 mg/ml 60,80 & 100 mg vials 2 mg/ml for intrathecal use	3-5 mg/kg/day IV or IM q8h

(continued)

Agent	Trade Names	Dosage Form	Usual Adult Regimen: Daily Dose, Route & Dose Interval
Griseofulvin	Grisactin Fulvicin U/F Grifulvin V Gris-PEG Grisactin Ultra Fulvicin P/G	microsize: 125;250 caps, 250;500 mg tab 125 mg/5 ml susp ultramicrosize: 125; 165;250;330 mg tab	500 mg - 1 gm po/day 330-750 mg po/day
Imipenem/ Cilastatin	Primaxin	0.25;0.5 gm vials	1-4 gm/day IV q6h
Iodoquinol	Yodoxin	210 mg tab 650 mg tab	650 mg/day po q8
Isoniazid	Laniazid Nydrazid	50;100;300 mg tab 50 mg/5 ml (oral solu) 1 gm vial (IM)	300 mg/day IM q24h 300 mg/day IM q12-24h
Kanamycin SO4	Kantrex Klebcil	.075;0.5; 1 gm vial 500 mg caps	15 mg/kg/day IV q8h
Ketoconazole	Nizoral	200 mg tab	200-400 mg/day po q12-24h up to 1.6 gm/day
Mefloquine	Lariam	250 mg tabs	1250 mg po x 1 (treatment); 250 mg po q wk (prophylaxis)
Mebendazole	Vermox	100 mg tab	100 mg po x 1-2 up to 2 gm/day
Methenamine hippurate	Hiprex	1 gm tabs	1-2 gm/day po q12h
Methenamine mandelate	Mandelamine	0.35;0.5;1 gm tab 250;500 mg/5 ml syrup 0.5; 1 gm granules	1-4 gm/day po q6h
Methicillin Na	Celbenin Staphcillin	1;4;6;10 gm vial	4-12 gm/day IV or IM q6h
Metronidazole	Flagyl, Metryl Metizol, Protostat Metric 21, Satric	250;500 mg tab 500 mg vial	0.75-2 gm/day po q12h 0.75-2 gm/day IV q6-12h
Mezlocillin Na	Mezlin	1;2;3;4 gm vial	6-24 gm/day IV q4-6h **(continued)**

7

Agent	Trade Names	Dosage Form	Usual Adult Regimen: Daily Dose, Route & Dose Interval
Miconazole	Monistat	200 mg amp	0.6-3.6 gm/day IV q8h
Minocycline HCl	Minocin	50;100 mg cap 50 mg/5 ml syrup 100 mg vial	200 mg/day po q12h 200 mg/day IV q6-8h
Moxalactam	Moxam	1;2;10 gm vial	2-8 gm/day IV q6-8h
Nafcillin Na	Unipen	250 mg caps; 500 mg tabs 250 mg/5 ml solu	1-2 gm/day po q6h
	Nafcil, Nallpen, Unipen	0.5;1;2 gm vial	2-12 gm/day IV or IM q4-6h
Nalidixic acid	NegGram	0.25;0.5;1 gm tab 250 mg/5 ml susp	1 gm po q6h
Neomycin SO4	Mycifradin	500 mg tab 125 mg/5 ml solu 500 mg vial for IM	3-12 gm po/day
Netilmicin	Netromycin	50;150 mg vial	4-6.5 mg/kg/day IV or IM q8h
Niclosamide	Niclocide	500 mg tabs	2 gm (single dose)
Nitrofurantoin	Macrodantin Furantoin Furaton Furalan Faran	macrocrystals: 25;50;100 mg caps microcrystals: 50;100 caps/tabs 25 mg/5 ml susp	50-100 mg po q6h
Norfloxacin	Noroxin	400 mg tabs	400 mg po bid
Novobiocin	Albamycin	250 mg caps	1-2 gm/day po q6-12h
Nystatin	Mycostatin Nystex Nilstat	100,000 units/ 500,000 units tab	0.5 ml-1 ml units po 3-5 x daily
Oxacillin	Bactocill, Prostaphlin	250; 500 mg caps 250 mg/5 ml solu 0.25;0.5;1;2;4;10 gm vials	2-4 gm/day po q6h 2-12 gm/day IV or IM q4-6h

(continued)

8

Agent	Trade Names	Dosage Form	Usual Adult Regimen: Daily Dose, Route & Dose Interval
Paromomycin SO4	Humatin	250 mg caps	3-4 gm/day po in 2-4 doses
Penicillin			
Crystalline G potassium	Pentids	0.2;0.25;0.4;0.5;0.8 million unit tabs 0.2;0.25;0.4 million units/5 ml	1-2 gm po/day q6h
	Penicillin G for injection	0.2;0.5;1;5;10;20 million unit vials	2-20 million units IV q4-6h
Crystalline G sodium	Penicillin G sodium for injection	5 million unit vial	2-20 million units IV q4-6h
Benzathine	Bicillin Bicillin L-A Permapen	200,000 unit tabs 300,000; 600,000 units/ml vial	Not recommended po 1.2-2.4 mil units IM
Benzathine+ procaine	Bicillin C-R	Benzathine: procaine/ml 150,000:150,000 units (10 ml) 300,000:150,000 (1,2,4 ml) 450,000:150,000 units (2 ml)	1.2-2.4 mil units IM
Procaine	Crysticillin Duracillin Pfizerpen Wycillin	300,000 units (10 ml) 500,000 units (12 ml) 600,000 units (1,2,4 ml syringe)	0.6-4.8 mil units/day IM q6-12h
Phenoxyethyl penicillin (V)	Beepen, Betapen, Pen-Vee K, V-Cillin K, Veetids, Ledercillin, Penapar VK	125;250;500 mg tabs 125;250 ml/5 ml susp	1-2 gm/day po q6h
Pentamidine	Pentam 300 Nebu Pent	300 mg vial 300 mg aerosol	4 mg/kg IV qd 300 mg/mo (prophylaxis)
Piperacillin	Pipracil	2;3;4;40 gm vials	6-24 gm/day IV q4-6h

(continued)

9

Agent	Trade Names	Dosage Form	Usual Adult Regimen: Daily Dose, Route & Dose Interval
Piperazine		250 mg tabs 500 mg/5 ml	3.5-5 gm/day
Polymyxin B	Aerosporin	500,000 unit vials 1 mg = 1,000 units	1.5-2.5 mg/kg/day IM or IV q4-6h
Praziquantel	Biltricide	600 mg tabs	20-75 mg/kg/day po in 3 doses
Primaquine		15 mg (base) tabs	15 mg po qd
Pyrantel	Antiminth	50 mg/ml susp	11 mg/kg x 1
Pyrazinamide		500 mg tabs	15-30 mg/kg/day po in 6-8 doses
Pyrimethamine	Daraprim	25 mg tabs	25 mg po q wk or daily
Pyrimethamine + sulfadoxine	Fansidar	Sulfa-500 mg plus pyrimeth-25 mg	1 tab/wk 3 tabs (1 dose)
Quinacrine HCl	Atabrine	100 mg	300-800 mg po/day
Quinine	Legatrin Quine 200,300 Quin-260 etc	130;200;300;325 mg caps 260;325 mg tabs	325 mg bid 650 mg q8h po
Quinine dihydrochloride		IV available from CDC	600 mg IV q8h
Rifampin	Rifadin	150;300 mg caps 600 mg vials	600 mg/day po (TB) 600-1200 mg/day po (other indications) 600 mg/day IV
Spectinomycin	Trobicin	2;4 gm vials	2 gm IM x 1
Streptomycin		1 & 5 gm vial	1-2 gm IM/day

Sulfonamides
  Trisulfa-
  pyrimidines
	Triple sulfa
	Neotrizine
		Sulfadiazine,
		Sulfamerazine
		& Sulfamethazine,
		167 mg (each) tabs and
		167 mg (each/5 ml susp
			2-4 gm/day po q4-8h

(continued)

10

Agent	Trade Names	Dosage Form	Usual Adult Regimen: Daily Dose, Route & Dose Interval
Sulfadiazine	Microsulfon	0.5 gm tabs	2-4 gm/day po q4-8h
Sulfamethox-azole	Gantanol	0.5; 1 gm tabs	1 gm po q8-12h
Sulfapyridine		0.5 gm tabs	1-4 gm/day po q6h
Sulfasalazine	Azulfidine	0.5 gm tabs 0.25 mg/5 ml susp	3-4 gm/day po q6h
Sulfisoxazole	Gantrisin	0.5 gm tabs	4-8 gm/day po q4-6h
Tetracyclines Demeclocycline	Dechlomycin	150 mg cap 150;300 mg tab	600 mg/day po q6-12h
Doxycycline	Vibramycin	50;100 mg tabs 50;100 mg caps 50 mg/5 ml susp 100 mg vials	100-200 mg/day po q12-24h 200 mg/day IV q12-24h
Minocycline	Minocin	50;100 mg caps 50;100 mg tabs 100 mg vials	100 mg/day po or IV q6-12
Oxytetracycline	Oxymycin; Terramycin EP Mycin	250 mg cap 500 mg vial (IV) 50;123 mg/ml with lidocaine (IM)	1-2 gm/day po q6h 0.5-1 gm/day IV q12h
Tetracycline	Achromycin; Brodspec; Cyclopar Sumycin, etc.	100;250;500 mg caps 250;500 mg tabs 125 mg/5 ml susp 250;500 mg vials (IV)	1-2 gm/day po q6h 0.5-1 gm/day IV q12h (up to 4 gm/day)
Thiabendazole	Mintezol	500 mg tab 500 mg/5 ml susp	1-3 gm po/day
Ticarcillin	Ticar	1;3;6;20;30 gm vials	4-24 gm/day IV q4-6h
Ticarcillin + clavulanic acid	Timentin	3 gm ticarcillin + 100 mg CA vials	3 gm (ticarcillin) IV q4-6h
Tobramycin	Nebcin	20;60;80 & 1200 mg vials	3-5 mg/kg/day IV or IM q8h **(continued)**

Agent	Trade Names	Dosage Form	Usual Adult Regimen: Daily Dose, Route & Dose Interval
Trimethoprim	Proloprim Trimpex	100;200 mg tabs	200 mg/day po q12-24h
Trimethoprim-sulfamethoxazole	Bactrim, Septra Cotrim	Trimethoprim:sulfa 40 mg:200 mg/5 ml susp 80 mg:400 mg tabs 160 mg:800 mg DS tabs 16 mg:80 mg/ml (IV)	2-20 mg/kg/day (trimethoprim) po or IV q6-8h
Vancomycin	Vancocin pulvules Vancocin HCl (oral solu) Vancocin HCl IV Lyphocin	125;250 mg caps 1;10 gm vials 0.5;1 gm vials (IV)	0.5-2 gm/day po q6h 1-2 gm/day IV q6-12h
Vidarabine	Vira-A, Ara-A	200 mg/ml	15 mg/kg/day IV
Zidovudine	Retrovir, AZT	100 mg caps; 50 mg/ 5 ml syrup 240 ml Infusion - 10 mg/ml (20 ml)	100 mg po q4h 1-2 mg/kg IV q4h

PREFERRED ANTIMICROBIAL AGENTS FOR SPECIFIC PATHOGENS

Organism	Usual Disease	Preferred Agent	Alternatives
Achromobacter xylosoxidans	Meningitis, septicemia	Antipseudomonad penicillin (2)	Cephalosporins - 3rd gen Sulfa-trimethoprim Imipenem Ticarcillin + clavulanic acid
Acinetobacter calcoaceticus var antitratum (Herellea vaginicola); var lwoffi (Mima polymorpha)	Sepsis (esp line sepsis) Pneumonia	Aminoglycoside (tobramycin or amikacin) + ceftazidime or antipseudomonad penicillin (3)	Imipenem Ciprofloxacin Cephalosporin - 3rd gen (5)
Actinobacillus actinomycetemcomitans	Actinomycosis	Penicillin	Clindamycin Tetracycline (4) Erythromycin Cephalosporins
	Endocarditis	Penicillin + aminoglycoside (1)	Cephalosporin + aminoglycoside
Actinomyces israelii (also A. naeslundii, A. viscosus, A. odontolyticus and Arachnia proprionica)	Actinomycosis	Penicillin G	Clindamycin Tetracycline (4) Erythromycin
Aeromonas hydrophila	Diarrhea	Ciprofloxacin/norfloxacin Sulfa-trimethoprim	Tetracycline (4)
	Bacteremia	Cephalosporin (3rd gen)	Sulfa-trimethoprim

(continued)

13

Organism	Usual Disease	Preferred Agent	Alternatives
Aeromonas hydrophila (cont.)	Cellulitis/myositis/ osteomyelitis	Ciprofloxacin	Aminoglycoside (1) Tetracycline (4) Imipenem Aztreonam Amoxicillin/Ticarcillin + clavulanic acid
Bacillus anthracis	Anthrax	Penicillin G	Erythromycin Tetracycline (4) Chloramphenicol
Bacillus cereus	Food poisoning	Not treated	
Bacillus species	Septicemia (comp host)	Vancomycin	Imipenem Aminoglycosides (1)
Bacteroides bivius	Female genital tract infections	Metronidazole Clindamycin Cefoxitin Cefotetan	Chloramphenicol Antipseudomonad penicillin (2) Imipenem Ticarcillin-clavulanic acid Ampicillin-sulbactam Cefmetazole
"B. fragilis group"	Abscesses Bacteremia Intra-abdominal sepsis	Metronidazole Clindamycin Cefoxitin	Cefotetan Chloramphenicol Antipseudomonad penicillin (2) Imipenem Ampicillin-sulbactam Ticarcillin-clavulanic acid Cefmetazole
"B. melaninogenicus group"	Oral-dental & pulmonary infections Female genital tract infections	Metronidazole Clindamycin Cefoxitin	Chloramphenicol Ampicillin-sulbactam Amoxicillin-clavulanic acid Ticarcillin-clavulanic acid Imipenem Cefotetan Cefmetazole (continued)

14

Organism	Usual Disease	Preferred Agent	Alternatives
Bartonella bacilliformis	Bartonellosis	Chloramphenicol Penicillin	Tetracycline + streptomycin
Bordetella pertussis	Pertussis	Erythromycin	Sulfa-trimethoprim Tetracycline
Borrelia burgdorferi	Lyme disease	Tetracycline (early disease) Ceftriaxone (late complications)	Penicillin G po or IV Amoxicillin Erythromycin
Borrelia recurrentis	Relapsing fever	Tetracycline (4)	Penicillin G Erythromycin Chloramphenicol
Branhamella catarrhalis (Moraxella catarrhalis)	Otitis, sinusitis, pneumonitis	Sulfa-trimethoprim	Amoxicillin-clavulanic acid Erythromycin Tetracycline (4) Cefaclor Cephalosporin (3rd gen) (5) Cefuroxime Ciprofloxacin Cefixime
Brucella	Brucellosis	Doxycycline (4) + rifampin	Doxycycline (4) + streptomycin Sulfa-trimethoprim Rifampin + doxycycline (4) or cephalosporin (3rd gen) (CNS involvement)
Calymmatobacterium granulomatis	Granuloma inguinale	Tetracycline (4)	Sulfa-trimethoprim Erythromycin (pregnancy) Gentamicin Chloramphenicol
Campylobacter jejuni	Diarrhea	Erythromycin	Tetracycline (4) Furazolidine Ciprofloxacin (continued)

Organism	Usual Disease	Preferred Agent	Alternatives
Campylobacter fetus	Septicemia, vascular infections, meningitis	Gentamicin	Chloramphenicol Erythromycin Clindamycin Tetracycline Imipenem
Capnocytophaga ochraceae	Periodontal disease Bacteremia in neutropenic host Tonsillitis (?)	Penicillins Clindamycin Erythromycin	Amoxicillin-clavulanic acid Imipenem Cefoxitin Cephalosporins (3rd gen) (5) Ciprofloxacin Tetracycline
Cardiobacterium	Bacteremia Endocarditis	Penicillin + aminoglycoside	Cephalosporin ± aminoglycoside
Chlamydia psittaci	Psittacosis	Tetracycline (4)	Chloramphenicol
Chlamydia pneumoniae (TWAR agent)	Pneumonia	Tetracycline (4) Erythromycin	
Chlamydia trachomatis	Urethritis Endocervicitis PID Epididymitis Urethral syndrome	Tetracycline (4)	Erythromycin
	Trachoma	Tetracycline (4) (topical + oral)	Sulfonamide (topical + oral)
	Lymphogranuloma venereum	Tetracycline (4)	Erythromycin
	Inclusion conjunctivitis	Erythromycin (topical or oral)	Sulfonamide
Citrobacter diversus	Urinary tract infections, pneumonia	Aminoglycoside (1) Cephalosporin (2nd & 3rd gen) (5) Sulfa-trimethoprim Imipenem	Tetracycline (4) Ciprofloxacin/Norfloxacin

(continued)

16

Organism	Usual Disease	Preferred Agent	Alternatives
Citrobacter freundii	Urinary tract infection, wound infection, septicemia, pneumonia	Imipenem Sulfa-trimethoprim Aminoglycoside	Tetracycline (4) Cephalosporin (3rd gen) (5) Antipseudomonad penicillin (2)
Clostridium difficile	Antibiotic-associated colitis	Vancomycin (oral) Metronidazole (oral)	Bacitracin (oral) Cholestyramine Lactobacilli Vancomycin + rifampin
Clostridium sp.	Gas gangrene Sepsis Tetanus Botulism Crepitant cellulitis	Penicillin G	Chloramphenicol Metronidazole Erythromycin Antipseudomonad penicillin (2) Clindamycin
Corynebacterium diphtheriae	Diptheria	Penicillin or erythromycin + antitoxin	
Corynebacterium JK strain	Septicemia	Vancomycin	Ciprofloxacin
Corynebacterium ulcerans	Pharyngitis	Erythromycin	
Coxiella burnetii	Q fever	Tetracycline (4)	Chloramphenicol Ciprofloxacin (?) Rifampin (?) (continued)

Organism	Usual Disease	Preferred Agent	Alternatives
Dysgonic fermenter type 2 (DF 2)	Septicemia (dog bite)	Penicillins	Cephalosporins Imipenem Vancomycin Ciprofloxacin Erythromycin Cephalosporin
	Wound infection	Penicillin	
Edwardsiella tarda	Gastroenteritis (usually not treated) Wound infection Bacteremia, liver abscesses	Ampicillin	Tetracycline (4) Cephalosporin (5) Aminoglycoside (1) Chloramphenicol
Ehrlichia	Ehrlichiosis	Tetracycline (4)	
Eikenella corrodens	Oral infections, bite wounds	Ampicillin/amoxicillin Penicillin G	Tetracycline (4) Erythromycin Amoxicillin-clavulanic acid Cephalosporin (5) Imipenem
Enterobacter aerogenes, E. cloacae	Sepsis, pneumonia, wound infections	Aminoglycoside (1) Sulfa-trimethoprim Ciprofloxacin	Aztreonam Imipenem Antipseudomonad penicillin (2) Cephalosporin-3rd gen (5)
	Urinary tract infection	Sulfa-trimethoprim Cephalosporin-3rd gen (5)	Antipseudomonad penicillin (2) Aminoglycoside Ciprofloxacin/Norfloxacin Imipenem
Enterococcus faecalis and E. faecium	Urinary tract infections	Ampicillin/amoxicillin	Penicillin + aminoglycoside Nitrofurantoin Ciprofloxacin
	Wound infections, intra-abdominal sepsis	Ampicillin	Penicillin + aminoglycoside Imipenem (E. faecalis) Vancomycin
	Endocarditis	Penicillin G/Ampicillin + gentamicin or streptomycin	Vancomycin + gentamicin or streptomycin (continued)

Organism	Usual Disease	Preferred Agent	Alternatives
Erwinia agglomerans	Urinary tract infections Bacteremia Pneumonia	Aminoglycosides (1)	Ciprofloxacin Chloramphenicol Cephalosporins
Erysipelothrix rhusiopathiae	Localized cutaneous	Penicillin	Erythromycin
	Endocarditis/ disseminated	Penicillin	Cephalosporins
E. coli	Septicemia Intra-abdominal sepsis Wound infection	Aminoglycoside (1) Cephalosporin (5) Ampicillin (if sensitive)	Sulfa-trimethoprim Imipenem Ciprofloxacin Aztreonam
	Urinary tract infection	Ampicillin (if sensitive) Tetracycline (4) Sulfa-trimethoprim (3) Aminoglycoside (1) Cephalosporin (5) Antipseudomonad penicillin (2)	Imipenem Aztreonam Ciprofloxacin/Norfloxacin Sulfonamide
Flavobacterium meningosepticum	Sepsis	Vancomycin	Sulfa-trimethoprim Clindamycin Imipenem Ciprofloxacin
Francisella tularensis	Tularemia	Streptomycin	Gentamicin Tetracycline (4) (?) Chloramphenicol (?)
Fusobacterium	Oral/dental/pulmonary infection; liver abscess	Penicillin G	Cefoxitin/cefotetan Chloramphenicol Imipenem Clindamycin Metronidazole (continued)

Organism	Usual Disease	Preferred Agent	Alternatives
Gardnerella vaginalis	Vaginitis	Metronidazole	Clindamycin
Haemophilus aphrophilus	Sepsis, endocarditis	Penicillin G + aminoglycoside (1)	Cephalosporin-3rd gen (5) + aminoglycoside (1)
H. ducreyi	Chancroid	Ceftriaxone Erythromycin	Sulfa-trimethoprim Amoxicillin + clavulanic acid Ciprofloxacin
H. influenzae	Meningitis	Cephalosporin, cefotaxime, ceftriaxone Chloramphenicol ± ampicillin	
	Epiglottitis Pneumonia Arthritis Cellulitis Otitis Sinusitis Bronchitis	Cephalosporin - 3rd gen (5) Sulfa-trimethoprim Cefamandole/cefuroxime Ampicillin (if sensitive) Sulfa-trimethoprim (3) Ampicillin/amoxicillin (if sens) Amoxicillin - clavulanic acid	Chloramphenicol ± ampicillin Ampicillin/ticarcillin - clavulanic acid Erythromycin - sulfonamide Cefaclor Tetracycline (4) Cefixime Ciprofloxacin

(continued)

Organism	Usual Disease	Preferred Agent	Alternatives
Hafnia alvei	Pneumonia, wound infection, urinary tract infection	Aminoglycosides (1)	Ciprofloxacin Chloramphenicol Antipseudomonad penicillin (2)
Helicobacter pyloris (Campylobacter pyloris)	Gastritis Recurrent duodenal ulcer disease	Bismuth subcitrate plus metronidazole plus tetracycline (or amoxicillin)	Bismuth plus metronidazole or amoxicillin
Kingella sp.	Endocarditis Septic arthritis	Penicillin + aminoglycoside	Cephalosporin + aminoglycoside
Klebsiella pneumoniae, K. oxytoca	Septicemia Pneumonia Intra-abdominal sepsis	Cephalosporin ± aminoglycoside (1)	Aminoglycoside (1) Sulfa-trimethoprim Piperacillin/mezlocillin Imipenem Ticarcillin - clavulanic acid Aztreonam Ampicillin-sulbactam Ciprofloxacin
	Urinary tract infection	Sulfa-trimethoprim Cephalosporin (5) Tetracycline (4)	Aminoglycoside (1) Amoxicillin/ticarcillin - clavulanic acid Ciprofloxacin/norfloxacin Piperacillin/mezlocillin Imipenem
Legionella sp.	Legionnaires' disease	Erythromycin ± rifampin	Sulfa-trimethoprim + rifampin Ciprofloxacin (7) + rifampin (continued)

21

Organism	Usual Disease	Preferred Agent	Alternatives
Leptospira	Leptospirosis	Penicillin G or ampicillin	Tetracycline (4)
Leptotrichia buccalis	Orodental infections	Penicillin G	Tetracycline (4) Clindamycin
Listeria monocytogenes	Meningitis Septicemia	Ampicillin or penicillin ± gentamicin (systemic and intrathecal)	Sulfa-trimethoprim Erythromycin Vancomycin (?)
Moraxella	Ocular infections Bacteremia	Aminoglycoside (1) Penicillins	Cephalosporin - 3rd gen (5) Imipenem Ciprofloxacin Antipseudomonad penicillin (2)
Moraxella catarrhalis (See Branhamella catarrhalis)			
Morganella morganii	Bacteremia Urinary tract infection Pneumonia Wound infection	Aminoglycoside Ciprofloxacin/norfloxacin	Imipenem Cephalosporin - 3rd gen (5) Sulfa-trimethoprim Aztreonam Antipseudomonad penicillin (2) Ticarcillin - clavulanic acid Amoxicillin - clavulanic acid Tetracycline (4)
Mycobacterium tuberculosis	Tuberculosis	INH + rifampin ± pyrazinamide	Streptomycin Cycloserine Ethambutol Ethionamide Kanamycin Capreomycin PAS

(continued)

Organism	Usual Disease	Preferred Agent	Alternatives
M. kansasii	Pulmonary infection	INH + rifampin + ethambutol ± streptomycin	Ethionamide Cycloserine
M. avium-intracellulare	Pulmonary infection	INH + rifampin + ethambutol + streptomycin	Clofazimine Capreomycin Ethionamide Amikacin Imipenem Cycloserine Ansamicin Ciprofloxain
	Disseminated infection	Rifampin + ethambutol + clofazimine ± ciprofloxacin ± amikacin	
M. chelonae	Pulmonary Cutaneous	Amikacin + cefoxitin	Kanamycin Erythromycin Doxycycline Ciprofloxacin
M. fortuitum	Soft tissue and wound infections	Amikacin + cefoxitin	Rifampin Erythromycin Sulfonamide Cefoxitin Doxycycline Ciprofloxacin
M. marinum	Soft tissue infections	Rifampin + ethambutol Sulfa-trimethoprim	Erythromycin Ciprofloxacin Doxycycline/minocycline Cycloserine (continued)

Organism	Usual Disease	Preferred Agent	Alternatives
M. leprae	Leprosy	Dapsone + rifampin ± clofazimine	Rifampin Ethionamide (Prothionamide) Cycloserine
Mycoplasma pneumoniae	Pneumonia	Erythromycin Tetracycline (4)	
Neisseria gonorrhoeae	Urethritis Salpingitis Cervicitis Arthritis-dermatitis	Ceftriaxone	Spectinomycin Ciprofloxacin Norfloxacin Cefuroxime axetil Cefotaxime Ceftizoxime Amoxicillin + probenecid (penicillin-sensitive strains)
N. meningitidis	Meningitis Bacteremia Pericarditis Pneumonia	Penicillin G	Ampicillin Chloramphenicol Sulfa-trimethoprim Cephalosporin-cefotaxime, ceftizoxime, ceftriaxone, cefuroxime
Nocardia asteroides	Nocardiosis: pulmonary infection, abscesses - skin, lung, brain	Sulfonamide (usually sulfadiazine)	Sulfa-trimethoprim Minocycline Amikacin Cycloserine

(continued)

Organism	Usual Disease	Preferred Agent	Alternatives
Pasteurella multocida	Animal bite wound	Penicillin G	Tetracycline (4) Ciprofloxacin Amoxicillin-clavulanic acid
	Septicemia Septic arthritis/ osteomyelitis	Penicillin	Cephalosporins Ampicillin-sulbactam Chloramphenicol
Peptostreptococcus	Oral/dental/pulmonary infection; intra-abdominal sepsis; gynecologic infection	Penicillin G Ampicillin/amoxicillin	Clindamycin Metronidazole Cephalosporin (5) Chloramphenicol Erythromycin Vancomycin Imipenem
Plesiomonas shigelloides	Diarrhea (usually not treated)	Sulfa-trimethoprim Tetracycline (4) Ciprofloxacin	Chloramphenicol Aminoglycosides (1)
	Extra-intestinal infection	Cephalosporin-3rd gen (3) Aminoglycoside (1)	Sulfa-trimethoprim Imipenem, ciprofloxacin
Propionibacterium acnes	Acne	Tetracycline	Clindamycin (topical)
Proteus mirabilis	Septicemia Urinary tract infection Intra-abdominal sepsis Wound infection	Ampicillin	Aminoglycosides (1) Cephalosporins (5) Sulfa-trimethoprim Antipseudomonad penicillin Aztreonam Imipenem Ciprofloxacin (continued)

Organism	Usual Disease	Preferred Agent	Alternatives
Proteus vulgaris	Septicemia	Cephalosporin-3rd gen (5)	Sulfa-trimethoprim
	Urinary tract infection	Aminoglycoside (1)	Antipseudomonad penicillin (2)
			Aztreonam
			Imipenem
			Amoxicillin/ticarcillin +
			clavulanic acid
			Ciprofloxacin
Providencia rettgeri	Septicemia	Cephalosporin-3rd gen (5)	Antipseudomonad penicillin (2)
	Urinary tract infection	Aminoglycoside (1)	Imipenem
			Aztreonam
			Sulfa-trimethoprim
Providencia stuartii	Septicemia	Aminoglycoside (1)	Antipseudomonad penicillin (2)
	Urinary tract infection	Cephalosporin-3rd gen (5)	Sulfa-trimethoprim
			Imipenem
			Aztreonam
			Ciprofloxacin
Pseudomonas aeruginosa	Septicemia, pneumonia	Aminoglycoside (tobramycin)	Aminoglycoside (1) ±
	Intra-abdominal sepsis	± antipseudomonas	cefoperazone, imipenem or
		penicillin (2)	ceftazidime
			Aztreonam
			Ciprofloxacin
	Urinary tract infections	Aminoglycoside (1)	Imipenem
		Antipseudomonad	Ceftazidime
		penicillin (2)	Cefoperazone
		Ciprofloxacin/norfloxacin	Aztreonam

(continued)

Organism	Usual Disease	Preferred Agent	Alternatives
Ps. cepacia	Septicemia Pneumonia	Sulfa-trimethoprim	Chloramphenicol Ceftazidime
Ps. mallei	Glanders	Streptomycin + tetracycline	Chloramphenicol + streptomycin
Ps. maltophilia (Xanthomonas maltophilia)	Septicemia	Sulfa-trimethoprim	Ticarcillin-clavulanic acid
Ps. pseudomallei	Melioidosis	Ceftazidime	Sulfa-trimethoprim Tetracycline (4) ± chloramphenicol Chloramphenicol ± aminoglycoside (1) Sulfonamide
Ps. putida	Septicemia, pneumonia, urinary tract infections	Aminoglycosides Ciprofloxacin/norfloxacin	
Rickettsia	Rocky Mountain spotted fever, Q fever, tick bite fever, murine typhus, scrub typhus, typhus, trench fever	Tetracycline (4) (>8 yrs)	Chloramphenicol
Salmonella typhi	Typhoid fever	Chloramphenicol	Sulfa-trimethoprim Ampicillin/amoxicillin Ciprofloxacin Cefotaxime/cefoperazone/ ceftriaxone

(continued)

27

Organism	Usual Disease	Preferred Agent	Alternatives
Salmonella sp. (other)	Enteric fever Mycotic aneurysm	Ampicillin/amoxicillin Sulfa-trimethoprim	Chloramphenicol Ciprofloxacin Cefotaxime/cefoperazone/ ceftriaxone
Serratia marcescens	Septicemia Urinary tract infection Pneumonia	Cephalosporin-3rd gen (5) Gentamicin or amikacin ± antipseudomonad penicillin or cephalosporin-3rd gen (5)	Cephalosporins-3rd gen (5) Sulfa-trimethoprim Antipseudomonad penicillin (2) Imipenem Ciprofloxacin Aztreonam
Shigella	Colitis	Sulfa-trimethoprim	Ampicillin Tetracycline (4) Ciprofloxacin/nalidixic acid
Spirillum minor	Rat bite fever	Penicillin G	Tetracycline (4) Streptomycin

Staphylococcus aureus
Methicillin sensitive
	Septicemia
	Pneumonia
	Wound infection
		Penicillinase resistant
		  penicillin (3) ± rifampin
		  or gentamicin
		Cephalosporins-1st gen (5)
		Cefuroxime/cefamandole
			Erythromycin/clindamycin
			Vancomycin
			Amoxicillin-clavulanic acid
			Ticarcillin-clavulanic acid
			Imipenem
			Ciprofloxacin
			Ampicillin-sulbactam
			  (continued)

Organism	Usual Disease	Preferred Agent	Alternatives
S. aureus (cont.) Methicillin resistant		Vancomycin ± rifampin or gentamicin	Sulfa-trimethoprim Ciprofloxacin Imipenem
Staph saprophyticus	Urinary tract infections	Sulfa-trimethoprim Ampicillin/amoxicillin	Cephalosporins Tetracycline (4) Ciprofloxacin/norfloxacin
Staph epidermidis	Septicemia Infected prosthetic devices	Vancomycin	Sulfa-trimethoprim Penicillinase resistant penicillin (3) Cephalosporin (5) Ciprofloxacin Imipenem
Streptococcus, Group A,B, C,G; bovis, milleri, pneumoniae, viridans, anaerobic	Pharyngitis Soft tissue infection Pneumonia Abscesses	Penicillin G	Cephalosporin (5) Clindamycin Vancomycin Erythromycin
	Endocarditis	Penicillin G ± streptomycin or gentamicin	Cephalosporin (5) Vancomycin
	Meningitis	Penicillin G	Chloramphenicol Cephalosporin-3rd gen (5)
Strep group D enterococcus (Enterococcus faecalis and E. faecium)	Urinary tract infection	Ampicillin/amoxicillin	Penicillin + aminoglycoside (1) Vancomycin Nitrofurantoin Ciprofloxacin/norfloxacin (continued)

29

Organism	Usual Disease	Preferred Agent	Alternatives
Strep group D (cont.)	Wound infection Intra-abdominal sepsis	Ampicillin/amoxicillin	Vancomycin Penicillin + aminoglycoside (1) Imipenem (not E. faecium)
	Endocarditis	Penicillin G/ampicillin + gentamicin or streptomycin	Vancomycin + gentamicin or streptomycin
Strep moniliformis	Rat bite fever Haverhill fever	Penicillin G	Tetracycline (4) Streptomycin
Treponema carateum	Pinta	Penicillin G	Tetracycline
Treponema pallidum	Syphilis	Penicillin G	Tetracycline (4) Erythromycin Ceftriaxone
Treponema pallidum ss erdemicum	Bejel	Penicillin	
Treponema pallidum ss pertenue	Yaws	Penicillin G	Tetracycline (4)
Ureaplasma urealyticum	Urethritis Endocervicitis PID (?)	Erythromycin	Tetracycline (4)
Vibrio cholerae	Cholera	Tetracycline (4)	Ampicillin Sulfa-trimethoprim Furazolidone
Vibrio vulnificus	Septicemia Wound infection	Tetracycline (4)	Chloramphenicol Penicillin G (continued)

Organism	Usual Disease	Preferred Agent	Alternatives
Yersinia enterocolitica	Enterocolitis (usually not treated)	Sulfa-trimethoprim	Cephalosporin-3rd gen (5)
	Mesenteric adenitis (usually not treated)		Ciprofloxacin
			Tetracycline (4)
	Septicemia	Aminoglycoside (gentamicin)	Chloramphenicol
			Cephalosporins-3rd gen (5)
Yersinia pestis	Plague	Streptomycin	Chloramphenicol
			Tetracycline (4)
Yersinia pseudotuberculosis	Mesenteric adenitis (usually not treated)	Aminoglycoside (1)	Sulfa-trimethoprim
	Septicemia	Ampicillin	Tetracycline (4)

1. Aminoglycosides = Gentamicin, tobramycin, amikacin, netilmicin
2. Antipseudomonad penicillin = Carbenicillin, ticarcillin, piperacillin, mezlocillin, azlocillin
3. Penicillinase resistant penicillins: Nafcillin, oxacillin, methicillin, cloxacillin, dicloxacillin
4. Tetracycline = Tetracycline, doxycycline, minocycline
5. Cephalosporins

   1st generation: Cefadroxil, cefazolin, cephalexin, cephapirin, cephradine
   2nd generation: Cefaclor, cefamandole, cefonicid, ceforanide, cefotetan, cefoxitin, cefuroxime, cefmetazole
   3rd generation: Cefotaxime, ceftizoxime, ceftazidime, cefoperazone, ceftriaxone, moxalactam, cefixime

31

ANTIMICROBIAL DOSING REGIMENS IN RENAL FAILURE

A. General Principles

1. The initial dose is not modified.
2. Adjustments in subsequent doses for renally excreted drugs may be accomplished by **a)** giving the usual maintenance dose at extended intervals, usually 3 half lives (extended interval method); **b)** giving reduced doses at the usual intervals (dose reduction method); or **c)** a combination of each.
3. Adjustments in dose are usually based on creatinine clearance that may be estimated as follows:

    a. <u>Formula</u>: Males: $\dfrac{\text{weight (kg) x (140-age in yrs)}}{72 \times \text{serum creatinine (mg/dl)}}$

    Females: above value x 0.85

    b. <u>Nomogram</u> (Kampmann J et al. Acta Med Scand 196:617,1974).

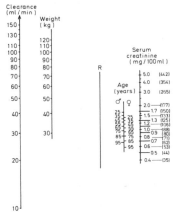

Use a straight edge to connect the patient's weight (2nd line on the left) and the patient's age (4th line). Mark intercept on R (3rd line) and swing straight edge to serum creatinine (5th line). Intercept on first line provides creatinine clearance

c. Pitfalls and notations with calculations
    (1) Elderly patient: Serum creatinine may be deceptively low with danger of overdosing) due to reduced muscle mass.
    (2) Pregnancy and volume expansion: GFR may be increased (with danger of underdosing) in third trimester of pregnancy and patients with normal renal function who receive massive parenteral fluids.
    (3) Obese patients: Use lean body weight.
    (4) Renal failure: Formulas assume stable renal function; for patients with anuria or oliguria assume CCr of 5-8 ml/min.

B. Aminoglycoside Dosing

1. Guidelines of Johns Hopkins Hospital Clinical Pharmacology Department

Agent	Loading dose (regardless of renal function)	Susequent doses (prior to level measurements) CCr>70 ml/mm	CCr<70 ml/mm	Therapeutic levels (1 hr after infusion over 20-30 min)
Gentamicin	2 mg/kg	1.7-2 mg/kg/8h	0.3 x CCr=mg/kg/8h	5-10 mcg/ml
Tobramycin	2 mg/kg	1.7-2 mg/kg/8h	0.3 x CCr=mg/kg/8h	5-10 mg/ml
Netilmicin	2.2 mg/kg	2-2.2 mg/kg/8h	0.3 x CCr=mg/kg/8h	5-10 mg/ml
Amikacin	8 mg/kg	7.5-8 mg/kg/8h	.12 x CCr=mg/kg/8h	20-40 mg/ml
Kanamycin	8 mg/kg	7.5-8 mg/kg/8h	.12 x CCr=mg/kg/8h	20-40 mg/ml

Note: 1. CCr = creatinine clearance.
2. Doses for gentamicin, tobramycin and netilmicin should be written in multiples of 5 mg; doses of amikacin and kanamycin should be written in multiples of 25 mg.
3. For obese patients use calculated lean body weight.
4. For patients who are oliguric or anuric use CCr of 5-8 ml/min.

2. Mayo Clinic guidelines (Van Scoy RE and Wilson WR, Mayo Clin Proc 62:1142, 1987)
a. Initial dose: Gentamicin, tobramycin, netilmicin: 1.5-2 mg/kg
   Amikacin, kanamycin, streptomycin: 5.0-7.5 mg/kg
b. Maintenance dose: Usual daily dose x CCr/100

3. Reduced dose nomogram developed for tobramycin

Weight		Usual dose (q8h)	
lbs	kg	1 mg/kg	1.7 mg/kg
264	120	120	200
242	110	110	185
220	100	100	165
198	90	90	150
176	80	80	135
154	70	70	115
132	60	60	100
110	50	50	85
88	40	40	65

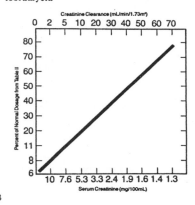

4. **Guidelines for AMA Drug Evaluations, 6th Edition, Chicago, 1986, p 1439 and Drug Information 88, American Hospital Formulary Service, 1988, p 58**

a. <u>Loading dose</u> based on estimated ideal body weight

Agent	Dose (mg/kg ideal wt)	Peak conc. (mcg/ml)
Tobramycin	1.5-2 mg/kg	4-10
Gentamicin	1.5-2 mg/kg	4-10
Netilmicin	1.3-3.25 mg/kg	4-12
Amikacin	5-7.5 mg/kg	15-30
Kanamycin	5-7.5 mg/kg	15-30

b. <u>Maintenance dose</u> as % of loading dose according to desired dosing interval and the corrected creatinine clearance CCr*

$$CCr \text{ (male)} = \frac{(140 - age)}{serum\ creatinine}$$

$$CCr \text{ (female)} = 0.85 \times CCr\ male$$

CCr (ml/min)	Half life (hrs)**	Dosing Interval (hr) 8	12	24
90	3.1	84%	-	-
80	3.4	80%	91%	-
70	3.9	76%	88%	-
60	4.5	71%	84%	-
50	5.3	65%	79%	-
40	6.5	57%	72%	92%
30	8.4	48%	63%	86%
25	9.9	43%	57%	81%
20	11.9	37%	50%	75%
17	13.6	33%	46%	70%
15	15.1	31%	42%	67%
12	17.9	27%	37%	61%
10***	20.4	24%	34%	56%
7	25.9	19%	28%	47%
5	31.5	16%	23%	41%
2	46.8	11%	16%	30%
0	69.3	8%	11%	21%

* From: Sarubbi FA Jr, Hull JH. Ann Intern Med 89:612,1978.
** Maintenance dose may be one half the loading dose at an interval approximately the estimated half life.
*** Serum concentrations should be measured to assist dose selection when the CCr is < 10 ml/min.

Drug Therapy Dosing Guidelines

(Adapted from Bennett WM, et al: Ann Intern Med 93:62,1980, AMA Drug Evaluations, 6th Ed., 1986, pp 1291-1631, and Drug Information 90, American Formulary Service, 1990, pp 31-466)

Drug	Major excretory route	Half life (hr) Normal	Half life (hr) Anuria	Usual regimen Oral	Usual regimen Parenteral	Maintenance regimen renal failure* Glomerular filtration rate in ml/min 50-80	10-50	<10
Acyclovir	Renal	2-2.5	20	200 mg 2-5 x daily	--	Usual	Usual	200 mg q12h
Amantidine	Renal	15-20	170	--	5-12 mg/kg q8h	Usual	5-12 mg/kg q12-24h	2.5-6 mg/kg q24h
				100 mg bid	--	100-150 mg q day	100-200 mg 2-3 x/wk	100-200 mg q wk
Amdinocillin	Renal	1.0	3.3	--	10 mg/kg q4-6h	Usual	10 mg/kg q6h	10 mg/kg q8h
Amikacin	Renal	2h	30h	--	7.5 mg/kg	See page 33,34		
Amoxicillin	Renal	1	15-20	250-500 mg q8h	--	.25-.5 gm q12h	.25-.5 gm q12-24h	.25-.5 gm q12-24h
Amoxicillin-clavulanic acid	Renal	1	8-16	250-500 mg q8h	--	Usual	0.25-0.5 gm q12h	0.25-0.5 gm q20-36h
Amphotericin B	Nonrenal	24	24	--	See pg 106,107	Usual	Usual	Usual
Ampicillin	Renal	1.0	8-12	.25-0.5 gm q6h	--	Usual	Usual	Usual
				--	1-3 gm q4-6h	Usual	1-2 gm IV q8h	1-2 gm IV q12h

(continued)

35

Drug	Major excretory route	Half life (hr)		Usual regimen		Maintenance regimen renal failure* Glomerular filtration rate in ml/min		
		Normal	Anuria	Oral	Parenteral	50-80	10-50	<10
Ampicillin-sulbactam	Renal	1.0	8-12h	--	1-2 gm q6h	1-2 gm IV q8h	1-2 gm IV q8h	1-2 gm IV q12h
Azlocillin	Renal	1	5	--	2-4 gm q4-6h	Usual	1.5-2 gm q8h	1.5-3 gm q12h
Aztreonam	Renal	1.7-2	6-9	--	1-2 gm q6h	1-2 gm q8-12h	1-2 gm q12-18h	1-2 gm q24h
Bacampicillin	Renal			0.4-0.8 gm q12h	--	Usual	Usual	
Capreomycin	Renal	4-6	50-100	1 gm q day-2x/wk	--	Usual	7.5 mg/kg q 1-2 days	7.5 mg/kg 2x/wk
Carbenicillin	Renal	1.0	13-16	.5-1 gm q6h / --	5-6 gm IV q4h	Usual / Usual	2-3 gm q6h	Avoid 2 gm q12h
Cefaclor	Renal	0.75	2.8	.25-0.5 gm q8h	--	Usual	Usual	Usual
Cefadroxil	Renal	1.4	20-25	.5-1 gm q12-24h	--	Usual	.5 gm q12-24h	.5 gm q36h
Cefamandole	Renal	0.5-1.0	10	--	0.5-2 gm q4-8h	.5-2 gm q6h	1-2 gm q8h	0.5-1 gm q12h
Cefazolin	Renal	1.8	18-36	--	0.5-2 gm q8h	0.5-1.5 gm q8h	.5-1 gm q8-12h	0.25-0.75 gm q18-24h

(continued)

36

Drug	Major excretory route	Half life (hr) Normal	Half life (hr) Anuria	Usual regimen Oral	Usual regimen Parenteral	Maintenance regimen renal failure* Glomerular filtration rate in ml/min 50-80	10-50	<10
Cefixime	Renal			400 mg/d	--	Usual	75% standard dose	400 mg q 2 days
Cefmetazole	Renal	1.2	↑	--	2 gm q6-12h	1-2 gm q12h	1-2 gm q16-24h	1-2 gm q 48h
Cefonicid	Renal	4-5	50-60	--	.5-2 gm q24h	8-25 mg/kg q24h	4-15 mg/kg q24-48h	3-15 mg/kg q3-5d
Cefoperazone	Gut	1.9-2.5	2-2.5	--	1-2 gm q 6-12h	Usual	Usual	Usual
Ceforanide	Renal	3	20-40	--	0.5-1 gm q12h	Usual	0.5-1 gm q24h	0.5-1 gm q48-72h
Cefotaxime	Renal	1.1	3	--	1-2 gm q8-12h	Usual	1-2 gm q12-24h	1-2 gm q24h
Cefotetan	Renal	3-4	12-30	--	1-2 gm q12h	Usual	1-2 gm q24h	1-2 gm q48h
Cefoxitin	Renal	0.7	13-22	--	1-2 gm q6-8h	1-2 gm q8-12h	1-2 gm q12-24h	0.5-1 gm q12-48h
Ceftazidime	Renal	1.5-2	15-25	--	1-2 gm q8-12h	Usual	1 gm q12-24h	0.5 gm q24-48h
Ceftizoxime	Renal	1.4-1.8	25-35	--	1-3 gm q6-8h	0.5-1.5 gm q8h	.25-1 gm q12h	.25 gm q24h

(continued)

Drug	Major excretory route	Half life (hr) Normal	Half life (hr) Anuria	Usual regimen Oral	Usual regimen Parenteral	Maintenance regimen renal failure* Glomerular filtration rate in ml/min 50-80	10-50	<10
Ceftriaxone	Renal & gut	6-9	12-15	--	0.5-1 gm q12-24h	Usual	Usual	Usual
Cefuroxime	Renal	1.3-1.7	20	--	.75-1.5 gm q8h	Usual	0.75-1.5 gm q8-12h	0.75 gm q24h
Cefuroxime axetil	Renal	1.2	20	250 mg q12h	--	Usual	Usual	250 mg q24h
Cephalexin	Renal	0.9	5-30	0.25-1.0 gm q6h	--	Usual	0.25-1.0 gm q8-12h	0.25-1 gm q24-48h
Cephalothin	Renal	0.5-0.9	3-8	--	.5-2 gm q4-6h	Usual	1.0-1.5 gm q6h	.5 gm q6h
Cephapirin	Renal	0.6-0.9	2.4	--	0.5-2 gm q4-6h	0.5-2 gm q6h	0.5-2 gm q8h	0.5-2 gm q12h
Cephradine	Renal	.7-1	8-15	0.25-1.0 gm q6h / --	-- / 0.5-2 gm q4-6h	Usual / 0.5-1 gm q6h	0.5 gm q6h / 0.5-1 gm q6-24h	0.25 gm q12h / 0.5-1 gm q24-72h
Chloramphenicol	Hepatic	2.5	3-7	0.25-0.75 gm q6h	.25-1 gm q6h	Usual	Usual	Usual
Chloroquine	Renal & metabolized	48-120	?	300-600 mg po qd	--	Usual	Usual	150-300 mg po qd

(continued)

38

Drug	Major excretory route	Half life (hr) Normal	Half life (hr) Anuria	Usual regimen Oral	Usual regimen Parenteral	Maintenance regimen renal failure* Glomerular filtration rate in mL/min 50-80	10-50	<10
Cinoxacin	Renal	1.5	8.5	.25-.5 gm q12h	--	.25 gm q6h	.25 gm q12h	.25 gm q24h
Ciprofloxacin	Renal & hepatic	4	5-10	.25-.75 gm q12h	--	Usual	.25-.5 gm q12h	.25-.5 gm q18h
Clindamycin	Hepatic	2-2.5	2-3.5	150-300 mg q6h	300-900 mg q6-8h	Usual	Usual	Usual
Clofazimine	Hepatic	8 days	8 days	50 mg qd 100 mg tid	--	Usual	Usual	Usual
Cloxacillin	Renal	0.5	0.8	0.5-1.0 gm q6h	--	Usual	Usual	Usual
Colistin	Renal	3-8	10-20	--	1.5 mg/kg q6-12h	2.5-3.8 mg/kg/day	1.5-2.5 mg/kg q24-36h	.6 mg/kg q24h
Cycloserine	Renal	8-12	?	250-500 mg bid	--	Usual	250-500 mg qd	250 mg qd
Dapsone	Hepatic metabolism	30	slight↑	50-100 mg/day	--	Usual	Usual	(No data)
Dicloxacillin	Renal	0.5-0.9	1-1.6	0.25-0.5 gm q6h	--	Usual	Usual	Usual
Dideoxyinosine (ddI)	Renal & nonrenal	1.3-1.6	?	167-375 mg bid	--	Usual	Excluded for creatinine > 2.5 mg/dl	

39

(continued)

Drug	Major excretory route	Half life (hr) Normal	Anuria	Usual regimen Oral	Parenteral	Maintenance regimen renal failure* Glomerular filtration rate in mL/min 50-80	10-50	<10
Doxycycline	Renal and gut	14-25	15-36	100 mg bid	100 mg bid	Usual	Usual	Usual
Erythromycin	Hepatic	1.2-2.6	4-6	.25-.5 gm q6h	1 gm q6h	Usual	Usual	Usual
Ethambutol	Renal	3-4	8	15-25 mg/kg q24h	--	15 mg/kg q24h	15 mg/kg q24-36h	15 mg/kg q48h
Ethionamide	Metabolized	4	9	.5-1 gm/day 1-3 doses	--	Usual	Usual	5 mg/kg q24h
Fluconazole	Renal	20-50		100-200 mg/day	100-200 mg/day	Usual	50-100 mg/day	25-50 mg/day
Flucytosine	Renal	3-6	70	37 mg/kg q6h	--	Usual	37 mg/kg q12-24h	Not recommended
Foscarnet	Renal	3-5		--	40 mg/kg / 60 mg/kg / 90 mg/kg	20-30 mg/kg / 40-50 mg/kg / 60-70 mg/kg	10-15 mg/kg / 20-30 mg/kg / 50-70 mg/kg	Contraindicated / Contraindicated / Contraindicated
Ganciclovir - induction doses (maintenance - 1/2 dose)	Renal	1.5-3	10	--	5.0 mg/kg IV bid	2.5 mg/kg bid	2.5 mg/kg qd	1.25 mg/kg qd
Gentamicin	Renal	2	48	--	1.7 mg/kg q8h	See pg 33,34		

(continued)

Drug	Major excretory route	Half life (hr) Normal	Anuria	Usual regimen Oral	Parenteral	Maintenance regimen renal failure* Glomerular filtration rate in mL/min 50-80	10-50	<10
Griseofulvin microsize ultramicrosize	Hepatic metabolism (Same)	24 (Same)	24 (Same)	.5-1 gm qd .33-.66 gm qd	-- --	Usual Usual	Usual Usual	Usual Usual
Imipenem	Renal	.8-1	3.5	--	0.5-1 gm q6h	0.5 gm q6-8h	0.5 gm q8-12h	0.25-0.5 mg q12h
Isoniazid	Hepatic	0.5-4	2-10	300 mg q24h	300 mg q24h	Usual	Usual	Slow acetylators 1/2 dose
Kanamycin	Renal	2-3	27-30	--	7.5 mg/kg	See pg 33,34		
Ketoconazole	Hepatic metabolism	1-4	1-4	200-400 mg q12-24h	--	Usual	Usual	Usual
Mefloquine	Hepatic	2-4 wks	2-4 wks	1250 mg x 1 250 mg q wk	--	Usual	Usual	Usual
Methenamine hippurate	Renal	3-6	?	1 gm q12h	--	Usual	Avoid	Avoid
mandelate	Renal	3-6	?	1 gm q12h	--	Usual	Avoid	Avoid
Methicillin	Renal (hepatic)	0.5	4	--	1-2 gm q4-6h	1-2 gm q6h	1-2 gm q8h	1-2 gm q12h
Metronidazole	Hepatic	6-14	8-15	.25-7.5 gm tid	.5 gm q6h	Usual	Usual	Usual

(continued)

41

Drug	Major excretory route	Half life (hr) Normal	Half life (hr) Anuria	Usual regimen Oral	Usual regimen Parenteral	Maintenance regimen renal failure* Glomerular filtration rate in ml/min 50-80	10-50	<10
Meztocillin	Renal	1	1.5	--	3-4 gm q4-6h	Usual	3 gm q8h	2 gm q8h
Miconazole	Hepatic	0.5-1	0.5-1	--	0.4-1.2 gm q8h	Usual	Usual	Usual
Minocycline	Hepatic & metabolized	11-26	17-30	100 mg q12h	100 mg q12h	Usual	Usual	Usual or slight decrease
Moxalactam	Renal	2	20	--	1-4 gm q8-12h	3 gm q8h	2-3 gm q12h	1 gm 12-24h
Nafcillin	Hepatic metabolism	0.5	1.2	0.5-1 gm q6h	0.5-2 gm q4-6h	Usual	Usual	Usual
Nalidixic acid	Renal & metabolized	1.5	21	1 gm q6h	--	Usual	Usual	Avoid
Netilmicin	Renal	2.5	35	--	2.0 mg/kg q8h	See pg 33,34		
Nitrofurantoin	Renal	0.3	1	50-100 mg q6-8h	--	Usual	Avoid	Avoid
Norfloxacin	Renal & metabolized	3.5	8	400 mg bid	--	Usual	400 mg qd	400 mg qd
Nystatin	Not absorbed	--	--	.4-1 mil units 3-5 x daily	--	Usual	Usual	Usual
Oxacillin	Renal	0.5	1	0.5-1 gm q6h	0.5-2 gm q4-6h	Usual	Usual	Usual

(continued)

Drug	Major excretory route	Half life (hr) Normal	Half life (hr) Anuria	Usual regimen Oral	Usual regimen Parenteral	Maintenance regimen renal failure* Glomerular filtration rate in ml/min 50-80	10-50	<10
Penicillin G crystalline	Renal	0.5	7-10	0.4-0.8 mil units q6h	1-4 mil units q4-6h	Usual	Usual	1/2 usual dose
procaine	Renal	24	↑	--	0.6-1.2 mil units IM q12h	Usual	Usual	Usual
benzathine	Renal	days	↑	--	0.6-1.2 mil units IM	Usual	Usual	Usual
V	Renal	0.5	7-10	0.4-0.8 mil units q6h	--	Usual	Usual	Usual
Pentamidine	Renal	6	↑	--	4 mg/kg q24h	Usual	4 mg/kg q24-36h	4 mg/kg q48h
Piperacillin	Renal	1.0	3.0	--	3-4 gm q4-6h	Usual	3 gm q8h	3 gm q12h
Polymyxin B	Renal	6	48	--	.8-1.2 gm IV q12h	1-1.5 mg/kg qd	1-1.5 mg/kg q12h	1 mg/kg q5-7d
Praziquantel	Hepatic metabolism	0.8-1.5	?	10-25 mg/kg · tid	--	Usual	Usual	Usual
Pyrazinamide	Metabolized	10-16	?	15-35 mg/kg daily	--	Usual	Usual	12-20 mg/kg/day
Pyrimethamine	Nonrenal	1.5-5 days	?	25-75 mg/day	--	Usual	Usual	Usual

(continued)

Drug	Major excretory route	Half life (hr)		Usual regimen		Maintenance regimen renal failure* Glomerular filtration rate in mL/min		
		Normal	Anuria	Oral	Parenteral	50-80	10-50	<10
Quinine	Hepatic metabolism	4-5	4-5	650 mg tid	7.5-10 mg/kg q8h	Usual	Usual	Usual
Quinacrine	Renal	5 days	↑	100-200 mg q6-8h	--	Usual	?	?
Rifampin	Hepatic	2-5	2-5	600 mg/kg day	600 mg/day	Usual	Usual	Usual
Spectinomycin	Renal	1-3	?	--	2 gm IM/day	Usual	Usual	Usual
Streptomycin	Renal	2.5	100-110	--	500 mg q12h	7.5 mg/kg q24h	7.5 mg/kg q24-72h	7.5 mg/kg q72-96h
Sulfadiazine	Renal	17	?	0.5-1.5 gm q4-6h	--	Usual	0.5-1.5 gm q8-12h	0.5-1.5 gm q12-24h
					30-50 mg/kg q6-8h	Usual	30-50 mg/kg q12-18h	30-50 mg/kg q18-24h
Sulfisoxazole	Renal	3-7	6-12	1-2 gm q6h	--	Usual	1 gm q8-12h	1 gm q12-24h
Tetracycline	Renal	8	50-100	.25-.5 gm q6h	.5-1 gm q12h	Usual	Use doxycycline	
Ticarcillin	Renal	1-1.5	16	--	3 gm q4h	Usual	2-3 gm q6-8h	2 gm q12h
Ticarcillin + clavulanic acid	Renal	1-1.5	16	--	3 gm q4h	Usual	2-3 gm q6-8h	2 gm q12h

(continued)

44

Drug	Major excretory route	Half life (hr)		Usual regimen		Maintenance regimen renal failure* Glomerular filtration rate in ml/min		
		Normal	Anuria	Oral	Parenteral	50-80	10-50	<10
Tobramycin	Renal	2.5	56	--	1.7 mg/kg q8h	See pg 33,34		
Trimethoprim	Renal	8-15	24	100 mg q12h	--	Usual	100 mg q18-24h	Avoid
Trimethoprim-sulfamethoxazole	Renal	T:8-15 S:7-12	T:24 S:22-50	2-4 tabs/d or 1-2 DS/day	--	Usual	Half dose	1 tab bid
					3-5 mg/kg q6-12h	3-5 mg/kg q 18h	3-5 mg/kg q24h	Avoid
Vancomycin	Renal	6-8	200-250	.125-.5 gm q6h	--	Usual dose	Usual dose	0.125 mg po
					15 mg/kg q12h	1 gm q24h	1 gm q3-10d	1 gm q5-10d
Vidarabine	Renal	3.5	↑	--	15 mg/kg/day	Usual	Usual	10 mg/kg/day
Zidovudine AZT	Hepatic	1	1.4	100 mg q4h	--	Usual	100 mg q6h	100 mg q6h

ANTIMICROBIAL DOSING REGIMENS DURING DIALYSIS
(Adapted from: Norris S, Nightengale CH and Mandell GL:
In: Principles and Practice of Infectious Diseases, 3rd Ed.,
Churchill Livingstone, NY 1990, pp 440-457, and American Formulary
Service 90, Amer Soc Hosp Pharmacists 1990, pp 31-466 .)

	Hemodialysis	Peritoneal dialysis
Acyclovir	0.5 gm post each dialysis (daily)	2.5 mg/kg/day
Amdinocillin	No extra dose	
Amikacin	2.5-3.75 mg/kg post dialysis	3-4 mg/2L dialysate removed
Amoxicillin	0.25 gm post dialysis	-
Amoxicillin + clavulanic acid	0.50 gm (amoxicillin) + .125 (CA) halfway through dialysis and another dose at end	-
Amphotericin B	Usual regimen	Usual regimen
Ampicillin	Usual dose post dialysis	Usual regimen
Ampicillin + sulbactam	2 gm ampicillin post dialysis	
Azlocillin	3 gm post dialysis and then 3 gm q12h	3 gm q12h
Aztreonam	One-eighth initial dose (60-250 mg) post dialysis	Usual loading dose, then one-fourth usual dose at usual intervals
Carbenicillin	.75-2.0 gm post dialysis	2 gm 6-12h
Cefaclor	Repeat dose post dialysis	
Cefadroxil	0.5-1 gm post dialysis	
Cefamandole	Repeat dose post dialysis	
Cefazolin	0.25-0.5 gm post dialysis	

(continued)

	Hemodialysis	Peritoneal dialysis
Cefixime	No extra dose	
Cefonicid	No extra dose	
Cefoperazone	Schedule dose post dialysis	
Cefotaxime	0.5-2 gm daily plus supplemental dose post dialysis	
Cefotetan	One-fourth usual dose q24h on non-dialysis days and one-half dose on dialysis days	
Cefoxitin	1-2 gm post dialysis	
Ceftazidime	1 gm loading 1 gm post dialysis	0.5-1 gm loading then 0.5 gm q24h or 250 mg in each 2L dialysate
Ceftizoxime	Scheduled dose post dialysis	3 gm q48h
Ceftriaxone	No extra dose	
Cefuroxime	Repeat dose post dialysis	15 mg/kg post dialysis
Cephalexin	0.25-1 gm post dialysis	
Cephalothin	Supplemental dose post dialysis	Option to add ≤ 6 mg/dL to dialysate
Cephapirin	7.5-15 mg/kg before dialysis and q12h after	
Cephradine	250 mg pre dialysis, then at 12 and 36-48 hr later	0.5 gm q6h
Chloramphenicol	Schedule dose post dialysis	Usual regimen
Ciprofloxacin	250-500 mg q24h post dialysis	250-500 mg q24h

(continued)

	Hemodialysis	Peritoneal dialysis
Clindamycin	Usual regimen	Usual regimen
Cloxacillin	Usual regimen	Usual regimen
Dicloxacillin	Usual regimen	Usual regimen
Doxycycline	Usual regimen	Usual regimen
Erythromycin	Usual regimen	Usual regimen
Ethambutol	15 mg/kg/day post dialysis	15 mg/kg/day
Flucytosine	20-37.5 mg/kg post dialysis	
Ganciclovir	1.25 mg/kg q24h given post dialysis on dialysis days	
Gentamicin	1.0-1.7 mg/kg post dialysis	1 mg/2L dialysate removed
Isoniazid	5 mg/kg post dialysis	Daily dose post dialysis
Imipenem	Supplemental dose post dialysis and q12h thereafter	
Kanamycin	4-5 mg/kg post dialysis	3.75 mg/kg/day
Ketoconazole	Usual regimen	Usual regimen
Metronidazole	Usual regimen	Usual regimen
Mezlocillin	2-3 gm post dialysis then 3-4 gm q12h	3 gm q12h
Minocycline	Usual dose	Usual dose
Moxalactam	1-2 gm post dialysis	
Nafcillin	Usual regimen	Usual regimen
Netilmicin	2 mg/kg post dialysis	
Oxacillin	Usual regimen	Usual regimen

(continued)

	Hemodialysis	Peritoneal dialysis
Penicillin G	500,000 units post dialysis	
Penicillin V	0.25 gm post dialysis	
Piperacillin	1 gm post dialysis, then 2 gm q8h	
Streptomycin	0.5 gm post dialysis	
Tetracycline	500 mg post dialysis	
Ticarcillin	3 gm post dialysis, then 2 gm q12h	3 gm q12h
Ticarcillin + clavulanic acid	3 gm (ticarcillin) post dialysis, then 2 gm q12h	3 gm (ticarcillin) q12h
Tobramycin	1 mg/kg post dialysis	1 mg/2L dialysate removed
Trimethoprim-sulfa	4-5 mg/kg (as trimethoprim) post dialysis	0.16/0.8 q48h
Vancomycin	1 gm/wk	0.5-1 gm/wk
Vidarabine	Scheduled dose post dialysis	

USE OF ANTIMICROBIAL AGENTS IN HEPATIC DISEASE

Many antimicrobial agents are metabolized by the liver and/or excreted via the biliary tract. Nevertheless, relatively few require dose modifications in hepatic disease; with the exceptions, doses are usually modified only if there is concurrent renal failure and/or the liver disease is either acute or is associated with severe hepatic failure as indicated by ascites or jaundice. The following recommendations are adopted from "Drug Information 88", American Hospital Formulary Service, Amer Soc Hosp Pharmacists, Bethesda, Md 1988.

Agent: Recommended dose modification

Aztreonam: Some recommend a dose reduction of 20-25%.

Carbenicillin: Maximum of 2 gm/day for patients with severe renal and hepatic insufficiency.

Cefoperazone: Maximum dose is 4 gm/day; if higher monitor levels; with coexisting renal impairment maximum dose is 1-2 gm/day.

Ceftriaxone: Maximum daily dose of 2 gm with severe hepatic <u>and</u> renal impairment.

Chloramphenicol: Use with caution with renal and/or hepatic failure; monitor serum levels to achieve levels of 5-20 ug/mL.

Clindamycin: Dose reduction recommended only for severe hepatic failure.

Isoniazid: Use with caution and monitor hepatic function for mild-moderate hepatic disease; acute liver disease or history of INH-associated hepatic injury is contraindication to INH.

Mezlocillin: Reduce dose by 50% or double the dosing interval.

Nafcillin: Metabolized by liver and largely eliminated in bile; nevertheless, dose modifications are suggested only for combined hepatic and renal failure.

Penicillin G: Dose reduction for hepatic failure only when accompanied by renal failure.

Rifampin: Induces hepatic enzymes responsible for inactivating methadone, corticosteroids, oral antidiabetic agents, digitalis, quinidine, cyclosporine, oral anticoagulants, estrogens, oral contraceptives and chloramphenicol. Concurrent use of these drugs with rifampin and use of rifampin in patients with prior liver disease requires careful review.

Ticarcillin: For patients with hepatic dysfunction and creatinine clearance < 10 mL/min, give 2 gm IV/day in one or two doses.

Ticarcillin/Clavulanate K: For patients with hepatic dysfunction and creatinine clearance < 10 mL/min give usual loading dose (3.1 gm) followed by 2 gm once daily.

ADVERSE REACTIONS TO ANTIMICROBIAL AGENTS

A. Adverse Reactions by Class

	Frequent	Occasional	Rare
Acyclovir	Irritation at infusion site; renal toxicity (esp with rapid IV infusion, prior renal disease and other nephrotoxic drugs); headache	Rash; nausea and vomiting; diarrhea; vertigo (oral); marrow suppression; metabolic encephalopathy; abnormal liver function tests; itching	CNS-agitation, lethargy, disorientation, transient hemiparesis, seizures; hallucinations; anemia; hypotension; neutropenia; thrombocytopenia
Amantadine	Insomnia, lethargy, dizziness, inability to concentrate	CNS-depression, confusion, slurred speech; congestive heart failure; GI intolerance, rash	CNS; psychosis, convulsions; eczematoid dermatitis; photosensitivity; oculogyric episodes; orthostatic hypotension; peripheral edema; bone marrow suppression
Aminoglycosides Tobramycin Gentamicin Amikacin Netilmicin Kanamycin	Renal failure	Vestibular and auditory damage	Fever; rash; blurred vision; neuromuscular blockage; eosinophilia
Aminosalicylic acid (PAS)	GI intolerance	Liver damage; allergic reactions; thyroid enlargement	Acidosis; vasculitis; hypoglycemia (diabetes); hypokalemia; encephalopathy; decreased prothrombin activity; myalgias; renal damage; gastric hemorrhage
Amoxicillin + clavulanic acid	(Similar to amoxicillin - See penicillins)		
Amphotericin B	Renal damage; hypokalemia; anemia; phlebitis and pain at injection site; nausea; vomiting; metallic taste; fever; chills; headache	Hypomagnesemia	Hypotension; rash; pruritus; blurred vision; peripheral neuropathy; convulsions; hemorrhagic gastroenteritis; arrhythmias; diabetes insipidus; hearing loss; pulmonary edema; anaphylaxis; acute hepatic failure; eosinophilia; leukopenia; thrombocytopenia (continued)

51

	Frequent	Occasional	Rare
Ampicillin + sulbactam	(Similar to those for ampicillin alone - See penicillins)		
Aztreonam	Eosinophilia	Phlebitis at infusion site; rash; diarrhea; nausea; eosinophilia; abnormal liver function tests	Thrombocytopenia; colitis; hypotension; unusual taste; seizures; chills
Bacitracin	Nephrotoxicity (proteinuria, oliguria, azotemia); pain with IM use		Rash; blood dyscrasias
Capreomycin	Renal damage (tubular necrosis esp in patients with prior renal damage	Ototoxicity (vestibular and auditory); electrolyte abnormalities; pain, induration and sterile abscesses at injection sites	Allergic reactions; leukopenia; leuko-cytosis; neuromuscular blockage (large IV doses - reversed with neostigmine); hypersensitivity reactions
Cephalosporins	Phlebitis at infusion sites; diarrhea (esp cefoperazone); pain at IM injection sites (less with cefazolin)	Allergic reactions (anaphylaxis rare); diarrhea and colitis; hypo-prothrombinemia (cefamandole, cefoperazone, moxalactam, cefmetazole and cefotetan); platelet dysfunction (moxalactam); eosinophilia; positive Coombs' test	Hemolytic anemia; interstitial nephritis (cephalothin); hepatic dysfunction; convulsions (high dose with renal failure); neutropenia; thrombocytopenia
Chloramphenicol	GI intolerance (oral); marrow suppression (dose related)		Fatal aplastic anemia; fever; allergic reactions; peripheral neuropathy; optic neuritis

(continued)

52

	Frequent	Occasional	Rare
Chloroquine		Visual disturbances (related to dose and duration of treatment); GI intolerance; pruritus	CNS-headache, confusion, psychosis; peripheral neuropathy; cardiac toxicity; hemolysis (G-6-PD deficiency); marrow suppression
Ciprofloxacin	(See quinolones)		
Clindamycin	Diarrhea	Rash; colitis; GI intolerance (oral)	Blood dyscrasias; hepatic damage; neutropenia; neuromuscular blockage; eosinophilia; fever; metallic taste; phlebitis at IV infusion sites
Clofazimine	Ichthyosis; discoloration of skin, cornea, retina and urine (with prolonged use); GI intolerance	Persistent abdominal pain, diarrhea and weight loss (high dose over 3 months); dry, burning, irritated eyes	Bowel obstruction; GI bleeding; splenic infarction; eosinophilic enteritis; vision loss
Colistimethate	(See Polymyxins)		
Cycloserine	CNS-anxiety, confusion depression, somnolence, disorientation, headache, hallucinations, tremor, hyperreflexia, increased CSF protein and pressure (dose related and reversible)	Liver damage; malabsorption; peripheral neuropathy; folate deficiency; anemia	Coma; seizures (contraindicated in epileptics); hypersensitivity reactions; heart failure, arrhythmias
Dapsone	Rash; headach (transient); GI intolerance; infectious mono-like syndrome	Blood dyscrasias (methemoglobulinemia and sulfahemoglobinemia); hemolytic anemia; nephrotic syndrome; allergic reactions; insomnia; irritability; uncoordinated speech; agitation; psychosis	Hypoalbuminemia; epidermal necrolysis; optic atrophy; agranulocytosis

(continued)

	Frequent	Occasional	Rare
Dideoxyinosine (ddI)		Pancreatitis (1%, not dose related); peripheral neuropathy (painful feet, dose related); nausea; vomiting; diarrhea, CNS changes - confusion, convulsions, agitation, dizziness; anemia; neutropenia; hyperuracemia; allergy	Dementia; coma; cardiac arrhythmias; hypokalemia, hypocalcemia, anaphylaxis
Emetine	Arrhythmias; precordial pain; muscle weakness; phlebitis	Diarrhea; vomiting; neuropathy; heart failure	
Erythromycins	GI intolerance (oral-dose related); phlebitis (IV)	Diarrhea; stomatitis; cholestatic hepatitis (esp estolate-reversible); phlebitis (IV administration); generalized rash	Allergic reactions; colitis; hemolytic anemia; reversible ototoxicity (esp high dose and renal failure)
Ethambutol		Optic neuritis; allergic reactions; GI intolerance; confusion; precipitation of acute gout	Peripheral neuropathy; thrombocytopenia; toxic epidermal necrolysis; lichenoid skin rash
Ethionamide	GI intolerance (improved with antacids); depression	Allergic reactions; peripheral neuropathy; liver damage; gynecomastia; menstrual irregularity	Optic neuritis; gouty arthritis; hypothyroidism; impotence; thyroid enlargement; poor diabetic control; rash; hepatitis
Fluconazole		Nausea; headache; rash; vomiting; diarrhea; prolonged protime with coumadin	Hepatitis; Stevens-Johnson syndrome

(continued)

54

	Frequent	Occasional	Rare
Flucytosine	GI intolerance (including nausea, vomiting, diarrhea and ulcerative colitis)	Rash; liver damage (dose related); marrow suppression (dose related, esp with renal failure or concurrent amphotericin); confusion	Hallucinations; eosinophilia; granulocytosis
Foscarnet	Renal failure (reversible); twitching	Anemia; electrolyte changes (calcium, magnesium, phosphorus); nausea	Hemolytic anemia (G-6-PD deficiency); hypotension; polyneuropathy; hypoglycemia; agranulocytosis
Furazolidone	GI intolerance	Allergic reactions; pulmonary infiltrates; headache	
Ganciclovir (DHPG) (Cytovene)	Neutropenia; thrombocytopenia	Anemia; fever; rash; changes in mental status; abnormal liver function tests	Psychosis; neuropathy; impaired reproductive function (?); hematuria; renal failure; nausea; vomiting; GI bleeding or perforation myocardiopathy; hypotension; ataxia; coma; somnolence
Griseofulvin	Headache (often resolves with continued treatment)	Photosensitivity	GI disturbances; allergic reactions; paresthesias; exacerbation of lupus; liver damage; lymphadenopathy; blood dyscrasias; thrush; transient hearing loss; fatigue; dizziness; insomnia; psychosis
Imipenem		Phlebitis at infusion sites; allergic reactions; nausea, vomiting and diarrhea; eosinophilia; hepatotoxicity (transient)	Seizures; myoclonus; colitis; bone marrow suppression; renal toxicity

(continued)

55

	Frequent	Occasional	Rare
Isoniazid	Hepatitis (patients over 35 yrs and usually reversible)	Allergic reactions; fever; peripheral neuropathy (reduce with pyridoxine)	CNS-optic neuritis; psychosis convulsions; toxic encephalopathy; twitching; coma; blood dyscrasias; hyperglycemia; lupus-like syndrome; keratitis; pellagra-like rash
Ketoconazole	GI intolerance (dose related)	Hepatic toxicity (usually reversible); endocrine-decreased steroid and testosterone synthesis with impotence, gynecomastia, reduced libido; menstrual abnormalities (prolonged use); headache; dizziness; asthenia; pruritus; rash	Fatal hepatic necrosis; anaphylaxis; lethargy; arthralgias; fever; marrow suppression
Mefloquine	Vertigo; light-headedness; nausea; nightmares; headache; visual disturbances	Confusion; psychosis; seizures	Prolong cardiac conduction
Methenamine	GI intolerance; dysuria	GI intolerance; dysuria (reduced dose or acidification)	Allergic reactions; edema; tinnitus; muscle cramps
Metronidazole	GI intolerance; metallic taste; headache	Peripheral neuropathy (prolonged use-reversible); phlebitis at injection sites; Antabuse-like reaction	Seizures; ataxic encephalitis; colitis; leukopenia; dysuria; pancreatitis; allergic reactions; mutagenic in Ames test
Miconazole		Phlebitis at injection sites; chills; pruritus; rash; dizziness; blurred vision; hyperlipidemia; nausea; vomiting; hyponatremia	Marrow suppression - anemia and thrombocytopenia; renal damage; anaphylaxis; psychosis; cardiac arrest

(continued)

56

	Frequent	Occasional	Rare
Nalidixic acid	(See Quinolones)		
Nitrofurantoin	GI intolerance	Hypersensitivity reactions; pulmonary infiltrates (acute, subacute or chronic; ± fever, eosinophilia, rash or lupus-like reaction)	Peripheral neuropathy; hepatitis; hemolytic anemia (G-6-PD deficiency); lactic acidosis; parotitis; pancreatitis
Nystatin		GI intolerance	Allergic reactions
Penicillins	Hypersensitivity reactions; rash (esp ampicillin and amoxicillin); diarrhea (esp ampicillin)	GI intolerance (oral agents); fever; Coombs' test positive; phlebitis at infusion sites and sterile abscesses at IM sites; Jarisch-Herxheimer reaction (syphilis or other spirochetal infections)	Anaphylaxis; leukopenia; thrombocytopenia; colitis (esp ampicillin); hepatic damage; renal damage; CNS-seizures, twitching (high doses in patients with renal failure); hyperkalemia (penicillin G infusion); abnormal platelet aggregation with bleeding diathesis (carbenicillin and ticarcillin)
Pentamidine	Nephrotoxicity; GI intolerance	Hypotension; hypoglycemia; rash (including Stevens-Johnson syndrome); marrow suppression (common in AIDS patients)	Increased liver function tests; pancreatitis; bronchospasm (inhalation); hyperglycemia, insulin-dependent diabetes
Polymyxins	Pain and phlebitis at injection sites; neurotoxicity (ataxia, paresthesias); nephrotoxicity		Allergic reactions; neuromuscular blockade
Primaquine		Hemolytic anemia (G-6-PD deficiency); GI intolerance	Headache; pruritus

(continued)

	Frequent	Occasional	Rare
Pyrazinamide		Hepatitis; hyperuricemia; arthralgias; GI intolerance	Rash; fever; porphyria; photosensitivity
Pyrimethamine		Folic acid deficiency with megaloblastic anemia and pancytopenia (dose related and reversed with leucovorin); allergic reactions	CNS-ataxia, tremors, seizures (dose related), fatigue)
Quinine		GI intolerance; cinchonism (tinnitus, headache, visual disturbances); hemolytic anemia (G-6-PD deficiency)	Arrhythmias; hypotension with rapid IV infusion; hypoglycemia; hepatitis; thrombocytopenia
Quinolones	(Animal studies show arthropathies in weight bearing joints of immature animals; significance in humans is not known, but this class is considered contraindicated in children and pregnancy	GI intolerance; CNS-headache; malaise; insomnia; dizziness; allergic reactions	Papilledema; nystagmus; visual disturbances; diarrhea; abnormal liver function tests; marrow suppression; photosensitivity
Rifampin	Orange discoloration of urine, tears (contact lens), sweat	Hepatitis; GI intolerance; hypersensitivity reactions; increases hepatic metabolism of steroids to increase steroid requirement in adrenal insufficiency and require alternative to birth control meds; flu-like syndrome with intermittent use	Thrombocytopenia; leukopenia; eosinophilia; renal damage; proximal myelopathy

58

(continued)

	Frequent	Occasional	Rare
Spectinomycin		Pain at injection site; urticaria; fever; insomnia; dizziness; nausea; headache	Anaphylaxis; fever; anemia; renal failure and abnormal liver function tests (multiple doses)
Sulfonamides	Allergic reactions - rash, pruritis, fever	Periarteritis nodosum, lupus, Stevens-Johnson syndrome, serum sickness; crystalluria with renal damage, urolithiasis and oliguria; GI intolerance; photosensitivity	Myocarditis; psychosis; neuropathy; dizziness; depression; hemolytic anemia (G-6-PD deficiency); marrow suppression; agranulocytosis
Tetracyclines	GI intolerance (dose-related); strains and deforms teeth in children up to 8 yrs; vertigo (minocycline); negative nitrogen balance and increased azotemia with renal failure (except doxycycline); vaginitis	Hepatotoxicity (dose-related, esp pregnant women); esophageal ulcerations; diarrhea; candidiasis (thrush and vaginitis); photosensitivity (esp demeclocycline); phlebitis with IV treatment and pain with IM injection	Malabsorptions; allergic reactions; visual disturbances; aggrevation of myasthenia; hemolytic anemia; colitis
Ticarcillin + clavulanic acid	Similar to those for ticarcillin alone (See Penicillins)		
Trimethoprim	GI intolerance (dose-related); rash	Marrow-megaloblastic anemia, neutropenia, thrombocytopenia	Pancytopenia
Trimethoprim-sulfamethoxazole	Fever, leukopenia, rash (AIDS patients); reactions noted above for sulfonamides and trimethoprim		

59

(continued)

	Frequent	Occasional	Rare
Vancomycin	Phlebitis at injections sites	"Red-man syndrome" (flushing over chest and face) or hypotension (infusion too rapid); rash; fever; neutropenia; eosinophilia; allergic reactions with rash	Anaphylaxis; ototoxicity and nephrotoxicity dose related); peripheral neuropathy; marrow suppression
Vidarabine		GI intolerance; phlebitis at infusion site; fluid overload	Blood dyscrasias; CNS-confusion and neurologic deterioration (esp with renal failure)
Zidovudine (AZT, Retrovir)	Anemia; leukopenia	Headache; malaise; insomnia; myalgias; myopathy; nausea; nail pigmentation	Seizures (reversible); allergy (rash, anaphylaxis); twitching

B. Penicillin Allergy

1. Cross reactions
Allergy to one penicillin indicates allergy to all.
Allergy to penicillins may indicate allergy to cephalosporins and imipenem.
There is no apparent cross reaction with aztreonam.

2. Skin testing:
This is considered a safe, rapid and effective method to exclude an IgE mediated response with $\geq$ 98% assurance.

Method (MMWR 38:S13,1989)

a. Patients with a history of severe reactions during the past year should be tested in the hospital setting with antigens diluted 100-fold; others may be tested in a physician staffed clinic.

b. Patients with a history of penicillin allergy and a negative skin test should receive penicillin, 250 mg po and be observed for one hour prior to treatment with therapeutic doses. Those with a positive skin test should be desensitized.

c. Penicillin allergy skin testing (adapted from Beall*)

Note: If there has been a severe, generalized reaction to penicillin in the previous year, the antigens should be diluted 100-fold, and patients should be tested in a controlled environment. Both major and minor determinants should be available for the tests to be interpretable. The patient should not have taken antihistamines in the previous 48 hours.

Reagents

Major determinants:
Benzylpenicilloyl-polylysine (major, Pre-Pen [Taylor Pharmacal Co., Decatur, Illinois], 6×10^{-5}M)
Benzylpenicillin (10^{-2} or 6000 U/mL)

Minor determinants:
Benzylpenicilloic acid (10^{-2}M)
Benzylpenilloic acid (10^{-2}M)

Positive control (histamine, 1 mg/mL)

Negative control (buffered saline solution)

Dilute the antigens 100-fold for preliminary testing if there has been an immediate generalized reaction within the past year.

Procedure

Epicutaneous (scratch or prick) test: apply one drop of material to volar forearm and pierce epidermis without drawing blood; observe for 20 minutes. If there is no wheal $\geq$ 4mm, proceed to intradermal test.

Intradermal test: Inject 0.02 ml intradermally with a 27- gauge short-bevelled needle; observe for 20 minutes.

Interpretation

For the test to be interpretable, the negative (saline) control must elicit no reaction and the positive (histamine) control must elicit a positive reaction.

Positive test: A wheal > 4mm in mean diameter to any penicillin reagent; erythema must be present.

Negative test: The wheals at the site of the penicillin reagents are equivalent to the negative control.

Indeterminate: All other results

---

*Reprinted with permission from Beall GN, Penicillins, pp 205-9. In: Saxon A, moderator. Immediate hypersensitivity reactions to beta-lactam antibiotics. Ann Intern Med 1987;107:204-15.

4. Penicillin desensitization (Adapted from the Medical Letter on Drugs and Therapeutics 30:77,1988 and MMWR 38:S13,1989).

   a. Penicillin densensitization should be done in a hospital because IgE mediated reactions can occur, although they are rare. Desensitization may be done orally or intravenously, although oral administration is often considered safer, simpler and easier.

   b. Parenteral desensitization: Give 1 unit penicillin IV and then double the dose at 15 minute intervals or increase the dose 10-fold at 20-30 minute intervals.

   c. Oral-desensitization protocol (from Wendel)

Dose*	Penicillin V Suspension (units/ml)	Amount†		Cumulative dose (units)
		ml	units	
1	1,000	0.1	100	100
2	1,000	0.2	200	300
3	1,000	0.4	400	700
4	1,000	0.8	800	1,500
5	1,000	1.6	1,600	3,100
6	1,000	3.2	3,200	6,300
7	1,000	6.4	6,400	12,700
8	10,000	1.2	12,000	24,700
9	10,000	2.4	24,000	48,700
10	10,000	4.8	48,000	96,700
11	80,000	1.0	80,000	176,700
12	80,000	2.0	160,000	336,700
13	80,000	4.0	320,000	656,700
14	80,000	8.0	640,000	1,296,700

Observation period: 30 minutes before parenteral administration of penicillin.

*Interval between doses, 15 minutes; elapsed time, 3 hours and 45 minutes; cumulative dose, 1.3 million units.
†The specific amount of drug was diluted in approximately 30 ml of water and then given orally.

Adapted with permission from the *New England Journal of Medicine* 1985;312:1229-32.

C. Adverse Reactions during Pregnancy (Adapted from Drug Evaluations, 6th Edition, AMA, Chicago, 1986, pp 44-46)

Agent	1st trimester (Embryonic development)	2nd & 3rd trimesters (Fetal development)	Labor-delivery
Antibacterial agents			
Aminoglycosides	8th nerve damage**	8th nerve damage**	-
Chloramphenicol	-	Gray-baby syndrome*	Gray-baby syndrome*
Dapsone	-	-	Carcinogenic*** Hemolytic reactions*
Metronidazole	Tumors***	-	-
Nitrofurantoin	-	Hyperbilirubinemia* Hemolytic anemia*	Hyperbilirubinemia* Hemolytic anemia*
Streptomycin	8th nerve damage multiple defects, micromelia*	8th nerve damage*	-
Sulfamethoxazole-trimethoprim	Malformations****	-	-
Sulfonamides	-	Hyperbilirubinemia*	Hyperbilirubinemia*
Tetracycline	Inhibit bone growth* Micromelia** Syndactyly**	Stain deciduous teeth* Inhibit bone growth* Enamel hypoplasia**	-
Antimalarial agents			
Chloroquine	8th nerve damage**	8th nerve damage**	-
Quinine	Malformations, abortions, 8th nerve damage*	Deafness Thrombocytopenia	-
Antituberculous agents			
Isoniazid	CNS effects***	-	-
Rifampin	CNS effects***	-	-
Streptomycin (see above)			

* Generally well documented in man   *** Documented in animals only
**Suspected in man   ****Questionable effects in man

D. Relative Safety during Pregnancy (Classification according to Medical Letter 29:61-64,1987)

	Probably safe	Caution	Contraindicated
Antibacterial agents	Aztreonam Cephalosporins Erythromycins (not estolate) Methenamine Penicillins Spectinomycin	Aminoglycosides Chloramphenicol Clindamycin Dapsone Imipenem Metronidazole Nitrofurantoin Sulfonamides Trimethoprim Trimethoprim-sulfa Vancomycin	Cinoxacin Ciprofloxacin Erythromycin (estolate) Nalidixic acid Norfloxacin Tetracyclines
Antifungal agents	Nystatin	Amphotericin B Fluconazole Flucytosine Ketoconazole Miconazole	Griseofulvin
Antiparasitic agents	Chloroquine Niclosamide Paromycin Praziquantel Pyrethrins	Diloxanide Furazolidone Iodoquinol Mebendazole Metronidazole Pentamidine Piperazine Pyrimethamine Pyrimethamine- sulfadoxine Quinacrine Quinine Suramin Thiabendazole	Emetine Lindane Mefloquine
Antituberculosis agents		Capreomycin Cycloserine Ethambutol Ethionamide Isoniazid Pyrazinamide Rifampin Streptomycin	
Antiviral agents		Acyclovir Ganciclovir Vidarabine Zidovudine (Retrovir, AZT)	Amantadine Ribavirin

DRUG INTERACTIONS

(Adapted from The Medical Letter Handbook of Adverse Drug Interactions. Medical Letter 1989:5-143)

Drug	Effect of interaction
Acyclovir	
Narcotics	Increased meperidine effect
Probenecid	Possible increased acyclovir toxicity
Amantadine	
Anticholinergics	Hallucination, confusion, nightmares
Aminoglycosides	
Amphotericin	Increased nephrotoxicity
Cephalosporins	Increased nephrotoxicity
Cisplatin	Increased nephrotoxicity
Cyclosporin	Increased nephrotoxicity
Ethacrynic acid	Increased ototoxicity
Furosemide	Increased oto and nephrotoxicity
MgSO$_4$	Increased neuromuscular blockage
Methotrexate	Possible decreased methotrexate activity with oral aminoglycosides
Vancomycin	Increased nephrotoxicity and possible increased ototoxicity
Aminosalicylic acid (PAS)	
Anticoagulants, oral	Increased hypoprothrombenia
Digitalis	Decrease digoxin effect
Probenecid	Increased PAS toxicity
Rifampin	Decreased rifampin effectiveness (give as separate doses by 8-12 hr)
Amphotericin B	
Aminoglycosides	Increased nephrotoxicity
Capreomycin	Increased nephrotoxicity
Corticosteroids	Increased hypokalemia
Cisplatin	Increased nephrotoxicity
Digitalis	Increased cardiotoxicity
Diuretics	Increased hypokalemia
Methoxyflurane	Increased nephrotoxicity
Skeletal muscle relaxants	Increased effect of relaxants
Vancomycin	Increased nephrotoxicity
Capreomycin	
Aminoglycosides	Increased oto and nephrotoxicity
Theophylline	Increased theophylline effect and toxicity
Cephalosporins	
Alcohol	Disulfiram-like reaction for those with tetrazolethiomethyl side chain: Cefamandole, cefoperazone, cefotetan, cefmetazole, moxalactam
Aminoglycosides	Possibly increased nephrotoxicity

Drug	Effect of interaction
Probenecid	Increased concentrations of cephalosporins

Chloramphenicol

Anticoagulants, oral	Increased hypoprothrombinemia
Chlorpropamide	Increased chlorpropamide activity
Dicumarol	Increased dicumarol activity
Phenobarbital	Decreased concentrations chloramphenicol
Phenytoin	Increased phenytoin activity
Rifampin	Decreased concentrations chloramphenicol
Tolbutamide	Increased tolbutamide activity

Ciprofloxacin (See Fluoroquinolones)

Cycloserine

Alcohol	Increased alcohol effect or convulsions
Ethionamide	Increased CNS toxicity
Isoniazid	CNS toxicity, dizziness, drowsiness
Phenytoin	Increased phenytoin effect (toxicity)

Erythromycins

Anticoagulants (oral)	Increased hypoprothrombinemia
Carbamazepine	Increased carbamazepine toxicity
Corticosteroids	Increased effect of methylprednisolone
Cyclosporine	Increased cyclosporine toxicity (nephrotoxicity)
Digoxin	Increased digitalis toxicity
Ergot alkaloids	Increased ergot toxicity
Phenytoin	Increased or decrease phenytoin effect
Theophylline	Increased theophylline effect

Ethionamide

Cycloserine	Increased CNS toxicity
Isoniazid	Increased CNS toxicity

Fluconazole

Anticoagulants, oral	Increased hypoprothrombinemia

Fluoroquinolones (ciprofloxacin, norfloxacin, etc)

Antacids	Decreased fluoroquinolone absorption with Mg, Ca or Al containing antacids or sucralfate
Anticoagulants (oral)	Increased hypoprothrombinemia
Caffeine	Increased caffeine effect
Nonsteroidal anti-inflammatory agents	Possible seizures and increased epileptogenic potential of theophylline, opiates, tricyclics and neuroleptics
Probenecid	Increased fluoroquinolone levels
Theophylline	Possible increased theophylline toxicity

Griseofulvin

Alcohol	Possibly potentiates effect of alcohol
Anticoagulant (oral)	Decreased anticoagulant effect
Contraceptive	Decreased contraceptive effect
Phenobarbital	Decreased griseofulvin levels

Drug	Effect of interaction
Isoniazid	
Alcohol	Increased hepatitis
	Decreased INH effects in some
Antacids	Decreased INH with Al containing antacids
Anticoagulants (oral)	Possible increased hypoprothrombinemia
Benzodiazepines	Increased effects of benzodiazepines
Carbamazepine	Increased toxicity of both drugs
Cycloserine	Increased CNS toxicity, dizziness, drowsiness
Disulfiram	Psychotic episodes, ataxia
Ethionamide	Increased CNS toxicity
Enflurane	Possible nephrotoxicity
Ketoconazole	Decreased ketoconazole effect
Phenytoin	Increased phenytoin toxicity
Rifampin	Possible increased hepatic toxicity
Ketoconazole	
Alcohol	Possible disulfiram-like reaction
Antacids	Decreased ketoconazole effect
Anticoagulants, oral	Increased hypoprothrombinemia
Corticosteroids	Increased methylprednisolone effect
Cyclosporine	Increased cyclosporine toxicity
H2 antagonists	Decreased ketoconazole effect
Isoniazid	Decreased ketoconazole effect
Phenytoin	Altered metabolism of both drugs
Rifampin	Decreased activity of both drugs
Theophylline	Decreased theophylline activity
Mebendazole	
Phenytoin and	
Carbamazepine	Decrease mebendazole concentrations: clinically significant only for extraintestinal helminthic infections
Metronidazole	
Alcohol	Disulfiram-like reaction
Anticoagulants, oral	Increased hypoprothrombinemia
Barbiturates	Decreased metronidazole effect with phenobarbital
Cimetidine	Possible increased metronidazole toxicity
Disulfiram	Organic brain syndrome
Flurouracil	Transient neutropenia
Lithium	Lithium toxicity
Miconazole	
Aminoglycosides	Possible decreased tobramycin levels
Anticoagulant, oral	Increased hypoprothrombinemia
Hypoglycemics	Severe hypoglycemia with sulfonylurea
Phenytoin	Increased phenytoin toxicity
Nalidixic acid	
Anticoagulants, oral	Increased hypoprothrombinemia

Drug	Effect of interaction
Nitrofurantoin	
Antacids	Possible decreased nitrofurantoin effect
Probenecid	Decreased nitrofurantoin effect (for UTI's)
Penicillins	
Allopurinol	Increased frequency of rash with ampicillin
Anticoagulants, oral	Decreased anticoagulant effect with nafcillin and dicloxacillin
Contraceptives	Possible decreased contraceptive effect with ampicillin or oxacillin
Lithium	Hypernatremia with ticarcillin
Methotrexate	Possible increased methotrexate toxicity
Probenecid	Increased concentrations of penicillins
Pentamidine	
Aminoglycosides	Increased nephrotoxicity
Amphotericin B	Increased nephrotoxicity
Capreomycin	Increased nephrotoxicity
Foscarnet	Increased nephrotoxicity
Piperazine	
Chlorpromazine	Possibly induces seizures
Polymyxin B and colistimethate	
Aminoglycoside	Increased nephrotoxicity; increased neruomuscular blockade
Neuromuscular blocking agents	Increased neuromuscular blockade
Vancomycin	Increased nephrotoxicity
Rifampin	
Aminosalicylic acid (PAS)	Decreased effectiveness of rifampin; give in separate doses by 8-12 h
Anticoagulants	Increased hypoprothrombinemia
Barbiturates	Decreased barbiturate effect
Benzodiazepines	Possible decreased benzodiazepine effect
B-adenergic blockers	Decreased B blocker effect
Chloramphenicol	Decreased chloramphenicol effect
Clofazimine	Reduced rifampin effect
Clofibrate	Decreased clofibrate effect
Contraceptives	Decreased contraceptive effect
Corticosteroids	Decreased corticosteroid effect
Cyclosporine	Decreased cyclosporine effect
Dapsone	Decreased dapsone effect
Digitalis	Decreased digitalis effect
Disopyramide	Decreased disopyramide effect
Estrogens	Decreased estrogen effect
Hypoglycemics	Decreased hypoglycemic effect of sulfonurea
Isoniazid	Increased hepatotoxicity
Ketoconazole	Decreased effect of ketoconazole and rifampin
Methadone	Methadone withdrawal symptoms
Mexiletine	Decreased antiarrhythmic effect

Drug	Effect of interaction
Rifampin (continued)	
Phenytoin	Decreased phenytoin effect
Progestins	Decreased norethindrome effect
Quinidine	Decreased quinidine effect
Theophyllines	Decreased theophylline effect
Verapamil	Decreased verapamil effect
Spectinomycin	
Lithium	Increased lithium toxicity
Sulfonamides	
Anticoagulants, oral	Increased hypoprothrombinemia
Barbiturates	Increased thiopental effect
Cyclosporine	Decreased cyclosporine effect with sulfamethazine
Digoxin	Decreased digoxin effect with sulfasalazine
Hypoglycemics	Increased hypoglycemic effect of sulfonylurea
Methotrexate	Possible increased methotrexate toxicity
Monoamine oxidase inhibitors	Possible increased phenelzine toxicity with sulfisoxazole
Phenytoin	Increased phenytoin effect except with sulfisoxazole
Tetracycline	
Alcohol	Decreased doxycycline effect in alcoholics
Antacids	Decreased tetracycline effect with antacids containing Ca^{++}, Al^{+++}, Mg^{++} and NAHCO3
Anticoagulants, oral	Increased hypoprothrombinemia
Antidepressants, tricyclic	Localized hemosiderosis with amitriptyline and minocycline
Anti-diarrhea agents	Agents containing kaolin and pectin or bismuth subsalicylate decrease tetracycline effect
Barbiturates	Decreased doxycycline effect
Bismuth subsalicylate (Pepto-Bismol)	Decreased tetracycline effect
Carbamazepine	Decreased doxycycline effect
Contraceptives, oral	Decreased contraceptive effect
Digoxin	Increased digoxin effect
Iron, oral	Decreased tetracycline effect (except with doxycycline) and decreased iron effect; give 3 hours before
Laxatives	Agents containing Mg^{++} decrease tetracycline effect
Lithium	Increased lithium toxicity
Methotrexate	Possible increased methotrexate toxicity
Methoxyflurane anesthesia	Possibly lethal nephrotoxicity
Molindone	Decreased tetracycline effect
Phenformin	Decreased doxycycline effect
Phenytoin	Decreased doxycycline effect

Drug	Effect of interaction
Rifampin	Possible decreased doxycycline effect
Theophylline	Possible increased theophylline toxicity
Zinc sulfate	Decreased tetracycline effect

Thiabendazole
Theophyllines	Increased theophylline toxicity

Trimethoprim
Azathioprine	Leukopenia
Cyclosporine	Increased nephrotoxicity
Digoxin	Possible increased digitalis effect
Phenytoin	Increased phenytoin effect
Thiazide diuretics	Possible increased hyponatremia with concomitant use of amiloride with thiazide diuretics

Trimethoprim-sulfamethoxazole
Anticoagulants, oral	Increased hypothrombinemia
Antidepressants, tricyclic	Reduced activity of antidepressants
Lidocaine	Methemoglobinemia
Mercaptopurine	Decrease mercaptopurine activity
Methotrexate	Megaloblastic anemia
Phenytoin	Increased phenytoin toxicity
Pimozide	Decreased pimozide effect

Vancomycin
Aminoglycosides	Increased nephrotoxicity and possible increased ototoxicity
Amphotericin B	Increased nephrotoxicity
Cisplatin	
Digoxin	Possible decreased digoxin effect
Paromomycin	Increased nephrotoxicity
Polymyxin	Increased nephrotoxicity

Vidarabine
Allopurinol	Increased neurotoxicity, nausea, pain and pruritus
Theophyllines	Increased theophylline effect

Zidovudine
Ganciclovir	Increased neutropenia and anemia

PREVENTATIVE MEDICINE

Vaccines available in the United States, by type and recommended routes of administration (MMWR 38:207,1989)

Vaccine	Type	Route
BCG (Bacillus of Calmette and Guérin)	Live bacteria	Intradermal or subcutaneous
Cholera	Inactivated bacteria	Subcutaneous or intradermal*
DTP (D = Diphtheria) (T = Tetanus) (P = Pertussis)	Toxoids and inactivated bacteria	Intramuscular
HB (Hepatitis B)	Inactive viral antigen	Intramuscular
Haemophilus influenzae b — Polysaccharide (HbPV)	Bacterial polysaccharide	Subcutaneous or intramuscular†
— or Conjugate (HbCV)	or Polysaccharide conjugated to protein	Intramuscular
Influenza	Inactivated virus or viral components	Intramuscular
IPV (Inactivated Poliovirus Vaccine)	Inactivated viruses of all 3 serotypes	Subcutaneous
Measles	Live virus	Subcutaneous
Meningococcal	Bacterial polysaccharides of serotypes A/C/Y/W-135	Subcutaneous
MMR (M = Measles) (M = Mumps) (R = Rubella)	Live viruses	Subcutaneous
Mumps	Live virus	Subcutaneous
OPV (Oral Poliovirus Vaccine)	Live viruses of all 3 serotypes	Oral
Plague	Inactivated bacteria	Intramuscular
Pneumococcal	Bacterial polysaccharides of 23 pneumococcal types	Intramuscular or subcutaneous
Rabies	Inactivated virus	Subcutaneous or intradermal‡
Rubella	Live virus	Subcutaneous
Tetanus	Inactivated toxin (toxoid)	Intramuscular§
Td or DT** (T = Tetanus) (D or d = Diphtheria)	Inactivated toxins (toxoids)	Intramuscular§
Typhoid	Inactivated bacteria	Subcutaneous††
Yellow fever	Live virus	Subcutaneous

*The intradermal dose is lower.
†Route depends on the manufacturer; consult package insert for recommendation for specific product used.
‡Intradermal dose is lower and used only for preexposure vaccination.
§Preparations with adjuvants should be given intramuscularly.
**DT = tetanus and diphtheria toxoids for use in children aged <7 years. Td = tetanus and diphtheria toxoids for use in persons aged ≥7 years. Td contains the same amount of tetanus toxoid as DTP or DT but a reduced dose of diphtheria toxoid.
††Boosters may be given intradermally unless acetone-killed and dried vaccine is used.

GUIDE FOR ADULT IMMUNIZATION
(Adapted from: Guide for Adult Immunization, American College of Physicians, 2nd Ed., Phil, PA 1-178,1990; MMWR 38:205-227,1989)

Category	Vaccine	Comments
AGE		
18-24 yrs	Td* (0.5 ml IM)	Booster every 10 yrs at mid-decades (age 25,35,45, etc) for those who completed primary series
	Measles** (MMR, 0.5 ml SC x 1 or 2	Post high school institutions should require two doses of live measles vaccine (separated by one month), the first dose preferably given prior to entry
	Mumps*** (MMR, 0.5 ml SC x 1)	Especially susceptible males
	Rubella*** (MMR, 0.5 ml SC x 1)	Especially susceptible females; pregnancy now or within 3 months post vaccination is contraindication to vaccination
	Influenza	Advocated for young adults at increased risk of exposure (military recruits, students in dorms, etc)
25-64 yrs	Td*	As above
	Mumps***	As above
	Measles** (MMR, 0.5 ml SC x 1)	Persons vaccinated between 1963 and 1967 may have received inactivated vaccine and should be revaccinated
	Rubella*** (MMR, 0.5 ml SC x 1)	Principally females ≤ 45 yrs with child-bearing potential; pregnancy now or within 3 months post vaccination is contraindication to vaccination
≥ 65 yrs	Td*	As above
	Influenza (0.5 ml IM)	Annually, usually in November
	Pneumococcal (23 valent, 0.5 ml IM)	Single dose; efficacy for elderly not established, but case control and epidemiology studies suggest 60-70% effectiveness in preventing pneumococcal bacteremia
SPECIAL GROUPS		
Pregnancy		All pregnant women should be screened for hepatitis B surface antigen (HBsAg) and rubella antibody
		Live virus vaccines**** should be avoided unless specifically indicated
		It is preferable to delay vaccines and toxoids until 2nd or 3rd trimester
		Immune globulins are safe; most vaccines are a theoretical risk only

(continued)

Category	Vaccine	Comments
	Td* (0.5 ml IM)	If not previously vaccinated - dose at 0, 4 wks (preferably 2nd and 3rd trimesters) and 6-12 mo.; boost at 10 yr intervals; protection to infant is conferred by placental transfer of maternal antibody
	Measles	Risk for premature labor and spontaneous abortion; exposed pregnant women who are susceptible** should receive immune globulin within 6 days and then MMR post delivery at least 3 months after immune globulin (MMR is contraindicated during pregnancy)
	Mumps	No sequelae noted, immune globulin is of no value and MMR is contraindicated
	Rubella	Rubella during 1st 16 wks carries great risk, e.g. 15-20% rate of neonatal death and 20-50% incidence of congenital rubella syndrome; history of rubella is unreliable indicator of immunity. Women exposed during 1st 20 weeks should have rubella serology and if not immune should be offered abortion.
	Hepatitis A	Immune globulin within two weeks of exposure
	Hepatitis B	All pregnant women should have prenatal screening for HBsAg; newborn infants of HBsAg carriers should receive HBIG and HBV vaccine; pregnant women who are HBsAg negative and at high risk should receive HBV vaccine
	Inactivated oral polio vaccine (0.5 ml SC)	Advised if exposure is imminent in women who completed the primary series over 10 yrs ago. Unimmunized women should receive 2 doses separated by 1-2 mo.; unimmunized women at high risk who need immediate protection should receive oral live polio vaccine
	Influenza Pneumococcal vaccine	Not routinely recommended, but can be given if there are other indications
	Varicella (VZIG, 12.5 U/kg IM)	Varicella-zoster immune globulin (VZIG) may prevent or modify maternal infection
<u>Family member exposure</u>		**Recommendations generally apply to household contacts**
	H. influenzae type B	H. influenzae meningitis: Rifampin prophylaxis for all household contacts in households with another child <4 yrs; contraindicated in pregnant women **(continued)**

Category	Vaccine	Comments
	Hepatitis A	Immune globulin within two weeks of exposure
	Hepatitis B	HBV vaccine (3 doses) for those with intimate contact and no serologic evidence of prior infection
	Influenza	Influenza case should be treated with amantadine to prevent spread; unimmunized high risk family members should receive amantadine (x 14 days) and vaccine.
	Meningococcal infection	Rifampin or sulfonamide for family contacts of meningococcal meningitis
	Varicella-zoster	No treatment unless immunocompromised: consider VZIG

ENVIRONMENTAL SETTINGS
Residents of nursing homes

	Influenza (0.5 ml IM)	Annually; vaccination rates of 80% required to prevent outbreaks
	Pneumococcal vaccine (23 valent, 0.5 ml IM	Single dose, efficacy not clearly established
	Td* (0.5 ml IM)	Booster dose at mid-decades

Residents of institutions for mentally retarded

	Hepatitis B	Screen all new admissions and long term residents: HBV vaccine for susceptibles (Seroprevalence rates are 30-80%)

Prison inmates	Hepatitis B	As above

Homeless	Td*	
	Measles, rubella, mumps	MMR 0.5 ml SC (young adults)
	Influenza	
	Pneumococcal vaccine	

OCCUPATIONAL GROUPS
Health care workers

	Hepatitis B (3 doses)	Personnel with contact with blood or blood products; serologic screening with vaccination only of seronegatives is optional; serologic studies show 5% are nonresponders (neg for anti-HBs) even with repeat vaccinations
	Influenza	Annual
	Rubella (MMR, 0.5 ml SC)	Personnel who might transmit rubella to pregnant patients or other health care workers should have documented immunity or vaccination

74   (continued)

Category	Vaccine	Comments
	Mumps (MMR, 0.5 ml SC)	Personnel with no documented history of mumps or mumps vaccine should be vaccinated
	Measles (MMR, 0.5 ml SC)	Personnel who do not have immunity** should be vaccinated; those vaccinated in or after 1957 should receive an additional dose and those who are unvaccinated should receive 2 doses separated by at least one month; during outbreak in medical setting vaccinate (or revaccinate) all health care workers with direct patient contact
	Polio	Persons with incomplete primary series should receive inactivated polio vaccine
Immigrants and refugees		
	Td*	Immunize if not previously done
	Rubella, Measles, Mumps	Most have been vaccinated or had these conditions, although MMR is advocated except for pregnant women
	Polio	Adults will usually be immune
	Hepatitis B	Screen for HBsAg and vaccinate family members and sexual partners of carriers; screening is especially important for pregnant women

LIFESTYLES

Homosexual men

	Hepatitis B	Prevaccination serologic screening advocated since 30-80% have serologic evidence of HBV markers

IV drug abusers

	Hepatitis B	As above; seroprevalence rates of HBV marker are 50-80%

IMMUNODEFICIENCY

HIV infection	Measles	Postexposure prophylaxis with immune globulin (0.25 ml/kg IM)
	Pneumococcal vaccine	Recommended
	H. influenzae b conjugate vaccine	Consider
	Influenza (0.5 ml IM)	Annual; consider amantadine during epidemics
Asplenia	Pneumococcal vaccine (23 valent, 0.5 ml IM)	Recommended, preferably given 2 weeks before elective splenectomy; revaccinate those who received the 14 valent vaccine and those vaccinated > 6 yrs previously

(continued)

Category	Vaccine	Comments
Renal failure	Hepatitis B	For patients whose renal disease is likely to result in dialysis or transplantation; double dose and periodic boosters advocated
	Pneumococcal vaccine	Pneumococcal vaccine
	Influenza	Annual
Alcoholics		
	Pneumococcal vaccine	
	Hepatitis B	Consider
TRAVEL* (Recommendations of Med Lett 32:33,1990)		For travelers to developed countries (Canada, Europe, Japan, Australia, New Zealand) the risk of developing vaccine-preventable disease is no greater than for traveling in the U.S.
		Each country has its own vaccine requirements
		Smallpox vaccination is no longer required and should not be given
	Yellow fever (see MMWR 39: RR6,1990)	Recommended for endemic area: Tropical S. America and most of Africa between 15° North & 15° South
		Available in U.S. only at sites designated by local or state health departments
		Contraindications: Immunocompromised host; pregnancy is a relative contraindication (live virus vaccine)
	Cholera	Consider only for travelers to highly endemic area and to countries that require vaccination because risk is low and vaccine has limited effectiveness (Lancet 1:270,1990)
	Typhoid fever	Recommended for travel to rural areas of countries where typhoid fever is endemic or any area of an outbreak. The live oral vaccine is preferred over the parenteral vaccine and is available from Berna Products (305-443-2900) (Lancet 1: 1049,1987)
	Hepatitis A	Immune globulin for susceptible travelers to areas with poor sanitation conditions; especially if contact with small children or work in health care areas; dose is 0.02 ml//kg (or 2 ml) IM for travel < 3 mo. and 0.06 ml/kg (or 5 ml) IM for travel > 3 mo. Repeat dose q 4-6 mo. while in endemic area. Susceptibility may be determined with tests for IgG antibody that are widely available (Lancet 1:1447,1988).

Category	Vaccine	Comments
	Hepatitis B	HBV vaccine if travel to endemic areas, and travel > 6 mo., sexual contact with local persons is likely or if contact with blood is likely. Major risk areas are Southeast Asia and sub-Saharan Asia.
	Rabies	Consider human diploid cell rabies vaccine (HDCV) or rabies vaccine absorbed (RVA) for extended travel to endemic area
	Japanese encephalitis (1 ml SC x 3 1-2 wks apart)	Vaccine recommended for prolonged travel to areas experiencing an epidemic, especially if there is likely to be extensive mosquito exposure. Potential problem countries include China, Korea, Taiwan, Thailand, Viet Nam, India, Nepal, Sri Lanka and the Philippines (NEJM 319:641,1988). Available through U.S. embassies in Asia
	Measles	Susceptible persons** should receive a single dose prior to travel
	Meningococcal vaccine	Recommended for travel to areas of epidemics, such as Kenya and Tanzania (MMWR 39:13,1990)
	Polio	Travelers to developing countries should receive a primary series of inactivated polio vaccine if not previously immunized

* Td - Diphtheria and tetanus toxoids absorbed (for adult use). Primary series is 0.5 ml IM at 0, 4 wks and 6-12 months; booster doses at 10 year intervals are single doses of 0.5 ml IM. Adults who have not received at least 3 doses of Td should complete the primary series.

** Persons are considered immune to measles if there is documentation of receipt of two doses of live measles vaccine after the first birthday, prior physician diagnosis of measles, laboratory evidence of measles immunity or birth before 1957.

*** Persons are considered immune to mumps if they have a record of adequate vaccination, documented physician diagnosed disease, laboratory evidence of immunity. Persons are considered immune to rubella if they have a record of vaccination after their first birthday or laboratory evidence of immunity. (A physician diagnosis of rubella is considered non-specific.)

** ***The preferred vaccine for persons susceptible to measles, mumps or rubella is MMR given as 0.5 ml SC for measles (one or two doses), mumps (one dose) or rubella (one dose). Pregnant women should not be vaccinated until after delivery.

**** Live virus vaccines = measles, rubella, yellow fever, oral polio vaccine

Influenza Vaccine (Recommendations of the Advisory Committee on Immunization Practice: MMWR 36:373-387,1987;37:361-373,1988; 38:183-185,297-311,1989, 39:293-296,1990; 39:RR-7,1-15,1990)

Preparations: Inactivated egg grown viruses that may be split (chemically treated to reduce febrile reactions in children) or whole. Preparations for the 1990-91 season contain 15 ug each of A/Taiwan/1/86 (H1N1), A/Shanghai/6/89 (H3N2) and B/Yamagata/16/89 per 0.5 ml dose. Product information available from Connaught (800) 822-2463, Parke Davis (800) 223-0432 and Wyeth (800) 321-2304. A history of prior vaccination in any prior year does not preclude the need for revaccination. Remaining 1989-90 season vaccine should not be used.

Administration (over 12 years): Whole or split virus vaccine, 0.5 ml x 1 IM in the deltoid muscle, preferrably in November and as early as September.

Target groups

1. Groups at greatest risk
   a. Adults and children with chronic disorders of the cardiovascular or pulmonary systems requiring regular medical following or hospitalization during the prior year.
   b. Residents of nursing homes or other chronic care facilities housing patients of any age with chronic medical conditions.

2. Groups at moderate risk
   a. Healthy individuals over 65 years.
   b. Persons who required regular medical following or hospitalization during prior year due to chronic metabolic disease (including diabetes mellitus), renal dysfunction, hemoglobinopathy or immunosuppression).
   c. Children (6 mo to 18 yrs) receiving long term aspirin treatment and therefore at risk for Reye's syndrome with influenza.

3. Persons capable of transmitting nosocomial influenza to high risk groups
   a. Physicians, nurses and other health care workers having extensive contact with high risk patients.
   b. Providers of care to high risk persons.
   c. Household members of high risk persons.

4. Persons with HIV infection

5. Others: Any persons who wish to reduce chances of influenza, especially those providing essential community services, students and others in institutional settings.

Contraindications
1. Severe allergy to eggs.
2. Persons with febrile illness (delay until symptoms abate).
3. Pregnancy is not viewed as a contraindication in women with high risk conditions, but it is preferred to vaccinate after the first trimester unless the first trimester corresponds to the influenza season.

Adverse reactions:
1. Soreness at the vaccination site for up to 2 days.
2. Fever, malaise, etc. - infrequent and most common in those not previously exposed in influenza antigens, e.g. young children.
3. Allergic reactions - rare and include hives, angioedema, asthma, anaphylaxis; usually allergy to egg protein.

Measles Prevention (Revised Recommendations of the Advisory Committee on Immunization Practices (MMWR 38:S-9, 1989)

Recommendations

Routine childhood schedule	Two doses*, 1st at 12 months (high risk area) or 15 months (most areas); 2nd dose at 4-6 yrs.
Colleges and other educational institutions	Documentation of receipt of two doses after first birthday or other evidence of immunity**
Medical personnel beginning employment	Documentation of two doses after first birthday or other evidence of immunity**
Outbreaks in institutions	Revaccinate all students, their siblings and school personnel who do not have proof of immunity
Outbreaks in medical facilities	Revaccinate all medical workers born after 1956 who have direct patient contact and do not have evidence of immunity; exposed personnel who are susceptible should avoid patient contact 5th to 21st day after exposure or, if infected, for 7 days.
Exposures	Vaccine preferred if given < 72 h after exposure. Alternative: immune globulin (0.25 ml/kg IM, maximum 15 ml) is acceptable if given within 6 days.

* Preferably as MMR.
** Born before 1957, physician diagnosed measles or laboratory evidence of measles immunity (persons with measles-specific antibody detected by any test are considered immune).

Rabies Vaccine (Recommendation of Advisory Committee on Immunization Practice) (MMWR 33:393-402,407-408,1984 and 37:217-218,1988)

Indications for post-exposure antirabies treatment

a. <u>Type of exposure</u>: Primarily bite; less frequently by saliva exposure to cuts, wounds of skin or mucous membranes; aerosol exposure is rare mechanism of transmission.

b. <u>Animal species</u>: Primarily carnivorous wild animals (especially raccoons, skunks, foxes and bats in the U.S.); dogs and cats are rarely infected in the U.S., but are common in some underdeveloped countries; rodents are rarely infected.

c. <u>Circumstances of exposure</u>: An unprovoked attack is most suspect.

Treatment

a. <u>Unimmunized persons</u>:
Rabies immune globulin (RIG) 20 IU/kg with 1/2 dose infiltrated into wound site and remainder IM in the gluteal area <u>plus</u> human diploid cell rabies vaccine (HDVC) IM (deltoid) in five 1 ml doses on days 0,3,7,14 and 28.

b. <u>Immunized persons</u> (pre-exposure immunization with any rabies vaccine and history of documented antibody response):
Two doses of HDVC IM (deltoid) in two 1 ml doses on days 0 and 3.

c. <u>Pre-exposure vaccination</u>: Three 1 ml doses HDVC IM in deltoid on days 0,7 and 28.

d. <u>Rabies Vaccine Adsorbed (RVA)</u> is a new cell culture-derived rabies vaccine licensed 3/88 for pre- and post-exposure prophylaxis. Timing of vaccination is identical to that for HDCV: **a)** pre-exposure - three 1.0 mL doses IM in deltoid on days 0,7 and 28; **b)** post-exposure - five 1.0 mL doses IM in deltoid on days 0,3,7,14 and 28. RIG is given as described above.

Side effects of HDVC and RVA

Local reactions are common.

Mild reactions (headache, abdominal pain, nausea, dizziness, etc): 10-20%

Allergic reactions (hives to anaphylaxis): 1/1000.

Tetanus Prophylaxis (MMWR 39:39,1990)

History of Tetanus toxoid	Clean, minor wounds		Other wounds**	
	Td*	TIG*	Td*	TIG*
Unknown or < 3 doses	Yes	No	Yes	Yes
≥ 3 doses	No, unless > 10 yrs since last dose	No	No, unless > 5 yrs since last dose	No

*Td = Tetanus toxoid; TIG = Tetanus immune globulin
**Wounds contaminated with dirt, stool, soil, saliva, etc;
  puncture wounds; avulsions; wounds from missiles, crushing,
  burns and frostbite.

Pneumococcal Vaccine - Advisory Committee on Immunization Practices, Center For Disease Control, American Thoracic Society, The Infectious Diseases Society of America, American College of Physicians: MMWR 38:64-76,1989 and Guide for Adult Immunization ACP (2nd Edition) - 91-96, 1990.

Vaccine: 23 valent polysaccharide vaccine for the S. pneumoniae serotypes responsible for 87% of bacteremic pneumococcal disease in the U.S.

Recommendations for adults
1. Immunocompetent adults at increased risk of pneumococcal disease or its complications due to chronic illness (e.g. cardiovascular disease, pulmonary disease, diabetes, alcoholism, cirrhosis, renal failure, chronic liver disease or cerebrospinal fluid leaks) or who are ≥ 65 years old.

2. Immunocompromised adults at increased risk of pneumococcal disease or its complications (e.g. splenic dysfunction or anatomic asplenia, lymphoma, Hodgkin's disease, multiple myeloma, cancer chemotherapy, organ transplant recipients, HIV infection and conditions associated with immunosuppression).

   Notations: 1) Vaccine should be given at least 2 weeks before elective splenectomy; 2) Vaccine should be given as long as possible before planned immunosuppressive treatment; 3) Hospital discharge is a convenient time for vaccination since 2/3's of patients with serious pneumococcal infections have been hospitalized within the prior 5 years; 4) May be given simultaneously with influenza vaccine (separate injection sites).

Adverse reactions
1. Pain and erythema at injection site: 50%
2. Fever, myalgia, severe local reaction: < 1%
3. Anaphylactoid reactions: 5/million

Revaccination: Should be strongly considered for high risk patients vaccinated 6 or more years previously; revaccination after 3-5 years is recommended for transplant recipients, patients with renal failure and patients with nephrotic syndrome.

Hepatitis Vaccine (Recommendations of the Advisory Council on Immunization Practices) (MMWR 39:RR-2, 1-26, 1990)

1. <u>HAV</u>: Immune globulin (IG)

	Dose ml/kg IM	<u>Frequency</u>
a. Pre-exposure		
Workers with non-human primates	0.06	q 4-6 mo.
Travelers to developing countries		
Visit less than 3 mo.	0.02	Once
Visit over 3 mo.	0.02	q 4-6 mo.

   b. Post-exposure (must be given within two weeks of exposure)

> Close personal contacts and sexual partners
>
> Day care centers: Staff and attendees when one case or at least two cases in families of attendees
>
> Institutions for custodial care: Residents with staff with close contact with cases
>
> Common source exposure: food and waterborne outbreaks if recognized within the 2 week post-exposure period of effectiveness
>
> Food handlers: Other food handlers, but not patrons unless uncooked food was handled without gloves and patrons can be located within 2 weeks of exposure
>
> Hospitals: Not recommended for hospital personnel

        0.02   Once

2. <u>Hepatitis B</u> (MMWR 36:353-366,1987; MMWR 37:342-351,1987; MMWR 39:1-26,1990):

   a. <u>Vaccine preparations</u>

       (1) Heptavax B: Plasma-derived vaccine available since 6/82; 20 ug HBsAg/ml; use is now restricted to hemodialysis patients, other immunocompromised hosts and persons with yeast allergy.

       (2) Recombivax HB: Recombinant vaccine produced by <u>Saccharomyces cerevisiae</u> (baker's yeast) and available since 7/86; 10 or 40 ug HBsAg/ml; usual adult dose is 3 1 ml doses (10 ug) at 0, 1 and 6 mo.

       (3) Engerix-B: Recombinant vaccine available since 1989; 20 ug HBsAg/ml; usual adult dose regimen is 3 1 ml doses (20 ug) at 0, 1 and 2 months; alternative schedule is 4 1 ml doses (20 ug) at 0, 1, 2 and 12 mo. (for more rapid induction of immunity)

   b. <u>Pre-exposure vaccination:</u>

       (1) <u>Regimen</u>: Three IM doses (deltoid) at 0 time, 1 month and 6 months. The usual adult dose is 1 ml (20 ug Engerix B or 10 ug of Recombivax HB); hemodialysis patients and possibly other immunocompromised patients should receive 2-4x the usual adult dose (usually 40 ug doses) or 4 doses.

(2) <u>Response rates</u>: > 90% of healthy adults develop adequate antibody response (> 10 milli Internat. Units/ml) and field trials show 80-95% efficacy.

(3) <u>Revaccination</u>: Revaccination of non-responders will produce response in 15-25% with one additional dose and in 30-50% with 3 doses. 30-50% of responders lose detectable antibody within 7 years, although implications for revaccination are unclear.

(4) <u>Prevaccination serologic testing</u>: Testing groups at highest risk is usually cost effective if the prevalence of HBV markers is > 20% (see table). Routine testing usually consists of one antibody test: either anti-HBc or anti-HBs. Anti-HBc detects both carriers (HBsAg) and non-carriers (anti-HBsAg), but does not distinguish between them.

<u>Prevalence of hepatitis B serologic markers</u>

Population group	Prevalence of serologic markers of HBV infection	
	HBsAg (%)	Any marker (%)
Immigrants/refugees from areas of high HBV endemicity	13	70-85
Alaskan Natives/Pacific Islanders	5-15	40-70
Clients in institutions for the developmentally disabled	10-20	35-80
Users of illicit parenteral drugs	7	60-80
Sexually active homosexual men	6	35-80
Household contacts of HBV carriers	3-6	30-60
Patients of hemodialysis units	3-10	20-80
Health-care workers - frequent blood contact	1-2	15-30
Prisoners (male)	1-8	10-80
Staff of institutions for the developmentally disabled	1	10-25
Heterosexuals with multiple partners	0.5	5-20
Health-care workers - no or infrequent blood contact	0.3	3-10
General population (NHANES II)		
Blacks	0.9	14
Whites	0.2	3

(5) <u>Candidates for vaccination</u>
Health care personnel exposed to blood and body fluids
Residents and staff of facilities for developmentally handicapped
Hemodialysis patients
IV drug abusers
Homosexual and bisexual men who are sexually active

Patients with hemoglobulinemias and clotting disorders
requiring long term use of high risk plasma derivatives
Household and sexual contacts of HBV carriers
Miscellaneous groups for whom vaccine should be considered:
inmates of long term correctional facilities; heterosexually
active persons with multiple sexual partners; international
travelers to HBV endemic areas

c. <u>Pregnant women</u>: All pregnant women should be tested for
HBsAg during an early prenatal visit; infants born to HBsAg
positive mothers should receive HBIG (0.5 ml) IM x 1
(preferably within 12 hours of delivery) and HB vaccine (0.5
ml) x 3 (10 ug plasma derived or 5 ug recombinant) at 0 time
(concurrent with HBIG), at 1 month and at 6 months. Test
infant for HBsAg and anti-HBs at 12-15 mo.

d. <u>Post-exposure vaccination</u>: (MMWR 39:RR-2,1990)
(1) Percutaneous or needlestick exposures

	Treatment when source is found to be:		
Exposed person	HBsAg-positive	HBsAg-negative	Source not tested or unknown
Unvaccinated	HBIG x 1* and initiate HB vaccine†	Initiate HB vaccine†	Initiate HB vaccine†
Previously vaccinated Known responder	Test exposed for anti-HBs 1. If adequate,$ no treatment 2. If inadequate, HB vaccine booster dose	No treatment	No treatment
Known nonresponder	HBIG x 2 or HBIG x 1 plus 1 dose HB vaccine	No treatment	If known high-risk source, *may treat as if source were HBsAg-positive*
Response unknown	Test exposed for anti-HBs 1. if inadequate,$ HBIG x 1 plus HB vaccine booster dose 2. If adequate, no treatment	No treatment	Test exposed for anti-HBs 1. If inadequate$, HB vaccine booster dose 2. If adequate, no treatment

*HBIG dose 0.06 ml/kg IM.
†HB vaccine dose - see 2a
$Adequate anti-HBs is ≥10 SRU by RIA or positive by EIA.

(2) Perinatal or sexual exposures

	HBIG		Vaccine	
Exposure	Dose	Recommended timing	Dose	Recommended timing
Perinatal	0.5 ml IM	Within 12 hours of birth	0.5 ml IM*	Within 12 hours of birth†
Sexual	0.06 ml/kg IM	Single dose within 14 days of last sexual contact	1.0 ml IM*	First dose at time of HBIG treatment†

* Dose is 0.5 ml of all three preparation (2a) for infants.
Adult dose is 1.0 ml of all three preparations for adults.
† Separate injection sites.

PROPHYLACTIC ANTIBIOTICS IN SURGERY

Antimicrobial Agents in Surgery (Adapted from the Medical Letter 31:105-108,1989 and Kaiser AB: N Engl J Med 315:1129-1138,1986)

Type of Surgery	Preferred regimen	Alternative	Comment
CARDIOTHORACIC			
Cardiovascular: Coronary by-pass; valve surgery	Cefazolin 1 gm IV pre-op (and 6qh x 48h)*	Vancomycin** 15 mg/kg IV pre-op, after initiation of by-pass (10 mg/kg) (and q8h x 48h)	Single doses appear to be as effective as multiple doses providing high serum concentrations are maintained throughout the procedure. Some specialists prefer cefamandole or cefuroxime to cefazolin.
Pacemaker insertion	Cefazolin as above (see comments)	No alternative	Single doses appear to be as effective as multiple doses. Prophylaxis advocated only for centers with high infection rates.
Peripheral vascular surgery	Cefazolin 1 gm IV pre-op (and q6h x 48h)*	Vancomycin** 15 mg/kg (and q8h x 48 h)	Recommended for procedures on abdominal aorta and procedures on leg that include groin incision. Some recommend prophylaxis for any implantation of prosthetic material or vascular access in hemodialysis.
Thoracic surgery: lobectomy, pneumonectomy	Cefazolin 1 gm IV pre-op (and q6h x 48h)*		Optimal duration is unknown. Antibiotic prophylaxis is not recommended for thoracic trauma or chest tube insertion.
GASTROINTESTINAL			
Gastric surgery	Cefazolin 1 gm IV pre-op	Clindamycin 600 mg IV + gentamicin 1.5 mg/kg	Advocated only for high risk - bleeding ulcer, gastric cancer, gastric by-pass and percutaneous endoscopic gastrostomy. Prophylactic antibiotics are not indicated for uncomplicated duodenal ulcer surgery. (continued)

85

Type of Surgery	Preferred regimen	Alternative	Comment
Biliary tract	Cefazolin 1 gm IV pre-op	Gentamicin 1.5 mg/kg pre-op and q8h x 3	Advocated only for high risk - acute cholecystitis, obstructive jaundice, common duct stones, age over 70 yrs.
Colorectal	Neomycin 1 gm po and erythromycin 1 gm po at 1 pm, 2 pm and 11 pm the day before surgery (19,18 and 11 hrs pre-op) or Clindamycin 600 mg IV plus gentamicin 1.5 mg/kg pre-op	Cefoxitin 1-2 gm IV or Clindamycin 600 mg IV plus gentamicin 1.5 mg/kg IV or Metronidazole 500 mg IV plus gentamicin 1.5 mg/kg IV	Some advocate the combined use of an oral and parenteral prep, especially for low anterior resection. Some advocate 3 subsequent doses of parenteral agents at 8 hr intervals.
Penetrating trauma abdomen	Cefoxitin 2 gm IV pre-op (and 1-5 days post-op - see comments)	Metronidazole 500 mg (see comments)	Patients with intestinal perforation should receive these agents for 2-5 days.
Appendectomy	Cefoxitin 1 gm IV pre-op (and 1-5 days post-op - see comments)	Metronidazole 500 mg (see comments)	For perforated or gangrenous appendix continue regimen for 3-5 days. For non-perforated appendix 1-4 doses are adequate.
Laparotomy, lysis of adhesions, splenectomy, etc. without GI tract surgery	None		
GYNECOLOGY AND OBSTETRICS Vaginal and abdominal hysterectomy	Cefazolin 1 gm IV pre-op (and q8h x 2)*	Doxycycline 200 mg IV	Single dose appears to be as effective as multiple doses.
Cesarean section	Cefazolin 1 gm IV after clamping cord (and q6h x 2)*	Metronidazole 500 mg IV or uterine irrigation with cefoxitin 2 gm in 1L normal saline	Advocated for high risk only - active labor, premature rupture of membranes.

(continued) |

86

Type of Surgery	Preferred regimen	Alternative	Comment
Abortion			
First trimester with prior PID	Aqueous penicillin G 1 million units IV pre-op	Doxycycline 300 mg po	Some advocate a second dose of penicillin at 3 hrs post procedure.
Second trimester	Cefazolin 1 gm IV pre-op	Metronidazole 500 mg po pre-op	Some advocate two additional doses.
Dilation and curettage	None		
Tubal ligation	None		
Cystocele or rectocele repair	None		
HEAD AND NECK			
Tonsillectomy ± adenoidectomy	None		
Rhinoplasty	None		
Major surgery with entry via oral cavity or pharynx	Cefazolin 2 gm IV pre-op	Clindamycin 600 mg IV plus gentamicin 1.5 mg/kg IV pre-op and q8h x 2	Controlled study shows cefazolin dose of 2 gm superior to 0.5 gm (Ann Surg 207:108,1988).
ORTHOPEDIC SURGERY			
Joint replacement	Cefazolin 1 gm IV pre-op (and q6h x 3 doses)*	Vancomycin** 1 gm IV	Cefazolin dose should be 2 gm for knee replacement with tourniquet.
Open reduction of fracture/ internal fixation	Cefazolin 1 gm IV (and q6h x 3 doses)*		Open fractures are considered contaminated and should be treated with cefazolin 1 gm IV/IM q8h x 10 days*. (continued)

87

Type of Surgery	Preferred regimen	Alternative	Comment
Amputation of leg	Cefoxitin 1 IV pre-op (and q6h x 48h)*		
NEUROSURGERY			
Cerebrospinal fluid shunt	Trimethoprim 160 mg plus sulfamethoxazole 800 mg IV pre-op and q12 h x 3 doses		Efficacy of antimicrobials not established.
Craniotomy	Vancomycin 1 gm IV plus gentamicin 1.5 mg/kg	Clindamycin 300 mg IV and at 4 hr	Efficacy not clearly established. Advocated for pre-op high risk procedures - re-exploration and microsurgery.
Spinal surgery	None		
Ocular	Gentamicin or tobramycin topically for 2-24 hrs before surgery	Neomycin, gramicidin and polymyxin B topically 2-24 hrs pre-op	Some give subconjunctival injection (gentamicin, 10-20 mg ± cefazolin 100 mg) at end of surgery.
UROLOGY			
Prostatectomy			
Sterile urine	None		
Infected urine	Continue agent active in vitro or give single pre-operative dose		Sterilization of urine before surgery is preferred.
Prostatic biopsy	None		
Dilation of urethra	None		

(continued)

88

Type of Surgery	Preferred regimen	Alternative	Comment
MISCELLANEOUS			
Inguinal hernia repair	None		One study showed benefit of cefonicid, 1 gm IV 30 min. pre-op (R. Platt et al. NEJM 322:153,1990).
Mastectomy	None		One study showed benefit of cefonicid for breast surgery (R. Platt et al. NEJM 322: 153,1990).
Traumatic wound	Cefazolin 1 gm IV q8h		

* Single dose generally considered adequate; for dirty surgery, treatment should be continued 5-10 days.

** Vancomycin preferred for hospitals with a high rate of wound infections caused by methicillin-resistant S. aureus or S. epidermidis, and for patients with allergy to penicillins or cephalosporins.

**PROPHYLACTIC ANTIBIOTICS TO PREVENT ENDOCARDITIS IN THE
SUSCEPTIBLE HOST**
**Recommendations based on guidelines from the Committee on Prevention of
Rheumatic Fever and Bacterial Endocarditis of the American Heart Association
(Circulation 70:1123A-1127A,1984) and Medical Letter consultants
(Medical Letter on Drugs and Therapeutics 29:107,1987)**

A. **Patients to receive prophylaxis** (list is not considered all inclusive)

1. Valvular heart disease

    a. Prosthetic valve (including biosynthetic valves)

    b. Rheumatic valve disease (history of rheumatic fever without
        valve disease is not an indication)

    c. Congenital valve disease; an exception is uncomplicated atrial
        septal defect

    d. Prior history of endocarditis

2. Mitral valve prolapse if associated with a mitral insufficiency
    murmur

3. Idiopathic hypertrophic subaortic stenosis

4. Surgically constructed systemic-pulmonary shunts

B. **Procedures with established or suspected risk**

1. Respiratory tract

    a. All dental procedures likely to cause gingival bleeding

    b. Tonsillectomy and/or adenoidectomy

    c. Surgical procedures or biopsy of the respiratory mucosa

    d. Bronchoscopy, especially with a rigid bronchoscope (risk with
        flexible bronchoscope is low)

    e. Incision and drainage of infected tissue

2. Gastrointestinal and genitourinary tract

    a. Surgery or instrumentation of the genitourinary tract and
        gastrointestinal tract

        (1) Urology: Cystoscopy, prostatic surgery, urethral
             catheterization (especially with urinary tract infection),
             GU tract surgery

        (2) Gastrointestinal tract: Esophageal dilatation, gallbladder
             surgery, scleral therapy of varices, colonic surgery

        (3) Endoscopy: Upper GI endoscopy with biopsy,
             proctosigmoidoscopy with biopsy

   b.   Incision and drainage of infected tissue

   c.   Prophylaxis is not recommended for percutaneous liver biopsy,
        GI endoscopy without biopsy, barium enema, uncomplicated
        vaginal delivery, brief ("in and out") urinary catheterization
        with sterile urine, cesarean section, therapeutic abortions,
        uterine dilatation and curettage, sterilization procedures,
        insertion of IUD.

   d.   The risk appears enhanced for patients with prosthetic valves
        or surgically constructed systemic-pulmonary shunts. The
        Committee recommends only parenteral regimens and more
        liberal use of prophylaxis for these patients.

C. **Regimens** (Medical Letter 31:112,1989)

   1.   Procedures involving dental work and the respiratory tract

            Pre-procedure   Subsequent doses

   a.   Parenteral
        (1) Ampicillin, 2 gm IM or   Options: Repeat parenteral
        IV 30 min pre-procedure   regimen 8 hrs later; give
        plus gentamicin, 1.5 mg/kg   penicillin V, 1 gm po 8
        IM or IV 30 min   hr later, or give no
        pre-procedure   further antibiotics
                                          (Medical Letter
                                          consultants do not
                                          recommend the second dose)

        (2) Penicillin allergy: None
        Vancomycin, 1 gm IV
        infused slowly over 1 hr
        starting 1 hr prior to
        procedure

   b.   Oral (not recommended for
        patients with prosthetic
        valves, prior endocarditis
        or patients receiving
        penicillin prophylaxis for
        rheumatic fever)

        (1) Amoxicillin, 3 gm po   Amoxicillin, 1.5 gm po 6
        1 hr pre-procedure   hr later

        (2) Penicillin allergy: Erythromycin, 500 mg po
        Erythromycin, 1 gm po   6 hr later
        2 hr pre-procedure

2. Procedures involving GI or GU tract

| | Pre-procedure | Subsequent doses |

a. Parenteral

    (1) Ampicillin, 2 gm IM or   None
IV 30 min pre-procedure
plus gentamicin, 1.5 mg/kg
IM or IV 30 min pre-
procedure

    (2) Penicillin allergy: None
Vancomycin, 1 gm infused
over 1 hr beginning 1 hr
pre-procedure plus
gentamicin, 1.5 mg/kg IM
or IV 30 min pre-procedure

b. Oral (not recommended for
patients with prosthetic
valves, prior endocarditis
or for patients receiving
oral penicillin prophylaxis
for rheumatic fever)

    Amoxicillin, 3 gm po   Amoxicillin, 1.5 gm po
    1 hr pre-procedure   6 hr later

D. Endocarditis Prophylaxis: Recommendations of the Endocarditis Working Party of the British Society for Antimicrobial Chemotherapy. (Lancet 1:88-89,1990)

    A. Dental extractions, scaling or periodontal surgery

        1. No anesthesia or local anesthesia

            a. Amoxicillin, 3 gm po 1 hr pre-procedure

           Penicillin allergy:

            b. Erythromycin stearate, 1.5 gm po 1-2 hrs pre-procedure or clindamycin, 600 mg po 1 hr pre-procedure

        2. General anesthesia

            a. Amoxicillin, 1 gm IM (in 2.5 ml 1% lidocaine) with induction and 0.5 gm po 6 hrs later or

            b. Amoxicillin, 3 gm po 4 hrs before induction and 3 gm po as soon as possible post-op or

            c. Amoxicillin, 3 gm plus probenecid, 1 gm po 4 hr pre-op

3. Special risk patients who should be referred to hospital:
(1) patients with prosthetic valves who are to have general anesthesia; (2) patients who are to have general anesthesia and are allergic to penicillin or who have received penicillin at least once during the previous month; (3) patients who had had endocarditis

   a. Amoxicillin, 1 gm IM (in 2.5 ml 1% lidocaine) plus gentamicin, 120 mg with induction of anesthesia; amoxicillin, 1.5 gm 6 hr later

   Penicillin allergic or penicillin within prior month:

   b. Vancomycin, 1 gm IV over 60 min followed by gentamicin, 120 mg IV with anesthesia

B. Surgery or instrumentation on upper respiratory tract: 1a or 3b, but post-operative antibiotic may have to be IM or IV if swallowing is painful

C. Genitourinary surgery or instrumentation:
Infected urine: Cover organism in urine
Sterile urine: Cover enterococcus, 3a or 3b

D. Obstetrical and gynecological procedures: PLUS prosthetic valve: 3a or 3b

E. Gastrointestinal procedures: PLUS prosthetic valve: 3a or 3b

TRAVELER'S DIARRHEA
(Adapted from NIH Consensus Development Panel, 1985, See JAMA 253:2700,1985;
and Medical Letter 32:33-34,1990)

Risk: High risk areas (incidence 20-50%): developing countries of Latin
America, Africa, Middle East and Asia

Intermediate risk: Southern Europe and some Caribbean islands

Low risk: Canada, Northern Europe, Australia, New Zealand, United
States

Agents

Bacteria	Viruses
E. coli (enterotoxigenic,* enteroinvasive, enteroadherent)	Norwalk agent
	Rotavirus (?)
Salmonella	
Shigella	Parasites
Campylobacter jejuni	Giardia lamblia
Aeromonas hydrophila	Entamoeba histolytica
Plesiomonas shigelloides	
Vibrio cholerae (non-01)	
Vibrio fluvialis	
Vibrio parahaemolytica	

* Most common

Prevention

Food and beverages: Risky foods - Raw vegetables, raw meat or raw seafood,
tapwater, ice, unpasteurized milk and dairy products and unpeeled fruit

Preventative agents with documented efficacy (efficacy of 50-85%)
Doxycycline: 100 mg po/day (photosensitivity reactions)
Sulfa-trimethoprim: 1 DS (double strength) tab po/day (serious skin
reactions and hematological reactions reported).
Trimethoprim: 200 mg po/day
Ciprofloxacin: 500 mg po/day
Norfloxacin: 400 mg po/day
Bismuth subsalicylate (Pepto-Bismol): 2 300 mg tabs qid

Treatment

Oral intake to maintain fluid and electrolyte balance:
Potable fruit juice, caffeine-free soft drinks, salted crackers.
For severe symptoms: WHO oral replacement solution that may be
formulated by -

Ingredients/L or qt. water
NaCl: 3.5 gm (3/4 tsp)
$NaHCO_3$ (baking soda): 2.5 gm (1 tsp)
KCl: 1.5 g (1 cup orange juice or 2 bananas)
Sucrose (table sugar): 40 gm (4 level tbsp)

Diphenoxylate (Lomotil) (2.5 mg tabs po 3-4 x daily)
Loperamide (Imodium) (4 mg, then 2 mg after each loose stool to
    maximum of 16 mg/day)
Bismuth subsalicylate (Pepto-Bismol) (30 ml or 2 tabs q 30 min x 8)

Antimicrobial agents (empiric selection)
Sulfa-trimethoprim: 1 DS tab bid x 5 days or 2 DS x 1
Trimethoprim: 200 mg po bid x 5 days
Doxycycline: 100 mg po bid x 5 days
Ciprofloxacin: 500 mg po bid x 5 days
Norfloxacin: 400 mg po bid x 5 days
Combination: Sulfa-trimethoprim, 1 DS bid x 3 days plus Loperamide
(above dose), appears more effective than either drug alone (JAMA
263:257,1990).

Panel Recommendations

1. Prophylactic drugs are not recommended (but prophylactic antimicrobial
    agents appear most cost-effective; see Reves RR et al: Arch Intern Med
    148:2421,1988).

2. Travelers to risk areas should carry antimotility drugs (diphenoxylate or
    loperamide) or bismuth subsalicylate and an antimicrobial agent (sulfa-
    trimethoprim, trimethoprim or doxycycline).

    a. Mild diarrhea (less than 3 stools/day, without blood, pus or fever):
        Loperamide, diphenyoxylate or bismuth subsalicylate in doses noted
        above

    b. Moderate or severe diarrhea: Antimicrobial agent (regimens noted above)
        Note: Recent report showed superior results with trimethoprim-
        sulfamethoxazole (1 DS bid po) x 3 days plus loperamide (4 mg loading
        dose, then 2 mg with each loose stool). (Ericsson CD et al. JAMA
        263:257,1990).

    c. Persistent diarrhea with serious fluid loss, fever or stools showing blood
        or mucus: Seek medical attention.

3. Instruct patients regarding
    Dietary precautions for prevention
    Oral rehydration
    Use of drugs including side effects

INTERNATIONAL TRAVELER'S HOTLINE

CDC 24 hr/day automated telephone system with advice for international
travelers concerning malaria, food and water precautions, traveler's diarrhea,
immunizations for children < 2 years, pregnant travelers disease outbreaks and
vaccine requirements by geographic area. Call (404) 332-4559. Health Information
for International Travel 1990 edition is available at $5.00/copy from
Superintendent of Documents, U.S. Government Printing Office, Washington, D.C.
20402, (202) 783-3238, stock no. 017-023-00187-6.

Immunizations: See page 76-77

Malaria Prophylaxis and Treatment (MMWR 39:1-10,1990 and The Medical Letter on Drugs and Therapeutics 31:13,1990)

Centers for Disease Control Malaria Hotline: (404) 332-4555

Risk areas: Most areas of Central and South America, Hispaniola, sub-Saharan Africa, the Indian Subcontinent, Southeast Asia, the Middle East and Oceania. During 1980-1988 there were 1,534 cases of P. falciparum in U.S. civilians: 1,222 (80%) acquired in sub-Saharan Africa; 112 (7%) in Asia; 100 (7%) in the Caribbean and South America, and 100 (7%) in other areas.

Drug resistance of P. falciparum to chloroquine (CRFP) is probable or confirmed in all countries with P. falciparum except the Dominican Republic, Haiti, Central America west of the Panama Canal, the Middle East and Egypt (Figure 1). Resistance to both chloroquine and Fansidar is widespread in Thailand, Burma, Cambodia and the Amazon basin area of South America, and has been reported in sub-Saharan Africa.

Advice to travelers
1. Personal protection:
    Transmission is most common between dusk and dawn.
    Precautions include remaining in well screened areas, use of mosquito nets, clothing that covers most of the body, insect repellent containing DEET on exposed areas, and pyrethrum-containing insect spray for environs and clothing.
2. Chemoprophylaxis (see Table 1 for doses)
    a. Travel to areas with no chloroquine-resistant P. falciparum:
        Chloroquine beginning 1-2 weeks before travel and 4 weeks after leaving risk area
        Alternative: Hydroxychloroquine (for persons who do not tolerate chloroquine)
    b. Travel to areas with chloroquine-resistant P. falciparum:
        Mefloquine (Figure 2). Note: Dosing recommendation for malaria prophylaxis with mefloquine was changed according to MMWR 39:63,1990 (Sept 14, 1990). The new regimen is a single dose taken weekly beginning one week before travel; prophylaxis is continued weekly during travel in malarious areas and for four weeks after leaving such areas.
        Alternatives: Doxycycline beginning 1-2 days before travel and for 4 weeks after leaving risk area. Chloroquine (for persons with contraindication to mefloquine and doxycycline, especially pregnant females and children. If chloroquine is used, the traveler should take a single dose (Table 2) of Fansidar to take for prompt use with a febrile illness if professional medical care is not available.

3. Primaquine: This drug may be given after the traveler has left the risk area to prevent relapses due to P. vivax and P. ovale. Primaquine prophylaxis is usually given during the last 2 weeks of the 4 week period of prophylaxis after exposure. Indications is not clear, but best advised when the traveler has prolonged exposure, such as missionaries and Peace Corp volunteers.

Figure 1: Malarious areas with _Plasmodium falciparum_

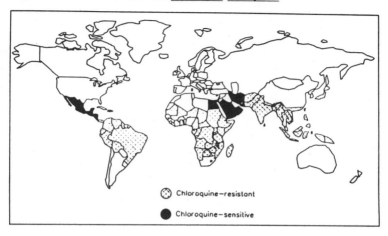

Figure 2: Recommended prophylactic regimen of mefloquine

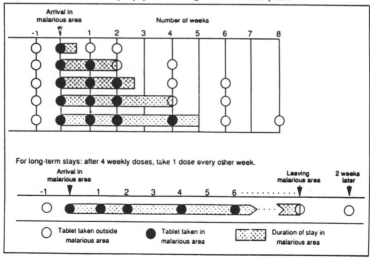

Doses of antimalarial agents for treatment
and prophylaxis

TABLE 1. Drugs used in the prophylaxis of malaria

Drug	Adult dose
Chloroquine phosphate (Aralen®)	300 mg base (500 mg salt) orally, once/week
Hydroxychloroquine sulfate (Plaquenil®)	310 mg base (400 mg salt) orally, once/week
Mefloquine (Lariam®)	228 mg base (250 mg salt) orally, once/week*
Doxycycline	100 mg orally, once/day
Proguanil	200 mg orally, once/day in combination with weekly chloroquine
Primaquine	15 mg base (26.3 mg salt) orally, once/day for 14 days

* The 250 mg dose should be taken once each week
  x 4 weeks followed by once dose every other week
  as indicated in Figure 2.

TABLE 2. Drug used in the presumptive treatment of malaria

Drug	Adult dose
Pyrimethamine-sulfadoxine (Fansidar®)	3 tablets (75 mg pyrimethamine and 1,500 mg sulfadoxine), orally as a single dose

TREATMENT OF FUNGAL INFECTIONS

Adapted from NIAID Mycosis Study Group Reports (Ann Intern Med 98:13,1983; Ann Intern Med 103:861,1985; Chest 93:848,1987), recommendations of the American Thoracic Society (Amer Rev Respir Dis 138:1078,1988) and consultants of the Medical Letter 32:58,1990

Fungus	Form	Preferred Treatment	Dose, alternative agent(s), comment
Aspergillus	Bronchopulmonary	Corticosteroids	
	Aspergilloma (fungus ball)	Usually none	Massive hemoptysis - surgical resection with perioperative amphotericin. Progressive invasive disease - amphotericin B IV, 30-40 mg/kg
	Invasive pulmonary or extrapulmonary	Amphotericin B IV	Total dose: 30-40 mg/kg. Most patients require rapid advance in daily dose to 0.5-1.0 mg/kg. Surgery often required for pulmonary cavities and sinus infections
Blastomyces	Acute pulmonary (immunocompetent)	Usually none	
	Acute pulmonary - severe or progressive	Ketoconazole po	400 mg/day; with unfavorable clinical response - increase to 600-800 mg/day. Alternative: Amphotericin B IV, 30-40 mg/kg. Itraconazole promising
	Chronic pulmonary	Ketoconazole po	As above
	Disseminated (immunocompetent without renal or CNS involvement)	Ketoconazole po	As above

(continued)

Fungus	Form	Preferred Treatment	Dose, alternative agent(s), comment
	Disseminated with GU involvement	Ketoconazole po	600-800 mg/day Alternative: Amphotericin B IV, 30-40 mg/kg
	Disseminated Immunosuppressed or CNS involvement	Amphotericin B IV	Total dose: 30-40 mg/kg
Candida	Localized - mucocutaneous		
	Oral (thrush)	Nystatin S&S Clotrimazole Ketoconazole	500,000 units 3-5x/day x 10-14 days 10 mg troches 3-5x/day x 10-14 days 200 mg po bid, 5-7 days AIDS: Continue any of above regimens indefinitely Fluconazole (100 mg po qd x 5-14 days) is equally effective, but not preferred due to expense
	Vaginal	Miconazole Nystatin Clotrimazole Ketoconazole	Intravaginal cream (2%) or suppository (100 mg) qd x 7 days Intravaginal cream or tablet (100,000 units) bid x 7 days Intravaginal cream (1%) or tablet (100 mg) qd x 7 days 200 mg po bid x 5-7 days
	Cutaneous - intertrigo balanitis, paronychia	Nystatin, ciclopirox, clotrimazole, miconazole,	Topical treatment, keep area dry and clean with maximum exposure to air
	Chronic mucocutaneous	Ketoconazole	200 mg po bid x 3-12 months Alternative: Intermittent amphotericin B ± topical anti-Candida agent (continued)

Fungus	Form	Preferred Treatment	Dose, alternative agent(s), comment
	Esophageal	Ketoconazole Fluconazole	200 mg po bid x 10-21 days 100-200 mg po qd (up to 400 mg/day) x 10-21 days Alternative: Amphotericin B (0.2-0.4 mg/kg/day) x 7-14 days AIDS: Maintenance ketoconazole 200 mg po bid or fluconazole 100-200 mg po qd
	Peritoneal (peritoneal dialysis)	Amphotericin B topical or IV	Topical treatment: 2-4 ug/L in dialysate fluid Catheter may require removal
	Peritoneal - (post op, perforated viscus, etc)	Amphotericin B IV	Total dose: 3-10 mg/kg (Indications to treat are often unclear)
	Urinary	None or amphotericin B topically	Remove catheter or use for bladder instillations of amphotericin B: 50 mg/L in D5W and infuse 1 L/day via closed triple lumen catheter x 5 days Alternative: Flucytosine or fluconazole Fungus ball: Surgical removal and amphotericin B IV
	Bloodstream Septicemia	Amphotericin B IV	Total dose: 3-10 mg/kg Remove or change IV lines Immunocompetent host: Remove line and treat only if fungemia persists Immunosuppressed: Remove line, but treatment with amphotericin B ± flucytosine often required (continued)

101

Fungus	Form	Preferred Treatment	Dose, alternative agent(s), comment
	Disseminated or metastatic (deep organ infection)	Amphotericin B IV ± flucytosine po	Total dose: 20-40 mg/kg (0.3-0.8 mg/kg/day) Indications for flucytosine: Normal marrow and renal function or clinical deterioration with amphotericin B Flucytosine dose: 150 mg/kg/day po Alternative: Ketoconazole or miconazole for patients who refuse or cannot tolerate amphotericin B
	Endocarditis	Amphotericin B IV ± flucytosine po	Total dose: 30-40 mg/kg 150 mg/kg/day (flucytosine) Surgery required
Chromoblastomycosis		Flucytosine po	100-150 mg/kg/day x 6-8 wks Alternatives: Ketoconazole po 400 mg/day x 3-6 mo, thiabendazole or intra-lesional amphotericin B Small lesions usually respond to flucytosine; large lesions should be surgically excised with perioperative flucytosine
Coccidioides	Pulmonary - acute	Usually none	
	Pulmonary - severe, cavitary or progressive infiltrate	Ketoconazole po or amphotericin B IV	400-600 mg/day x 6-18 mo. 15-40 mg/kg (amphotericin) Itraconazole promising
	Pulmonary cavitary disease - giant cavities (>5 cm), subpleural location, serious hemoptysis and secondary infection	Surgical excision	Perioperative amphotericin B often advocated (500 mg) (continued)

102

Fungus	Form	Preferred Treatment	Dose, alternative agent(s), comment
	Disseminated (non-meningeal, immunocompetent)	Amphotericin B IV or ketoconazole	Total dose: 30-40 mg/kg (amphotericin) Ketoconazole in dose of 200-800 mg/day (usually 400-600 mg) x 6-18 mo. or longer Note: relapses appear more common with ketoconazole
	Disseminated - immunosuppressed non-meningeal	Amphotericin B IV	Total dose: 30-40 mg/kg Itraconazole promising
	Meningitis	Amphotericin B IV and topically	Total dose: 30-40 mg/kg IV Intrathecal: 0.5-0.7 mg 2x/wk Alternative: Miconazole or ketoconazole (800-1200 mg/day) (experience limited)
Cryptococcus	Pulmonary - stable and immunocompetent	Usually none	Exclude extrapulmonary disease: culture blood, urine and CSF; follow x-rays q 1-2 mo. x 1 yr
	Pulmonary - progressive and/or immunosuppressed host	Amphotericin B IV ± flucytosine	Total dose: 15-20 mg/kg (amphotericin) Alternative for immunocompetent host with progressive pulmonary or extrapulmonary non-meningeal is ketoconazole 200-800 mg po/day
	Extrapulmonary non-meningeal	Amphotericin B ± flucytosine	Total dose: 2-3 gm (amphotericin B) Alternative for immunocompetent patient is ketoconazole 400 mg/day or fluconazole 200 mg/day (up to 400 mg/day)
	Disseminated including meningeal	Amphotericin B ± flucytosine	Standard: Amphotericin (0.3 mg/kg/day) + flucytosine (150 mg/kg/day) x 6 weeks Four week regimen: Immunocompetent host without neurologic complications, pretreatment CSF WBC > 20/mm3 + Ag < 1:32; and post therapy CSF Ag < 1:8 + neg India ink (continued)

Fungus	Form	Preferred Treatment	Dose, alternative agent(s), comment
			Fluconazole: 200-400 mg po qd x 10-12 wks after CSF culture is negative AIDS: Amphotericin B, 0.4-0.6 mg/kg/day ± flucytosine x 6-10 wks; maintenance therapy (after 15 mg/kg amphotericin B and CSF culture negative): fluconazole 200 mg po qd (up to 400 mg/day) indefinitely; maintenance dose of amphotericin B for fluconazole failures is 1 mg/kg/wk
Histoplasma	Pulmonary - acute	Usually none	Severe acute: Some recommend amphotericin B (500 mg over 2-3 wks) or ketoconazole (400 mg/day) x 6 mo.
	Pulmonary - chronic	Amphotericin B Ketoconazole	Total dose: 35-40 mg/kg 400-600 mg/day x 6 mo. Relapses more common with ketoconazole Itraconazole promising
	Pulmonary - cavitary Stable, minimal Sx, thin wall cavity	None	
	Persistent, thick walled cavity (>2mm) or progressive Sx	Ketoconazole po	400-800 mg/day x 6-12 mo. Alternative: Amphotericin B IV, 30-40 mg/kg Surgery for intractable hemoptysis despite medical Rx Itraconazole promising
	Disseminated - immuno-competent, without CNS involvement	Ketoconazole po	As above Patients with severe illness, AIDS or immunosuppression should receive amphotericin B (continued)

Fungus	Form	Preferred Treatment	Dose, alternative agent(s), comment
	Disseminated - CNS involvement or immunosuppressed	Amphotericin B IV	Total dose: 30-40 mg/kg AIDS: Amphotericin in dose of 0.5-1.0 gm, then maintenance ketoconazole po 400 mg/day or amphotericin B IV 1 mg/kg/wk
	Mediastinal granuloma or fibrosis	Surgical resection if symptomatic	Invasive disease into airways, esophagus, etc (rare): Treat with ketoconazole or amphotericin B
	Ocular	Laser photocoagulation Intraocular steroids Retinal irradiation	Appears to be immune-mediated disease
Paracoccidioides	Pulmonary or mucocutaneous	Ketoconazole po	200-400 mg/day x 6-12 mo. Alternative: Amphotericin B IV, 30-40 mg/kg (preferred for severe disease) or sulfonamides Itraconazole promising
Phycomycetes Absidia Mucor (Mucormycosis) Rhizopus	Pulmonary and extrapulmonary including rhinocerebral	Amphotericin B IV	Total dose: 30-40 mg/kg Most patients require rapid increase to daily dose of 0.5-1.0 mg/kg Rhinocerebral: Surgical debridement required
Pseudallescheria boydii	Sinusitis, endophthalmitis	Ketoconazole po or miconazole IV	200-600 mg/day x 1-12 mo. 200-1200 mg q8h
Sporothrix (Sporotrichosis)	Lymphocutaneous	SSKI po Heat	1 ml (1 gm/ml) tid increasing to 12-15 ml/day x 6-8 wks Alternative: Ketoconazole
	Extracutaneous	Amphotericin B IV	Total dose: 30-40 mg/kg

Antifungal Agents

Amphotericin B

A. **Activity:** Active vs. most fungi including Aspergillus, Blastomyces, Candida (all species), Cryptococcus, Histoplasma, Coccidioides, Phycomycetes (Absidia, Rhizopus, Mucor), and Sporothrix. Resistance has been noted in strains of Coccidioides, Candida, Pseudoallescheria and Phycomycetes.

B. **Administration**

1. IV administration: Dissolve in D5W in concentration less than 0.1 mg/ml and deliver by slow infusion over 4-6 hrs with or without
   1) heparin (50 units/dl in the infusion) to reduce phlebitis,
   2) hydrocortisone (25-50 mg IV) to reduce fever and chills,
   3) premedication with ASA (15-20 mg/kg po), diphenhydramine (Benadryl 25 mg po) and meperidine HCl (15-20 mg IV)

   a. Initial dose: 1 mg in 50-100 mL D5W infused IV over 20 hrs with monitoring over 4 hrs of vital signs to detect hyper-sensitivity reaction, hypotension, etc. (Some simply start with a 5-10 mg dose.)

   b. Standard regimen: .25 mg/kg in 500 ml D5W over 2-6 hrs with subsequent dose increases of 5-10 mg/day to maintenance doses.

   c. "Rapid regimen": Follow initial dose by 0.3 mg/kg at 4 hrs after test done and then 2-3 at 8 hr intervals, but no more than 0.6 mg/kg/day.

   d. Maintenance: Usual dose is 0.3-0.7 mg/kg/day or 0.6-1.2 mg/kg qod given over 2-6 hours depending on tolerance; maintenance doses for serious infections (Mucor, invasive aspergillosis) may be .8-1.2 mg/kg/day; the dose for less serious infections (Candida esophagitis) is 0.3 mg/kg/day. Doses should be reduced or interval extended when serum creatinine exceeds 2.5 ug/dl. Usual total dose for deep seated mycotic infection is 1.5-3 gm; "low dose maintenance regimen" is 0.3 mg/kg/day x 10 days.

   e. Monitoring during treatment: Serum creatinine daily or every other day; serum potassium, magnesium, and complete blood count 1-2x/wk.

2. Local administration

   a. Intrathecal or intraventricular: Dissolve in D5W to give 0.25 mg/ml; 1st dose is 0.05 mg (50 ug) followed by 0.2-0.5 mg 1-3x weekly. Addition of dexamethasone 0.25 mg/ml may reduce local toxic effect. Volume of CSF equal to volume injected should be withdrawn before intrathecal administration. Usual method of administration is intraventricular via Ommaya reservoir.

106

      b.   Intravesicular: Continuous irrigation via triple lumen catheter using 50 mg/L D5W/day.

      c.   Intra-articular: 5-15 mg infusions.

      d.   Intra-ocular: Up to 10 μg.

C.   <u>Pharmacokinetic properties</u>: Poor absorption with topical therapy (oral, bladder, joint instillations, etc). Peak serum levels are 1-3 μg/ml with usual dose (1 mg/kg 3x/wk). Stored in body and slowly released so that after discontinuation therapeutic serum levels are detectable up to 9 days, urinary excretion continues 2-4 months and tissue levels are detectable for 1 yr. Serum half life is 24-48 hrs. Only 3-5% is excreted in urine so that renal failure has minimal effect on dosing recommendations. Penetration into the eye and CNS are poor. Due to unusual pharmacokinetic properties this is one of the few antimicrobial agents in which the recommended treatment strategies are given in terms of total dose rather than daily dose.

D.   <u>Side effects</u>

      a.   Chills, fever, headache, nausea, and vomiting: 50% of patients: reduced with slow infusion and aspirin, corticosteroids, antiemetics, IV meperidine, etc. Tolerance usually improves with continued treatment.

      b.   Nephrotoxicity: Early nephrotoxicity is reversible and dose related; late more irreversible damage is due to total dose. When renal function is normal at start the incidence of residual renal disease with 2 gm is low, and with over 4 gm it is expected. Usual manifestations are increasing creatinine, K loss, proteinuria and renal tubular acidosis.

      c.   Phlebitis at infusion site; reduce with concurrent heparin slow infusion or central line.

      d.   Anemia due to suppression of erythropoiesis; dose related and reversible. Leukopenia and thrombocytopenia also common.

      e.   Hypokalemia: K supplementation with alkalinizing salt (bicarbonate, gluconate, etc) often necessary.

      f.   Drug interaction with granulocytic transfusions (pulmonary infiltrates).

Flucytosine

A. <u>Activity</u>: Active vs. most strains of Phialophora, Cladosporium, Candida and Cryptococcus; activity vs. Aspergillus is variable.

B. <u>Indications</u>: Chromomycosis (caused by Phialophora and Cladosporium) is the only indication for flucytosine alone usually used in combination with amphotericin.

C. <u>Administration</u>: 25-40 mg/kg (usually 37.5 mg/kg) po q6h; dosing interval is extended in renal failure:
   Creatinine clearance > 40 ml/min - usual dose q6h.
   Creatinine clearance 20-40 ml/min - usual dose q12h.
   Creatinine clearance 10-20 ml/min - usual dose q24h.
   Creatinine clearance < 10 - maintain level 100 mg/ml.
   Peritoneal dialysis: usual dose q24h.
   Hemodialysis: usual dose post dialysis.

D. <u>Pharmacokinetics</u>: Absorption 80-90% with oral dosing, usual peak serum level = 50-75 ug/ml; widely distributed with good penetration to eye and CNS. 90% eliminated unchanged in urine; half life of 3-5 hr increases to 100 hr in renal failure.

E. <u>Side effects</u>: Avoid or use with extreme caution in patients with renal failure (especially with concurrent amphotericin B) or marrow suppression (cancer chemotherapy, AIDS, AZT therapy, etc).

   1. Nausea and/or diarrhea (6%); fatal enterocolitis with diarrhea and cramps reported.

   2. Leukopenia and thrombocytopenia: Dose related, especially with levels over 100 mg/ml; concurrent cytosine arabinoside contraindicated. Monitoring serum levels is advocated, especially if given with renal failure or with nephrotoxic or marrow toxic drugs.

   3. Hepatic dysfunction in 5-10%, reversible.

   4. Teratogenic: Contraindicated in pregnancy.

   5. When combined with amphotericin B, there may be toxic blood levels due to the renal toxicity of amphotericin.

Ketoconazole (Nizoral)

A.   <u>Activity</u>: Candida sp, Blastomyces, Coccidioides, Histoplasma, Paracoccidioides, Cryptococcus, Pseudoallescheria boydii and dermatophytes.

B.   <u>Administration</u>: 200 mg tablets; usual dose is 200-400 mg/day, but doses up to 800-1200 mg/day have been given for 6 months or longer depending on infection (see treatment of fungal infections). Drug is well absorbed only in persons with normal gastric acidity so achlorhydria or concurrent use of antacids or H2 blocking agents interferes with absorption; patients with achlorhydria should receive the drug as one 200 mg tab dissolved in 4 ml of 0.2 N HCl and those requiring antacids, H2 blockers or anticholinergics should receive them at least 2 hours after ketoconazole. Dose should be reduced in liver disease, but specific guidelines are not available.

C.   <u>Pharmacokinetics</u>: Mean peak serum levels with 200 and 400 mg doses are 2 and 4 ug/ml, respectively. Penetrates into body fluids and tissues well except CNS. Serum half life is 1.5-9 hours depending on dose and is not altered by renal failure. Metabolized in the liver and inactive metabolites are excreted in the bile; urine levels are nil.

D.   <u>Side effects</u>

1.   Gastrointestinal: Nausea, vomiting, anorexia are common and dose dependent.

2.   Inhibition of testosterone synthesis with impotence, decreased libido, gynecomastia; dose related.

3.   Interfers with cortisol synthesis although hypoadrenalism is rare.

4.   Hepatic toxicity with increased aminotransferase levels is common (2-10%) and usually reversible with continued use; 1 in 15,000 develops symptomatic hepatitis that may be fatal and is not dose related. The patient should report any symptoms of liver disease such as unusual fatigue, nausea, vomiting, jaundice, dark urine, or pale stools. It is recommended that liver function tests be examined before and at 1-2 month intervals during treatment.

5.   Miscellaneous: Menstrual irregularities, pruritus, rash, headache, fever, dizziness, diarrhea, constipation.

6.   Interactions: Avoid concurrent use of antacids, H^2 blocking agents, anticholinergics, antiparkinsonism drugs, rifampin, isoniazid and phenytoin.

<u>Fluconazole</u> (Medical Letter 32:50-52,1990)

A. <u>Activity:</u> Active in clinical trials vs. <u>Candida albicans</u> and <u>Cryptococcus neoformans;</u> active in animal models vs. <u>Aspergillus, Blastomyces dermatitidis, Coccidioides immitis</u> and <u>Histoplasma capsulatum</u>. There is no reliable method to evaluate in vitro activity.

B. <u>Indications:</u> Oropharyngeal candidiasis, esophageal candidiasis, cryptococcosis and maintenance treatment of cryptococcal meningitis in patients with AIDS.

C. <u>Administration</u> (available for po or IV use)

   1. Oropharyngeal and esophageal candidiasis: 200 mg po x 1, then 100 mg po/day x 14-21 days (or longer).

   2. Cryptococcal meningitis: 400 mg po x 1, then 200-400 mg/day; AIDS patients: Amphotericin B is preferred for initial treatment until 15 mg/kg and CSF culture is neg; fluconazole is preferred for maintenance treatment with usual dose of 200 mg/day.

D. <u>Pharmacokinetics:</u> Absorption with oral dosing is 90% and independent of gastric acidity. Fluconazole is widely distributed with good penetration into CSF and eye. About 80% of oral dose is excreted unchanged in the urine (compared to 5% for ketoconazole). Serum half life of 20-30 hours with normal renal function increases to 40-60 hours or longer in renal failure.

E. <u>Side effects</u>

   1. Gastrointestinal intolerance, i.e. nausea, vomiting, diarrhea and abdominal pain.

   2. Headache, rash, and occasional mild increase in aminotransferases.

   3. Rare severe reactions: Stevens-Johnson syndrome, toxic epidermal necrolysis and acute hepatic necrosis.

   4. Expensive (but comparable to amphotericin). The Red Book 1990 wholesale price is about $7/100 mg tab, $11/200 mg tab and $81/200 mg for intravenous use.

F. <u>Compared with ketoconazole and fluconazole</u>

   1. Is absorbed independently of gastric acid.

   2. Penetrates CSF well, accounting for utility in cryptococcal meningitis.

   3. Most is excreted unchanged in the urine (80% vs. 5% for ketoconazole).

   4. Serum half life is about 30 hours compared to 8 hrs for ketoconazole.

   5. Toxicity does not include inhibition of adrenal steroidogenesis.

   6. Price comparison shows fluconazole is 5-10 x more expensive (depending on dose).

TREATMENT OF VIRAL INFECTIONS

A. Herpesvirus Group

Virus	Regimen	Comment
Herpes simplex		
Genital-primary	Acyclovir: Oral - 200 mg 5 x daily x 7-10 days; IV - 15 mg/kg/day x 5-7 days	Mild lesions and symptoms are usually not treated
Genital-recurrent	Acyclovir: Oral - 200 mg 5 x daily x 5-7 days	Initiate during prodrome or at first site of lesions
Genital-prophylaxis	Acyclovir: 200 mg 2-5 po x/day or 400 mg po bid	Indicated only with $\geq$ 6 recurrences/yr FDA approved for up to one year, but good safety profile with treatment up to 5 yrs Contraindicated in pregnancy
Perirectal	Acyclovir: 400 mg po 5 x daily x 10 days	
Encephalitis	Acyclovir: IV - 10 mg/kg q8h x 10-14 days	
Mucocutaneous progressive	Acyclovir: IV - 5-10 mg/kg q8h x 7-14 days; oral - 200-400 mg po 5 x/day x 7-14 days	AIDS patients often require preventative therapy with acyclovir 200-400 mg po 3-5 x/day indefinitely
Burn wound	Acyclovir: IV - 5 mg/kg q8h x 7 days; oral - 200 mg 5 x/day x 7-14 days	
Prophylaxis - high risk patients	Acyclovir: IV - 5 mg/kg q8h; oral - 200 mg 3-5 x/day	Organ transplant recipients (renal and marrow): treat seropositive patients for 1-3 mo. post transplant
Keratitis	Trifluridine: Topical (1%) or Vidarabine: topical (3%) x 7-21 days	
Acyclovir - resistant strains	Vidarabine: IV 10-15 mg/kg over 12-24 hr Foscarnet: IV 60 mg/kg q8h (investigational)	Thymidine kinase deficient strains, usually in HSV-2 strains from immuno-suppressed patients previously treated with acyclovir

Virus	Regimen	Comment
Varicella-zoster		
Pneumonia	**Acyclovir:** IV - 10-12 mg/kg q8h x 7 days; oral - 800 mg 5 x daily x 10 days	Efficacy not clearly established; IV preferred for serious infections
Dermatomal	**Acyclovir:** IV 10-12 mg/kg q8h x 7 days; oral 800 mg 5 x daily x 7-10 days	Indications to treat are greater for severe disease, early disease or zoster in immunosuppressed host Acyclovir and/or cortico-steroids (prednisone 40 mg/ day x 7 days, then taper over 10-14 days) may reduce post-herpetic neuralgia Acyclovir should be started $\leq$ 4 days from onset Post-herpetic neuralgia: Amitriptyline
Ophthalmic zoster	**Acyclovir:** Oral 600-800 mg 5 x daily x 10 days	Consult ophthalmologist
Disseminated zoster or varicella (immuno-suppressed host)	**Acyclovir:** IV 10-12 mg/kg q8h x 7 days	Alternative is vidarabine: 10 mg/kg/day IV x 5-7 days
Cytomegalovirus		
Immunocompetent	None	
Immunosuppressed Retinitis	Ganciclovir 5 mg/kg IV bid x 14-21 days	Efficacy established; maintenance therapy usually required using ganciclovir, 5 mg/kg/day IV Alternative: Foscarnet 90-180 mg/kg/day IV
Colitis, enteritis and esophagitis	Ganciclovir 5 mg/kg IV bid x 10-21 days	Efficacy probable Alternative: Foscarnet 90-180 mg/kg/day IV (investigational)
Pneumonitis	Ganciclovir 7.5-10 mg/kg/day IV x 10-21 days	Efficacy not established Organ transplant recipients: consider ganciclovir plus IV gamma globulin, 500 mg/kg qod x 10 doses
Prophylaxis: Renal transplant (see comment)	CMV immune globulin (investigational) 150 mg/kg within 72 hr, then 100 mg/kg at 2,4,6 & 8 wks, then 50 mg/kg at 12 & 16 wks	Indicated for CMV sero-negative renal transplant recipient and CMV sero-negative donors

B. Influenza A: Amantadine

A. <u>Recommendations</u> (Advisory Council on Immunization Practices: MMWR 37:361,1988; 39:RR-7; 1-15,1990)
1. <u>Prophylaxis</u>: 70-90% effective in preventing influenza A infection. Highest priority - Control presumed influenza A outbreaks in institutions with high risk persons; administer to all residents regardless of vaccination status as soon as possible after outbreak recognized and as long as there is influenza activity in community. This form of prophylaxis should also be offered to unvaccinated staff who provide care for high risk patients.

   Other recommendations - 1) As adjunct to late vaccination of high risk persons (two weeks required for vaccine response); 2) Unvaccinated persons providing care to high risk persons in the home or in care facilities; continue until vaccine induces immunity (2 wks) or continue throughout epidemic if employee cannot be vaccinated or; 3) Consider for vaccinated health care personnel if outbreak involves strain not covered in the vaccine; 4) Immunodeficient persons who are expected to have a poor antibody response to the vaccine, especially high risk persons with contraindications to influenza vaccine.

2. <u>Treatment</u>: Amantadine can reduced the severity and duration of influenza, but is not known to prevent complications in high risk patients. Consequently, no specific recommendation is made. If given, it should be started within 48 hrs of the onset of symptoms and should be discontinued when clinically warranted, usually within 3-5 days. In closed populations, persons who have influenza and are treated should be separated from those receiving amantadine for prophylaxis.

B. <u>Dose</u> (MMWR 37:373,1988)

1. <u>Prophylaxis</u>: 100 mg/day (all adults)
2. <u>Treatment</u>: Age 10-64 - 200 mg/day in one or two doses; Age > 65 yrs - 100 mg/day as single daily dose; Seizure disorder - 100 mg/day
3. Creatinine clearance in ml/min/1.73 M^2 (<u>use 1/2 dose when 100 mg/day indicated</u>).
   > 80: 200 mg/day
   60-80: 200 mg alternating with 100 mg/day
   40-60: 100 mg/day
   30-40: 200 mg twice weekly
   20-30: 100 mg three times weekly
   10-20: 200 mg alternating with 100 mg weekly

C. <u>Side effects</u> (dose related): Anxiety, insomnia, dizziness, drunk feeling, slurred speech, ataxia, depression, lightheadedness, inability to concentrate. Incidence is 5-10% for healthy young adults taking 200 mg/day; lower prophylactic dose presumably decreases side effects and retains efficacy. Less frequent side effects include seizures and confusion; seizures and behavioral change are most common in the elderly, those with poor renal function and patients with a pre-existing seizure disorder or psychiatric condition.

D. <u>Information source (CDC)</u>: Technical Information Services, Center for Prevention Services, Mailstop E06, CDC, Atlanta, GA 30333 (404) 639-1819.

C. AZT (Retrovir, Zidovudine)

Indications: CD4 count <500/cu mm; patients with borderline values should have two measurements <500/cu mm at least one week apart. In absence of CD4 count the indication is symptomatic HIV infection. Use with caution with granulocytopenia (<1000/mm^3) or anemia (hemoglobin <9.5 g/dL).

Usual dose: 100 mg po q4h (5-6x/day) for total daily dose of 500-600 mg. Some authorities advocate 200 mg po q4h (1000-1200 mg/day) for the first month of treatment of symptomatic HIV infection and 1000-1200 mg/day as the maintenance dose in the presence of HIV related CNS complications. There are insufficient data for dosage adjustment recommendations with impaired hepatic or renal function.

Pharmacokinetics: Bioavailability with oral administration is 50-75%. No parenteral form is available. The drug is rapidly metabolized to GAZT and 90% is recovered in urine as AZT (10-20%) or GAZT (70-80%). Mean half life is 1.0 hr and 1.4 hr in anuric patients; for GAZT the half life is 1.0 hr and 8.0 hr in anuric patients. Levels in CSF are about .5x peak serum levels.

Toxicity: Hematologic toxicity is related to dose and stage of disease when treatment was initiated. Major side effects are anemia and neutropenia.*

Patient group	Dose (mg/day)	CD4 count (/mm^3)	Anemia (Hgb <8 g/dL)	Neutropenia (<750/mm^3)
Asymptomatic	500	200-500	1%	2%
Early symptomatic	1200	>200	1%	4%
Advanced symptomatic	1200	>200	3%	10%
	1200	<200	29%	47%

*See Richman DD et al. NEJM 317:192,1987, Fischl MA et al. Ann Intern Med 112:727,1990, Volberding PA et al. NEJM 322:941,1990.

Dose adjustment: For anemia, reduce dose, discontinue treatment (Hgb <7.5 gm/dL) and/or give recombinant human erythropoietin (4000 units/day sc; 24,000 units/wk) (See Fischl M et al. NEJM 322:1488,1990). For neutropenia (<750/mm^3), reduce dose, discontinue treatment or give G-CSF or GM-CSF.

Other side effects include severe headache, nausea, insomnia, myalgia, seizures, myopathy, abnormal liver function tests, and nail pigmentation.

Drug interactions: Agents that cause anemia or neutropenia should be avoided or co-administered with caution, i.e. ganciclovir, pentamidine, flucytosine, vinblastine and adriamycin.

Monitoring: With usual dose of 500-600 mg/day obtain CBC q 3 months if stable; with dose of 1000-1200 obtain CBC q 2-4 wks.

D. Hepatitis Viruses

Interferon alpha-2b (Medical Letter 32:1-2,1990)

Chronic hepatitis C: Two studies showed interferon alfa-2b (2-3 million units SC 3x/wk x 6 mo) led to normal or near-normal transaminase levels in about 50% of treated patients compared to 10% of controls. About 50% of responders relapsed within 6 months after treatment was discontinued (DiBisceglie AM et al. New Engl J Med 321:1506,1989). Indications for treatment and therapeutic regimen to use are controversial. Some authorities suggest initial treatment with 2-5 million units 3x/wk, treatment for at least 2 months to determine response according to serum aminotransferase levels and continued treatment for 6-12 months in responders.

Hepatitis B: Initial studies show interferon alfa-2b (5 million units SC daily x 4 mo) led to sustained loss of HBV DNA and HBeAg in one-third and return of liver function tests to normal in 40% (Perrillo RP et al. New Engl J Med 323:295,1990). Indications for treatment are controversial, but some authorities suggest interferon alfa for chronic HBV patients with serum aminotransferase levels over 2x normal, low-to-moderate levels of serum HBV DNA, and presence of HBeAg (Hoofnagle JH, New Engl J Med 323:337,1990).

Adverse reactions: About 50% experience flu-like symptoms of fever, malaise, myalgias and headache; Sx often respond to acetaminophen and decrease with continued treatment. Later side effects include granulocytopenia and thrombocytopenia (dose related), psychiatric symptoms, thyroid disorders and alopecia. Long term effects are unknown and treatment requires subcutaneous injections. Wholesale cost to pharmacist is $25/3 mil units.

TREATMENT OF TUBERCULOSIS
Official statement of the American Thoracic Society and the Centers for Disease Control (Amer Rev Resp Dis 134:355-363,1986; 136:492-496,1987)

A. Initial treatment regimens (ATS and CDC recommendations)

   1. Six month regimen
     Initial phase: INH, rifampin plus pyrazinamide given daily for 2 months (augment with ethambutol when INH resistance is suspected).

     Second phase: INH plus rifampin given daily or twice weekly for 4 months.

   2. Nine month regimen
     INH plus rifampin for 9 months
     (augment with ethambutol when INH resistance is suspected; INH and rifampin should be given daily for 1-2 months and then daily or twice/wk).

   3. Special considerations: Extrapulmonary tuberculosis, pregnancy, lactation, treatment failure, resistant strains, relapse and HIV infection: See F. Special Considerations (pg 118,119).

B. Recommended first line agents (see next page)

C. Second line antituberculous drugs

Agent	Forms	Daily dose (maximum)	Adverse reactions	Monitoring
Capreomycin	Vials: 1 gm	15-30 mg/kg IM (1 gm)*	Auditory, vestibular, and renal toxicity	Audiometry, vestibular function, renal function
Kanamycin	Vials: 75 mg, 500 mg and and 1 gm	13-30 mg/kg IM (1 gm)*	Auditory, vestibular (rare), and renal toxicity	Audiometry, vestibular function, renal failure
Ethionamide	Tabs: 250 mg	15-20 mg/kg PO (1 gm)*	Gastrointestinal intolerance, hepatotoxicity, hypersensitivity	Hepatic enzymes
PAS	Tabs: 500 mg 1 gm	12 gm	Gastrointestinal intolerance, hepatotoxicity, sodium load, hypersensitivity	
Cycloserine	Caps: 250 mg	1 gm	Psychosis, rash, convulsions	Assess mental status

* Usual daily dose of adult

B. Recommended first line agents
(Amer Rev Resp Dis 134:355-363,1986 and Medical Letter 30:43,1988)

Agent	Forms	Daily dose (maximum)	Twice weekly dose (maximum)	Cost/mo. (daily regimen)	Adverse reactions	Comment
Isoniazid	Tabs: 100 mg, 300 mg; Syrup: 50 mg/5 ml; Vials: 1 gm	5 mg/kg po or IM (300 mg)*	15 mg/kg (900 mg)*	$1	Elevated hepatic enzymes, peripheral neuropathy, hepatitis, hypersensitivity	Oral or parenteral pyridoxine 15-50 mg/day to prevent neuropathy
Rifampin	Caps: 150 mg, 300 mg; Vials: 600 mg IV	10-20 mg/kg po (600 mg)* IV (600 mg)	10 mg/kg (600 mg)*	$13-21	Orange discoloration of secretions & urine, nausea, vomiting, hepatitis, fever, purpura (rare)	May be given as 10 mg/ml suspension or intravenously
Pyrazinamide	Tabs: 500 mg	15-30 mg/kg po (2 gm)*	50-70 mg/kg	$19-48	Hepatotoxicity, hyperuricemia, arthralgias, rash, GI intolerance	
Streptomycin	Vials: 1 gm, 4 gm	15 mg/kg IM (1 gm)* pts > 40 yrs: 10 mg/kg IM (500-750 mg)*	25-30 mg/kg pts > 40 yrs: 20 mg/kg	$23-27	Ototoxicity and possible nephrotoxicity	Decrease dose for renal failure
Ethambutol	Tabs: 100 mg, 400 mg	15-25 mg/kg po (2.5 gm)*	50 mg/kg	$27-72	Optic neuritis, skin rash	25 mg/kg/day 1st 1-2 months or if strain is INH resistant. Decrease dose for renal failure

* Usual daily dose for adults.

D. Monitoring for adverse reactions

1. Baseline tests: Hepatic enzymes, bilirubin, serum creatinine or BUN, CBC, platelet count or estimate.
   Pyrazinamide: uric acid; ethambutol: visual acuity.

2. During treatment: Clinical monitoring with assessment at least once monthly; laboratory monitoring is not recommended except for symptoms suggesting toxicity and in patients with pre-existing liver disease. (Hepatotoxicity from antituberculous drugs is not known to be more common in patients with prior liver disease).

E. Evaluation of response

1. Sputum examination (smear and culture): Monthly until conversion is documented; minimum is exam at 2-3 months post treatment.
   Positive sputum at 3 months: Review compliance and drug susceptibility.

   a. Resistant organisms: Change regimen to include at least two active drugs and evaluate sputum monthly until sputum conversion.

   b. Susceptible organisms: Review compliance.

2. Radiologic studies: At completion of treatment as baseline for comparison for future films; x-ray at 2-3 months of treatment may be useful.

3. Routine follow-up after treatment (sensitive organisms):
   Nine month regimen with good response: None.
   Six month regimen: Follow-up at 6 and 12 months.

F. Special considerations

1. Extrapulmonary tuberculosis

   a. Nine month two-drug regimen recommended for sensitive strains; consider longer treatment for lymphadenitis, bone and joint tuberculosis.

   b. Six month regimen is "probably effective".

   c. Some authorities recommend corticosteroids for tuberculosis pericarditis and meningitis.

2. Pregnancy and lactation

   a. INH plus rifampin; ethambutol should be added for suspected resistant strains.

   b. Streptomycin is only antituberculous drug with established fetal toxicity (interferes with ear development and causes congenital deafness); kanamycin and capreomycin presumably share this toxic potential.

   c. Breast feeding should not be discouraged.

3. Treatment failures (persistent positive cultures after 5-6 months)

   a. Susceptibility tests on current isolate while continuing same regimen or augmenting this with two additional drugs.

   b. Sensitive strain: Consider treatment under direct observation.
   Resistant strain: Two active drugs.
   INH resistance: Rifampin and ethambutol ± pyrazinamide for 12 months.

4. Relapse after treatment

   a. INH + rifampin regimen previously: Organism at time of relapse is usually sensitive if the original strain was. Therefore, give same regimen initially, measure susceptibility, modify the regimen accordingly and consider observed treatment.

   b. Regimen not containing INH and rifampin: Presume new isolate is resistant to agents used. See 3b above.

5. HIV infection (Recommendations of the Centers for Disease Control and The American Thoracic Society: Amer Rev Resp Dis 136:492,1987)

   a. All patients with tuberculosis should have HIV serology.

   b. Antituberculous treatment should be started when acid-fast bacilli are found in a patient with HIV infection pending cultures.

   c. Standard treatment (pulmonary TB)
      (1) Initial 2 mo: INH (300 mg/day), rifampin (600 mg/day or 450 mg/ day for patients < 50 kg) + pyrazinamide (20-30 mg/kg/day)
      (2) Duration: INH + rifampin to complete minimum of 9 months or at least 6 months after documented culture conversion; some authorities advocate continuing INH for lifetime.

   d. Disseminated disease, CNS involvement or suspected resistance:
   Add ethambutol (25 mg/kg/day) for initial treatment.

   e. Inability to include INH or rifampin: Treat for minimum of 18 months and for at least 12 months after documented culture conversion.

PREVENTATIVE TREATMENT FOR TUBERCULOSIS
INFECTION IN THE U.S.
(Recommendations of the Advisory Committee for Elimination
of Tuberculosis, MMWR 39:#RR-8, pp 9-15, 1990)

A. **Indications**

1. High risk groups (persons in any category should be treated regardless of age unless previously treated).

   a. Persons with HIV infection with PPD $\geq$ 5 mm and persons at risk for HIV whose serologic status is unknown but HIV is suspected.
   b. Close contacts of newly diagnosed cases with PPD $\geq$ 5 mm. Children and adolescents with neg PPD who have been close contacts with infectious persons within past 3 months are candidates until there is a negative repeat PPD at 12 weeks post contact.
   c. Recent seroconverters with PPD $\geq$ 10 mm increase within 2 yr period for persons < 35 yrs and $\geq$ 15 mm increase for persons over 35 years.
   d. Persons with x-ray showing fibrotic lesions likely to represent healed TB and PPD $\geq$ 5 mm.
   e. Intravenous drug abusers known to be HIV seronegative and PPD $\geq$ 10 mm.
   f. Persons with medical conditions that have been associated with increased risk of TB and PPD $\geq$ 10 mm: silicosis; diabetes mellitus (esp if poorly controlled); corticosteroid treatment ($\geq$ 15 mg/day prednisone for over 2-3 wks); other immunosuppressive treatment; hematologic and lymphoproliferative diseases such as leukemia and Hodgkin's disease; end stage renal disease, and conditions associated with rapid weight loss or chronic malnutrition including gastrectomy, jejunoileal by-pass and weight loss of 10% or more below ideal body weight.

2. Persons under 35 years with PPD $\geq$ 10 mm.

   a. Foreign born persons from high prevalence countries.
   b. Medically underserved low-income populations including blacks, Hispanics and Native Americans.
   c. Residents of long term care facilities.

B. **Preventative treatment**

1. Usual regimen: Isoniazid, 300 mg/day for 6-12 months.

   a. Persons with HIV infection and those with stable chest x-rays compatible with past TB should be treated for 12 months.
   b. Others: 6-12 months

2. Directly observed therapy: Isoniazid in dose of 15 mg/kg (up to 900 mg) twice weekly.

C. **Monitoring**: Patients should be monitored in person by trained personnel at monthly interval. Black and Hispanic women, especially postpartum, may be at greatest risk for serious or fatal reaction and should be monitored more frequently.

SCREENING FOR TUBERCULOSIS
(Recommendations of Advisory Committee for Elimination
of Tuberculosis, MMWR 39:#RR-8, pp 1-8,1990)

A. **Background**

   1. It is estimated that > 90% of patients with active tuberculosis have harbored <u>M</u>. <u>tuberculosis</u> for over one year.
   2. The estimated number of persons in the U.S. with latent infection is 10-15 million.
   3. Preventative treatment with isoniazid is 90-95% effective when compliance is good.

B. **Populations to be screened**

   1. Persons with HIV infection.
   2. Close contacts with persons known or suspected to have tuberculosis.
   3. Persons with medical risks known to increase the risk of disease if infection has occurred.
   4. Foreign born persons from countries with high prevalence of TB.
   5. Medically underserved low income populations, e.g., blacks, Hispanics and Native Americans.
   6. Alcoholics and IV drug abusers.
   7. Residents of long term care facilities including correctional facilities, nursing homes, mental institutions, etc.

C. **Screening**

   1. PPD: 5 units given intracutaneously is the preferred test.
   2. Persons with signs or symptoms of pulmonary tuberculosis should have chest x-ray regardless of skin test results.

Agent	Condition	Treatment
M. kansasii	Major: Pulmonary Infrequent: Lymphaden- opathy; disseminated	3 drugs x 18 mo.: INH, rifampin and ethambutol or these 3 agents for 12 mo. plus strepto- mycin (1 gm IM 2x/wk) x 3 mo.
M. avium- intracellulare	Immunocompetent: Pulmonary	3-5 drugs: INH, rifampin, ethambutol x 18-24 mo plus streptomycin x 2-4 mo; also consider pyrazinamide and ethionamide
	AIDS: Disseminated disease	Efficacy of treatment debated; consider 4-5 drugs: rifampin, (or rifabutin), ethambutol, clofazimine ± ciprofloxacin ± amikacin; also consider cycloserine and ethionamide
M. marinum	Skin	Rifampin + ethambutol or trimethoprim-sulfa x 6 wks; also consider doxycycline, minocycline, ciprofloxacin and rifampin (alone) Excision of lesions
M. ulcerans	Skin	Rifampin + amikacin, minocycline + trimethoprim-sulfa x 4-6 Excision of lesions with grafting
M. fortuitum & M. chelonei	Post-operative sites (especially augmentation mammoplasty and median sternotomy); pulmonary; skin; lymphadenopathy; bone; keratitis	Cefoxitin + amikacin IV, then sulfonamide, rifampin, doxycycline or erythromycin orally (select by sensitivity tests) M. chelonae ss abscessus is usually sensitive to amikacin, cefoxitin and erythromycin; M. chelonei ss chelonae is usually sensitive to amikacin, tobramycin, erythromycin and doxycycline. Excision of lesions including removal of associated devices Ciprofloxacin, cefmetazole and imipenem are active vs. some M. fortuitum, but role in treatment is unknown.
M. gordonae	Pulmonary	INH, rifampin + ethambutol

TREATMENT OF PARASITIC INFECTIONS
(Reprinted from The Medical Letter on Drugs and Therapeutics 32:23,1990 with permission)

Infection	Drug	Adult Dosage*
AMEBIASIS (Entamoeba histolytica)		
asymptomatic		
Drug of choice:	Iodoquinol[1]	650 mg tid x 20d
Alternatives:	Diloxanide furoate[2]	500 mg tid x 10d
	Paromomycin	25-30 mg/kg/d in 3 doses x 7d
mild to moderate intestinal disease		
Drugs of choice:	Metronidazole[3,4]	750 mg tid x 10d
	followed by iodoquinol[1]	650 mg tid x 20d
Alternative:	Paromomycin	25-30 mg/kg/d in 3 doses x 7d
severe intestinal disease		
Drugs of choice:	Metronidazole[3,4]	750 mg tid x 10d
	followed by iodoquinol[1]	650 mg tid x 20d
Alternatives:	Dehydroemetine[2,5]	1 to 1.5 mg/kg/d (max. 90 mg/d) IM for up to 5d
	followed by iodoquinol[1]	650 mg tid x 20d
	OR Emetine[5]	1 mg/kg/d (max. 60 mg/d) IM for up to 5d
	followed by iodoquinol[1]	650 mg tid x 20d
hepatic abscess		
Drugs of choice:	Metronidazole[3,4]	750 mg tid x 10d
	followed by iodoquinol[1]	650 mg tid x 20d
Alternatives:	Dehydroemetine[2,5]	1 to 1.5 mg/kg/d (max. 90 mg/d) IM for up to 5d
	followed by chloroquine phosphate	600 mg base (1 gram)/d x 2d, then 300 mg base (500 mg)/d x 2-3 wks
	plus iodoquinol[1]	650 mg tid x 20d
	OR Emetine[5]	1 mg/kg/d (max. 60 mg/d) IM for up to 5d
	followed by chloroquine phosphate	600 mg base (1 gram)/d x 2d, then 300 mg base (500 mg)/d x 2-3 wks
	plus iodoquinol[1]	650 mg tid x 20d
AMEBIC MENINGOENCEPHALITIS, PRIMARY		
Naegleria		
Drug of choice:	Amphotericin B[6,7]	1 mg/kg/d IV, uncertain duration
Acanthamoeba		
Drug of choice:	see footnote 8	
Ancylostoma duodenale, see HOOKWORM		
ANGIOSTRONGYLIASIS		
Angiostrongylus cantonensis		
Drug of choice:	Mebendazole[7,9,10]	100 mg bid x 5d
Angiostrongylus costaricensis		
Drug of choice:	Thiabendazole[7,9]	75 mg/kg/d in 3 doses x 3 d[11] (max. 3 grams/day)
ANISAKIASIS (Anisakis)		
Treatment of choice:	Surgical removal	
ASCARIASIS (Ascaris lumbricoides, roundworm)		
Drug of choice:[12]	Mebendazole	100 mg bid x 3d
	OR Pyrantel pamoate	11 mg/kg once (max. 1 gram)
BABESIOSIS (Babesia)		
Drugs of choice:[13]	Clindamycin[7]	1.2 grams bid parenteral or 600 mg tid oral x 7d
	plus quinine	650 mg tid oral x 7d

123

Infection	Drug	Adult Dosage*
BALANTIDIASIS (Balantidium coli)		
Drug of choice:	Tetracycline[7]	500 mg qid x 10d
Alternatives:	Iodoquinol[1,7]	650 mg tid x 20d
	Metronidazole[3,7]	750 mg tid x 5d
BAYLISASCARIASIS (Baylisascaris procyonis)		
Drug of choice:	See footnote 15	
BLASTOCYSTIS hominis infection		
Drug of choice:	See footnote 16	
CAPILLARIASIS (Capillaria philippinensis)		
Drug of choice:	Mebendazole[7]	200 mg bid x 20d
Alternative:	Albendazole	200 mg bid x 10d
	Thiabendazole[7]	25 mg/kg/d in 2 doses x 30d
Chagas' disease, see TRYPANOSOMIASIS		
Clonorchis sinensis, see FLUKE infection		
CRYPTOSPORIDIOSIS (Cryptosporidium)		
Drug of choice:	See footnote 17	
CUTANEOUS LARVA MIGRANS (creeping eruption)		
Drug of choice:[18]	Thiabendazole	Topically and/or 50 mg/kg/d in 2 doses (max. 3 grams/d) x 2-5d[11]
Cysticercosis, see TAPEWORM infection		
DIENTAMOEBA fragilis infection		
Drug of choice:	Iodoquinol[1]	650 mg tid x 20d
	OR Paromomycin	25-30 mg/kg/d in 3 doses x 7d
	OR Tetracycline[7]	500 mg qid x 10d
Diphyllobothrium latum, see TAPEWORM infection		
DRACUNCULUS medinensis (guinea worm) infection		
Drug of choice:	Metronidazole[3,7,19]	250 mg tid x 10d
Alternative:	Thiabendazole[7,19]	50-75 mg/kg/d in 2 doses x 3d[11]
Echinococcus, see TAPEWORM infection		
Entamoeba histolytica, see AMEBIASIS		
ENTAMOEBA polecki infection		
Drug of choice:	Metronidazole[3,7]	750 mg tid x 10d
ENTEROBIUS vermicularis (pinworm) infection		
Drug of choice:[12]	Pyrantel pamoate	11 mg/kg once (max. 1 gram); repeat after 2 weeks
	OR Mebendazole	A single dose of 100 mg; repeat after 2 weeks
Fasciola hepatica, see FLUKE infection		
FILARIASIS		
Wuchereria bancrofti, Brugia (W.) malayi		
Drug of choice:[20]	Diethylcarbamazine[21]	Day 1: 50 mg, oral, p.c.
		Day 2: 50 mg tid
		Day 3: 100 mg tid
		Days 4 through 21: 6 mg/kg/d in 3 doses

(continued)

Infection	Drug	Adult Dosage*
FILARIASIS (continued)		
Loa loa		
Drug of choice:	Diethylcarbamazine[21]	Day 1: 50 mg, oral, p.c.
		Day 2: 50 mg tid
		Day 3: 100 mg tid
		Days 4 through 21: 9 mg/kg/d in 3 doses
Mansonella ozzardi		
Drug of choice:	See footnote 20	
Mansonella perstans		
Drug of choice:[22]	Mebendazole[7]	100 mg bid x 30d
Tropical eosinophilia		
Drug of choice:	Diethylcarbamazine	6 mg/kg/d in 3 doses x 7-10d
Onchocerca volvulus		
Drug of choice:	Ivermectin[2,7]	150 µg/kg oral once, repeated every 6 to 12 months

Infection	Drug	Adult Dosage*

FLUKE, hermaphroditic, infection
Clonorchis sinensis (Chinese liver fluke)

Drug of choice:	Praziquantel	75 mg/kg/d in 3 doses x 2d

Fasciola hepatica (sheep liver fluke)

Drug of choice:[23]	Bithionol[2]	30-50 mg/kg on alternate days x 10-15 doses

Fasciolopsis buski (intestinal fluke)

Drug of choice:	Praziquantel[7]	75 mg/kg/d in 3 doses x 1d
OR	Niclosamide[7]	a single dose of 4 tablets (2 g), chewed thoroughly

Heterophyes heterophyes (intestinal fluke)

Drug of choice:	Praziquantel[7]	75 mg/kg/d in 3 doses x 1d

Metagonimus yokogawai (intestinal fluke)

Drug of choice:	Praziquantel[7]	75 mg/kg/d in 3 doses x 1d

Nanophyetus salmincola

Drug of choice:	Praziquantel	60 mg/kg/d in 3 doses x 1d

Opisthorchis viverrini (liver fluke)

Drug of choice:	Praziquantel	75 mg/kg/d in 3 doses x 1d

Paragonimus westermani (lung fluke)

Drug of choice:	Praziquantel[7]	75 mg/kg/d in 3 doses x 2d
Alternative:	Bithionol[2]	30-50 mg/kg on alternate days x 10-15 doses

GIARDIASIS (Giardia lamblia)

Drug of choice:	Quinacrine HCl	100 mg tid p.c. x 5d
Alternatives:	Metronidazole[3,4,7]	250 mg tid x 5d
	Furazolidone	100 mg qid x 7-10d

GNATHOSTOMIASIS (Gnathostoma spinigerum)

Treatment of choice:	Surgical removal	
OR	Mebendazole[7]	200 mg q3h x 6d

HOOKWORM infection (Ancylostoma duodenale, Necator americanus)

Drug of choice:[24]	Mebendazole	100 mg bid x 3d
OR	Pyrantel pamoate[7]	11 mg/kg (max. 1 gram) x 3d

Hydatid cyst, see TAPEWORM infection

Hymenolepis nana, see TAPEWORM infection

ISOSPORIASIS (Isospora belli)

Drug of choice:	Trimethoprim-sulfa-methoxazole[7,25]	160 mg TMP, 800 mg SMX qid x 10d, then bid x 3 wks

LEISHMANIASIS
L. braziliensis, L. mexicana (American cutaneous and mucocutaneous leishmaniasis)

Drug of choice:[26]	Stibogluconate sodium[2]	20 mg/kg/d (max. 800 mg/d) IV or IM x 20d, may be repeated or continued until response
Alternative:	Amphotericin B[7]	0.25 to 1 mg/kg by slow infusion daily or every 2d for up to 8 wks

L. donovani (kala azar, visceral leishmaniasis)

Drug of choice:[27]	Stibogluconate sodium[2,28]	20 mg/kg/d (max. 800 mg/d) IV or IM x 20d (may be repeated)
Alternative:	Pentamidine isethionate	2-4 mg/kg/d IM for up to 15 doses

L. tropica, L. major (oriental sore, cutaneous leishmaniasis)

Drug of choice:[29]	Stibogluconate sodium[2]	10 mg/kg/d (max. 600 mg/d) IV or IM x 6-10d (may be repeated)
Alternative:	Topical treatment[30]	

LICE infestation (Pediculus humanus, capitis, Phthirus pubis)[31]

Drug of choice:	1% Permethrin[32]	Topically
OR	0.5% malathion	Topically
Alternatives:	Pyrethrins with pi-peronyl butoxide	Topically[33]
	Lindane	Topically[33]

Loa loa, see FILARIASIS

Infection	Drug	Adult Dosage*

MALARIA, Treatment of (*Plasmodium falciparum, P. ovale, P. vivax,* and *P. malariae*)
All *Plasmodium* except Chloroquine-Resistant *P. falciparum*
  ORAL

Drug of choice:	Chloroquine phosphate[34,35]	600 mg base (1 gram), then 300 mg base (500 mg) 6 hrs later, then 300 mg base (500 mg) at 24 and 48 hrs

  PARENTERAL

Drug of choice:	Quinine dihydrochloride[36]	600 mg in 300 ml normal saline IV over 2 to 4 hrs; repeat q8h until oral therapy can be started (max. 1800 mg/d)
	OR Quinidine gluconate[7,37]	10 mg/kg loading dose (max. 600 mg) in normal saline slowly over 1 hr, followed by continuous infusion of 0.02 mg/kg/min for 3 days maximum
Alternative:	Chloroquine HCl[35]	200 mg base (250 mg) IM q6h if oral therapy cannot be started

Chloroquine-resistant *P. falciparum*[39]
  ORAL

Drugs of choice:	Quinine sulfate[40,41]	650 mg tid x 3d
	plus pyrimethamine-sulfadoxine[42]	3 tablets at once
	OR **plus** tetracycline[7,14]	250 mg qid x 7d
	OR **plus** clindamycin[7]	900 mg tid x 3d
Alternative:	Mefloquine[43]	1250 mg once

(continued)

MALARIA, Treatment of Chloroquine-resistant *P. falciparum* (continued)
  PARENTERAL

Drug of choice:	Quinine dihydrochloride[36]	same as above
	OR Quinidine gluconate[7,37]	same as above

Prevention of relapses: *P. vivax* and *P. ovale* only

Drug of choice:	Primaquine phosphate[44]	15 mg base (26.3 mg)/d x 14d or 45 mg base (79 mg)/wk x 8 wks

MALARIA, Prevention of[45]

Drug of choice:	Chloroquine phosphate[46]	300 mg base (500 mg salt) orally, once/week beginning 1 wk before and continuing for 4 wks after last exposure

Chloroquine-Resistant Areas[39]

Drug of choice:	Mefloquine[46,47]	250 mg oral once/week x 4 wks, then every other week continuing for 4 weeks after last exposure
	OR Chloroquine phosphate[46]	as above
	plus pyrimethamine-sulfadoxine[42] for presumptive treatment[48]	Carry a single dose (3 tablets) for self-treatment of febrile illness when medical care is not immediately available
	plus proguanil[49] (in Africa south of the Sahara)	200 mg daily during exposure and for 4 weeks afterwards
	OR Doxycycline[46,50]	100 mg daily during exposure and for 4 weeks afterwards

Mites, see SCABIES

MONILIFORMIS moniliformis infection

Drug of choice:	Pyrantel pamoate[7]	11 mg/kg once, repeat twice 2 wks apart

Infection	Drug	Adult Dosage*

Naegleria species, see AMEBIC MENINGOENCEPHALITIS, PRIMARY

Necator americanus, see HOOKWORM infection

Onchocerca volvulus, see FILARIASIS

Opisthorchis viverrini, see FLUKE infection

Paragonimus westermani, see FLUKE infection

Pediculus capitis, humanus, Phthirus pubis, see LICE

Pinworm, see ENTEROBIUS

PNEUMOCYSTIS carinii pneumonia[51]

Drug of choice:	Trimethoprim-sulfamethoxazole	TMP 20 mg/kg per day, SMX 100 mg/kg/d, oral or IV in 4 doses x 14-21d
Alternative:	Pentamidine isethionate	4 mg/kg/d IV x 14-21d

Roundworm, see ASCARIASIS

SCABIES (Sarcoptes scabiei)

Drug of choice:	5% Permethrin	Topically
Alternatives:	Lindane	Topically
	10% Crotamiton	Topically

SCHISTOSOMIASIS

  S. haematobium

Drug of choice:	Praziquantel	40 mg/kg/d in 2 doses x 1d

  S. japonicum

Drug of choice:	Praziquantel	60 mg/kg/d in 3 doses x 1d

  S. mansoni

Drug of choice:	Praziquantel	40 mg/kg/d in 2 doses x 1d
Alternative:	Oxamniquine	15 mg/kg once[52]

  S. mekongi

Drug of choice:	Praziquantel	60 mg/kg/d in 3 doses x 1d

Sleeping sickness, see TRYPANOSOMIASIS

STRONGYLOIDIASIS (Strongyloides stercoralis)

Drug of choice:[53]	Thiabendazole	50 mg/kg/d in 2 doses (max. 3 grams /d) x 2d[11,54]

TAPEWORM infection — Adult (intestinal stage)

  Diphyllobothrium latum (fish), Taenia saginata (beef), Taenia solium (pork) Dipylidium caninum (dog)

Drug of choice:	Niclosamide	A single dose of 4 tablets (2 grams), chewed thoroughly
	OR Praziquantel[7]	10-20 mg/kg once

  Hymenolepis nana (dwarf tapeworm)

Drug of choice:	Praziquantel[7]	25 mg/kg once
Alternative:	Niclosamide	A single daily dose of 4 tablets (2 g), chewed thoroughly, then 2 tablets daily x 6d

  — Larval (tissue stage)

  Echinococcus granulosus (hydatid cysts)

Drug of choice:	Albendazole[55]	400 mg bid x 28 days, repeated as necessary

  Echinococcus multilocularis

Treatment of choice:	See footnote 56	

  Cysticercus cellulosae (cysticercosis)

Drug of choice:[57]	Praziquantel[7]	50 mg/kg/d in 3 doses x 14d
	OR Albendazole	15 mg/kg/d in 3 doses x 30d, repeated as necessary
Alternative:	Surgery	

Infection	Drug	Adult Dosage*
Toxocariasis, see VISCERAL LARVA MIGRANS		
TOXOPLASMOSIS (Toxoplasma gondii)[58]		
Drugs of choice:	Pyrimethamine[59]	25 mg/d x 3-4 wks
	plus	
	trisulfapyrimidines	2-6 grams/d x 3-4 wks
OR	**plus** sulfadiazine	2-6 grams/d x 3-4 wks
Alternative:	Spiramycin	2-4 grams/d x 3-4 wks
TRICHINOSIS (Trichinella spiralis)		
Drugs of choice:	Steroids for severe symptoms	
	plus mebendazole[7,61]	200-400 mg tid x 3d, then 400-500 mg tid x 10d
TRICHOMONIASIS (Trichomonas vaginalis)		
Drug of choice:[62]	Metronidazole[3]	2 grams once or 250 mg tid orally x 7d
TRICHOSTRONGYLUS infection		
Drug of choice:[12]	Pyrantel pamoate[7]	11 mg/kg once (max. 1 gram)
Alternative:	Thiabendazole[7]	50 mg/kg/d (max. 3 grams/d) in 2 doses[11]
TRICHURIASIS (Trichuris trichiura, whipworm)		
Drug of choice:[12]	Mebendazole	100 mg bid x 3d
TRYPANOSOMIASIS		
T. cruzi (South American trypanosomiasis, Chagas' disease)		
Drug of choice:	Nifurtimox[2]	8-10 mg/kg/d orally in 4 doses x 120d
Alternative:	Benznidazole[63]	5-7 mg/kg/d x 30-120d
T. brucei gambiense; T. b. rhodesiense (African trypanosomiasis, sleeping sickness) hemolymphatic stage		
Drug of choice:[64]	Suramin[2]	100-200 mg (test dose) IV, then 1 gram IV on days 1,3,7,14, and 21
Alternative:	Pentamidine isethionate	4 mg/kg/d IM x 10d
late disease with CNS involvement		
Drug of choice:[64]	Melarsoprol[2,65]	2-3.6 mg/kg/d IV x 3 doses; after 1 wk 3.6 mg/kg per day IV x 3 doses; repeat again after 10-21 days
Alternatives:	Tryparsamide	One injection of 30 mg/kg (max. 2g) IV every 5d to total of 12 injections; may be repeated after 1 month
	plus suramin[2]	One injection of 10 mg/kg IV every 5d to total of 12 injections; may be repeated after 1 month
VISCERAL LARVA MIGRANS[66]		
Drug of choice:[67]	Diethylcarbamazine[7]	6 mg/kg/d in 3 doses x 7-10d
OR	Thiabendazole	50 mg/kg/d in 2 doses x 5d (max. 3 grams/d)[11]
Alternative:	Mebendazole[7]	100-200 mg bid x 5d[68]
Whipworm, see TRICHURIASIS		
Wuchereria bancrofti, see FILARIASIS		

* The letter d indicates day.

1. Dosage and duration of administration should not be exceeded because of possibility of causing optic neuritis; maximum dosage is 2 grams/day.

2. In the USA, this drug is available from the CDC Drug Service, Centers for Disease Control, Atlanta, Georgia 30333; telephone: 404-639-3670 (evenings, weekends, and holidays: 404-639-2888).

3. Metronidazole is carcinogenic in rodents and mutagenic in bacteria; it should generally not be given to pregnant women, particularly in the first trimester.

4. Outside the USA, ornidazole and tinidazole are also used.

5. Dehydroemetine is probably as effective and probably less toxic than emetine. Because of its toxic effects on the heart, patients receiving emetine should have electrocardiographic monitoring and should remain sedentary during therapy.

6. One patient with a Naegleria infection was successfully treated with amphotericin B, miconazole, and rifampin (JS Seidel et al, N Engl J Med, 306:346, 1982).

7. Considered an investigational drug for this condition by the U.S. Food and Drug Administration.

8. Experimental infections with Acanthamoeba sp. have been reported to respond to sulfadiazine (CG Culbertson, Annu Rev Microbiol, 25:231, 1971). Amebic keratitis due to Acanthamoeba sp. has been reported to respond to topical miconazole, propamidine isethionate, and antibiotics (MB Moore et al, Am J Ophthalmol, 100:396, 1985).

9. Effectiveness documented only in animals.

10. Analgesics, corticosteroids, and careful removal of CSF at frequent intervals can relieve symptoms. Albendazole and ivermectin have been used successfully in animals.

11. This dose is likely to be toxic and may have to be decreased.

12. Concurrent use of pentamidine and trimethoprim-sulfamethoxazole has been reported to cure an infection with B. divergens (O Raoult et al, Ann Intern Med, 107:944, 1987).

13. Limited clinical results suggest a decrease in diarrhea with therapy. Infection is self-limiting in immunocompetent patients.

14. Several reports indicate that ivermectin may be effective for treatment of W. bancrofti (S Diallo et al, Lancet, 1:1030, 1987) and M. ozzardi (TB Nutman et al, J Infect Dis, 156:662, 1987).

15. Diethylcarbamazine should be administered with special caution in heavy infections with Loa loa because it can provoke ocular problems or an encephalopathy. Antihistamines or corticosteroids may be required to decrease allergic reactions due to disintegration of microfilariae in treatment of all filarial infections, especially those caused by Onchocerca and Loa loa. Surgical excision of subcutaneous Onchocerca nodules is recommended by some authorities before starting drug therapy.

16. Ivermectin may also be effective.

17. Ivermectin in a dose of 200 µg/kg has been reported to be as effective as diethylcarbamazine in decreasing the number of microfilaria and causes fewer adverse ophthalmologic reactions (BM Greene et al, N Engl J Med, 313:133, 1985; AT White et al, J Infect Dis, 156:463, 1987). Semiannual to annual prophylaxis appears to be effective in keeping microfilarial counts at low levels.

18. Some Medical Letter consultants use suramin only if ocular microfilariae persist after diethylcarbamazine therapy and nodulectomy.

19. Unlike infections with other flukes, fasciola hepatica infections may not respond to praziquantel. Limited data indicate that albendazole may be effective in this condition.

20. Given on empty stomach. Although approved for human use, it is available currently only as a veterinary product. No alcoholic beverage should be consumed before or for 12 hours after therapy. Keep patient at bedrest for 4 hours after treatment.

21. In felines, ancylol (2, 6, diodo-4-nitrophenol) by subcutaneous injection has been effective against migrating larvae.

22. Albendazole is also effective (RNG Pugh, Ann Trop Med Parasitol, 80:565, 1986).

23. In sulfonamide-sensitive patients, such as some patients with AIDS, pyrimethamine 50-75 mg daily has been effective. In immunocompromised patients, it may be necessary to continue therapy indefinitely.

24. Limited data indicate that ketoconazole, 400 to 600 mg daily for 28 days, may be effective for treatment of L. panamensis and L. mexicana (cutaneous).

25. For the African form of visceral leishmaniasis, therapy may have to be extended to at least 30 days and may have to be repeated.

26. Ketoconazole, 400 mg daily for four to eight weeks, has also been reported to be effective (J Vallet et al, Am J Trop Med Hyg, 35:491, 1986).

27. Application of heat 39˚ to 42˚C directly to the lesion for 20 to 32 hours over a period of 10 to 12 days has been reported to be effective in L. tropica minor (FA Neva et al, Am J Trop Med Hyg, 33:800, 1984).

28. For infestation of eyelashes with crab lice, use petrolatum.

29. FDA-approved for head lice only

30. Some consultants recommend a second application one week later to kill hatching progeny.

31. AIDS patients may need longer duration of therapy. For AIDS patients who develop hypersensitivity or resistance to both TMP/SMX and pentamidine, trimetrexate with leucovorin rescue or a combination of dapsone and trimethoprim may be effective. Aerosolized pentamidine has been tried for both treatment and prophylaxis (Medical Letter, 29:103, 1987).

32. 5% permethrin, not yet marketed in the USA, could prove to be the drug of choice when it becomes available.

33. In East Africa, the dose should be increased to 30 mg/kg/d, and in Egypt and South Africa, 30 mg/kg/d x 2d. Neuropsychiatric disturbances and seizures have been reported in some patients (H Stokvis et al, Am J Trop Med Hyg, 35:330, 1986).

34. Albendazole or ivermectin have also been effective.

35. In disseminated strongyloidiasis, thiabendazole therapy should be continued for at least five days. In immunocompromised patients it may be necessary to continue therapy or use other agents (see footnote 34).

36. Niclosamide is effective for the treatment of T. solium but, since it causes disintegration of segments and release of viable eggs, its use creates a theoretical risk of causing cysticercosis. It should therefore be followed in three or four hours by a purge. Quinacrine is preferred by some clinicians because it expels T. solium intact.

37. Surgical resection of cysts is the treatment of choice. When surgery is contraindicated, or cysts rupture spontaneously during surgery, mebendazole (experimental for this purpose in the USA) can be tried (JF Wilson and RL Rausch, Ann Trop Med Parasitol, 76:165, 1982; ADM Bryceson et al, Trans R Soc Trop Med Hyg, 76:510, 1982). Albendazole has also been reported to be effective (DL Morris et al, JAMA, 253:2053, 1985). Flubendazole has also been used with some success (E Tellez-Giron et al, Am J Trop Med Hyg, 33:627, 1984). Praziquantel and albendazole will kill protoscolices and may be useful in case of spill during surgery.

38. Surgical excision is the only reliable means of treatment although recent reports have been encouraging about use of albendazole or mebendazole (JF Wilson et al, Am J Trop Med Hyg, 37:162, 1987; A Davis et al, Bull WHO, 64:383, 1986).

39. Corticosteroids should be given for two to three days before and during praziquantel therapy. Praziquantel should not be used for ocular or spinal cord cysticercosis. Metrifonate 7.5 mg/kg x 5d, repeated six times at two-week intervals, has been reported to be effective for ocular as well as cerebral and subcutaneous disease. Albendazole, 15 mg/kg x 30d, which can be repeated, has been used successfully (F Escobedo et al, Arch Intern Med, 147:738, 1987).

40. In ocular toxoplasmosis, corticosteroids should also be used for anti-inflammatory effect on the eyes.

41. Pyrimethamine is teratogenic in animals. To prevent hematological toxicity from pyrimethamine, it is advisable to give leucovorin (folinic acid), about 10 mg/day, either by injection or orally. Pyrimethamine alone 50-75 mg daily has been used to treat CNS toxoplasmosis after sulfonamide sensitivity develops. In AIDS patients treatment should continue indefinitely.

42. Every two to three days for infants. Most authorities would treat congenitally infected newborns for about one year.

43. The efficacy of thiabendazole for trichinosis is not clearly established; it appears to be effective during the intestinal phase but its effect on larvae that have migrated is questionable. In the tissue phase, mebendazole 200-400 mg tid x 3 days, then 400-500 mg tid x 10 days, may be effective. Albendazole may also be effective for this indication.

44. Sexual partners should be treated simultaneously. Outside the USA, ornidazole and tinidazole have been used for this condition. Metronidazole-resistant strains have been reported; higher doses of metronidazole for longer periods of time are sometimes effective against these strains.

45. Limited data

46. For prevention of attack after departure from areas where P. vivax and P. ovale are endemic, which includes almost all areas where malaria is found (except Haiti), some experts in addition prescribe primaquine phosphate 15 mg base (26.3 mg)/d or, for children, 0.3 mg base/kg/d during the last two weeks of prophylaxis. Others prefer to avoid the toxicity of primaquine and rely on surveillance to detect cases when they occur, particularly when exposure was limited or doubtful. See also footnote 44.

47. Beginning one week before travel and continuing for the duration of stay and for two more doses after leaving. For a stay of two weeks or less, Medical Letter consultants recommend four weekly doses followed by one more dose two weeks later. The pediatric dosage has not been approved by the FDA, and the drug has not been approved for use during pregnancy. Women should take contraceptive precautions while taking mefloquine and for two months after the last dose. Mefloquine is not recommended for children weighing less than 15 kg, or for patients taking beta-blockers, calcium-channel blockers, or other drugs that may prolong or otherwise alter cardiac conduction. Patients with a history of seizures or psychiatric

disorders and those whose occupation requires fine coordination or spatial discrimination probably should avoid mefloquine (Medical Letter, 31:13, Feb 9, 1990).

48. Resistance to *Fansidar* is widespread in Southeast Asia and the Amazon basin and is frequent in east Africa. Use of *Fansidar* is contraindicated in patients with a history of sulfonamide or pyrimethamine intolerance, in pregnancy at term, and in infants less than two months old.

49. Proguanil (*Paludrine* – Ayerst, Canada; ICI, England), which is not available in the US but is widely available overseas, is recommended mainly for use in Africa south of the Sahara. In addition, concurrent use of proguanil and sulfisoxazole (*Gantrisin*; and others) has been effective prophylactically in areas of mefloquine resistance in Thailand, particularly in young children for whom tetracycline is contraindicated (LW Pang et al, WHO Bull, 67:51, 1989).

50. The FDA considers use of tetracyclines as antimalarials to be investigational. Use of tetracyclines is contraindicated in pregnancy and in children less than eight years old. Physicians who prescribe doxycycline as malaria chemoprophylaxis should advise patients to use an appropriate sunscreen (Medical Letter, 31:59, 1989) to minimize the possibility of a photosensitivity reaction and should warn women that Candida vaginitis is a frequent adverse effect.

51. AIDS patients should be treated for 21 days. For AIDS patients who develop hypersensitivity or resistance to both TMP/SMX and pentamidine, trimetrexate with leucovorin rescue (Medical Letter, 31:5, 1989) or a combination of dapsone and trimethoprim may be effective. Oral TMP/SMX or aerosolized pentamidine is recommended for prophylaxis (Medical Letter, 31:91, 1989; JA Kovacs and H Masur, J Infect Dis, 160:882, Nov 1989).

52. In east Africa, the dose should be increased to 30 mg/kg/d, and in Egypt and South Africa, 30 mg/kg/d x 2d. Neuropsychiatric disturbances and seizures have been reported in some patients (H Stokvis et al, Am J Trop Med Hyg, 35:330, 1986).

53. In immunocompromised patients it may be necessary to continue therapy or use other agents. Albendazole or ivermectin has also been effective.

54. In disseminated strongyloidiasis, thiabendazole therapy should be continued for at least five days.

55. Some patients may benefit from or require surgical resection of cysts. Albendazole may also be useful preoperatively or in case of spill during surgery.

56. Surgical excision is the only reliable means of treatment, although some reports have suggested use of albendazole or mebendazole (JF Wilson et al, Am J Trop Med Hyg, 37:162, 1987; A Davis et al, Bull WHO, 64:383, 1986).

57. Corticosteroids should be given for two to three days before and during drug therapy. Metrifonate, 7.5 mg/kg x 5d, repeated six times at two-week intervals, has been reported to be effective for ocular as well as cerebral and subcutaneous disease. Any cysticercocidal drug, however, may cause irreparable damage when used to treat ocular or spinal cysts, even when corticosteroids are used.

58. In ocular toxoplasmosis, corticosteroids should also be used for anti-inflammatory effect on the eyes.

59. Pyrimethamine is teratogenic in animals. To prevent hematological toxicity from pyrimethamine, it is advisable to give leucovorin (folinic acid), about 10 mg/day, either by injection or orally. Some clinicians have used pyrimethamine 50 to 100 mg daily with a sulfonamide to treat CNS toxoplasmosis in patients with AIDS and, when sulfonamide sensitivity developed, have given clindamycin 1.8 to 2.4 g/d in divided doses instead of the sulfonamide. In AIDS patients, treatment should continue indefinitely.

60. Congenitally infected newborns should be treated with pyrimethamine every two or three days and a sulfonamide daily for about one year.

61. Albendazole or flubendazole may also be effective for this indication.

62. Sexual partners should be treated simultaneously. Outside the USA, ornidazole and tinidazole have been used for this condition. Metronidazole-resistant strains have been reported; higher doses of metronidazole for longer periods are sometimes effective against these strains.

63. Limited data

64. In T. b. gambiense infections, eflornithine (difluoromethylornithine; DFMO – Merrell Dow) has been effective in both the hemolymphatic and CNS stages. Its effectiveness in T. b. rhodesiense infections has been variable. Some clinicians have given 400 mg/kg/d IV in 4 divided doses for 14 days, followed by oral treatment with 300 mg/kg/d for 3-4 wks (F Doua et al, Am J Trop Med Hyg, 37:525, 1987).

65. In frail patients, begin with as little as 18 mg and increase the dose progressively. Pretreatment with suramin has been advocated for debilitated patients.

66. For severe symptoms or eye involvement, corticosteroids can be used in addition.

67. Ivermectin and albendazole may also be effective (D Stürchler et al, Ann Trop Med Parasitol, 83:473, 1989).

68. One report of a cure using 1 gram tid for 21 days has been published (IA Bekhti, Ann Intern Med, 100:463, 1984).

ADVERSE EFFECTS OF SOME ANTIPARASITIC DRUGS*

ALBENDAZOLE (Zentel)
Occasional: diarrhea; abdominal pain
Rare: leukopenia; alopecia; increased serum transaminase levels

BENZNIDAZOLE (Rochagan)
Frequent: allergic rash; dose-dependent polyneuropathy; gastrointestinal disturbance; psychic disturbance

BITHIONOL (Bitin)
Frequent: photosensitivity reactions; vomiting; diarrhea; abdominal pain; urticaria
Rare: leukopenia; toxic hepatitis

CHLOROQUINE HCl and CHLOROQUINE PHOSPHATE (Aralen; and others)
Occasional: pruritus; vomiting; headache; confusion; depigmentation of hair; skin eruptions; corneal opacity; weight loss; partial alopecia; extraocular muscle palsies; exacerbation of psoriasis, eczema and other exfoliative dermatoses; myalgias; photophobia
Rare: irreversible retinal injury (especially when total dosage exceeds 100 grams); discoloration of nails and mucous membranes; nerve-type deafness; peripheral neuropathy and myopathy; heart block; blood dyscrasias, hematemesis

CROTAMITON (Eurax)
Occasional: skin rash; conjunctivitis

DEHYDROEMETINE – Similar to emetine, but possibly less severe

DIETHYLCARBAMAZINE CITRATE USP (Hetrazan)
Frequent: severe allergic or febrile reactions due to the filarial infection; GI disturbances
Rare: encephalopathy; loss of vision in onchocerciasis

DILOXANIDE FUROATE (Furamide)
Frequent: flatulence
Occasional: nausea; vomiting; diarrhea
Rare: urticaria; pruritus

EFLORNITHINE (Difluoromethylornithine; DFMO; Ornidyl)
Frequent: diarrhea; anemia
Occasional: thrombocytopenia
Rare: seizures; hearing loss

EMETINE HCl
Frequent: cardiac arrhythmias; precordial pain; muscle weakness; cellulitis at site of injection
Occasional: diarrhea; vomiting; peripheral neuropathy; heart failure

FLUBENDAZOLE – similar to mebendazole, but frequent inflammation at IM injection site

FURAZOLIDONE (Furoxone)
Frequent: nausea; vomiting
Occasional: allergic reactions, including pulmonary infiltration, hypotension, urticaria, fever, vesicular rash; hypoglycemia; headache
Rare: hemolytic anemia in G-6-PD deficiency and neonates; disulfiram-like reaction with alcohol; MAO-inhibitor interactions; polyneuritis

IODOQUINOL (Yodoxin)
Occasional: rash; acne; slight enlargement of the thyroid gland; nausea; diarrhea; cramps; anal pruritus
Rare: optic atrophy, loss of vision, peripheral neuropathy after prolonged use in high dosage (for months); iodine sensitivity

IVERMECTIN (Mectizan)
Occasional: fever; pruritus; tender lymph nodes; headache; joint and bone pain
Rare: hypotension

LINDANE (Kwell; and others)
Occasional: eczematous skin rash; conjunctivitis
Rare: convulsions; aplastic anemia

MALATHION (Ovide)
Occasional: local irritation

MEBENDAZOLE (Vermox)
Occasional: diarrhea; abdominal pain
Rare: leukopenia; agranulocytosis; hypospermia

MEFLOQUINE (Lariam)
Frequent: vertigo; lightheadedness; nausea; other gastrointestinal disturbances; nightmares; visual disturbances; headache
Occasional: confusion; psychosis
Rare: convulsions; coma

MELARSOPROL (Mel B; Arsobal)
Frequent: myocardial damage; albuminuria; hypertension; colic;

Herxheimer-type reaction; encephalopathy; vomiting; peripheral neuropathy
Rare: shock

METRIFONATE (Bilarcil)
Frequent: reversible plasma cholinesterase inhibition
Occasional: nausea; vomiting; abdominal pain; headache; vertigo

METRONIDAZOLE (Flagyl; and others)
Frequent: nausea; headache; dry mouth; metallic taste
Occasional: vomiting; diarrhea; insomnia; weakness; stomatitis; vertigo; paresthesia; rash; dark urine; urethral burning; disulfiram-like reaction with alcohol
Rare: seizures; encephalopathy; pseudomembranous colitis; ataxia; leukopenia; peripheral neuropathy; pancreatitis

NICLOSAMIDE (Niclocide)
Occasional: nausea; abdominal pain

NIFURTIMOX (Bayer 2502; Lampit)
Frequent: anorexia; vomiting; weight loss; loss of memory; sleep disorders; tremor; paresthesias; weakness; polyneuritis
Rare: convulsions; fever; pulmonary infiltrates and pleural effusion

ORNIDAZOLE (Tiberal)
Occasional: dizziness; headache; gastrointestinal disturbances
Rare: reversible peripheral neuropathy

OXAMNIQUINE (Vansil)
Occasional: headache; fever; dizziness; somnolence; nausea; diarrhea; rash; insomnia; hepatic enzyme changes; ECG changes; EEG changes; orange-red discoloration of urine
Rare: convulsions; neuropsychiatric disturbances

PAROMOMYCIN (Humatin)
Frequent: GI disturbance
Rare: eighth-nerve damage (mainly auditory); renal damage

PENTAMIDINE ISETHIONATE (Pentam 300)
Frequent: hypotension; hypoglycemia often followed by diabetes mellitus; vomiting; blood dyscrasias; renal damage; pain at injection site; GI disturbances

Occasional: may aggravate diabetes; shock; hypocalcemia; liver damage; cardiotoxicity; delirium; rash
Rare: Herxheimer-type reaction; anaphylaxis; acute pancreatitis; hyperkalemia

PERMETHRIN (*Nix; Elimite*)
Occasional: burning; stinging; numbness; increased pruritus; pain; edema; erythema; rash

PIPERAZINE CITRATE USP
Occasional: dizziness; urticaria; GI disturbances
Rare: exacerbation of epilepsy; visual disturbances; ataxia; hypotonia

PRAZIQUANTEL (*Biltricide*)
Frequent: malaise; headache; dizziness
Occasional: sedation; abdominal discomfort; fever; sweating; nausea; eosinophilia; fatigue
Rare: pruritus; rash

PRIMAQUINE PHOSPHATE USP
Frequent: hemolytic anemia in G-6-PD deficiency
Occasional: neutropenia; GI disturbances; methemoglobinemia in G-6-PD deficiency
Rare: CNS symptoms; hypertension; arrhythmias

PROGUANIL (*Paludrine*)
Occasional: oral ulceration; vomiting; abdominal pain; diarrhea (with large doses); hair loss; scaling of palms and soles
Rare: hematuria (with large doses)

PYRANTEL PAMOATE (*Antiminth*)
Occasional: GI disturbances; headache; dizziness; rash; fever

PYRETHRINS and PIPERONYL BUTOXIDE (*RID*; others)
Occasional: allergic reactions

PYRIMETHAMINE USP (*Daraprim*)
Occasional: blood dyscrasias; folic acid deficiency
Rare: rash; vomiting; convulsions; shock; possibly pulmonary eosinophilia

QUINACRINE HCl USP (*Atabrine*)
Frequent: dizziness; headache; vomiting; diarrhea
Occasional: yellow staining of skin; toxic psychosis; insomnia; bizarre dreams; blood dyscrasias; urticaria; blue and black nail pigmentation; psoriasis-like rash
Rare: acute hepatic necrosis; convulsions; severe exfoliative dermatitis; ocular effects similar to those caused by chloroquine

QUININE DIHYDROCHLORIDE and SULFATE
Frequent: cinchonism (tinnitus, headache, nausea, abdominal pain, visual disturbance)
Occasional: hemolytic anemia; other blood dyscrasias; photosensitivity reactions; hypoglycemia; arrhythmias; hypotension; drug fever
Rare: blindness; sudden death if injected too rapidly

SPIRAMYCIN (*Rovamycine*)
Occasional: GI disturbances
Rare: allergic reactions

STIBOGLUCONATE SODIUM (*Pentostam*)
Frequent: muscle pain and joint stiffness; nausea and vomiting
Occasional: colic; diarrhea; rash; pruritus; myocardial damage; liver damage; bradycardia
Rare: hemolytic anemia; renal damage; shock; sudden death

SURAMIN SODIUM (*Germanin*)
Frequent: vomiting; pruritus; urticaria; paresthesias; hyperesthesia of hands and feet; photophobia; peripheral neuropathy
Occasional: kidney damage; blood dyscrasias; shock; optic atrophy

THIABENDAZOLE (*Mintezol*)
Frequent: nausea; vomiting; vertigo
Occasional: leukopenia; crystalluria; rash; hallucinations; olfactory disturbance; erythema multiforme; Stevens-Johnson syndrome
Rare: shock; tinnitus; intrahepatic cholestasis; convulsions; angioneurotic edema

TINIDAZOLE (*Fasigyn*) `
Occasional: metallic taste; nausea; vomiting; rash

TRIMETREXATE (with "leucovorin rescue")
Occasional: rash; peripheral neuropathy; increased serum aminotransferase concentrations

TRYPARSAMIDE
Frequent: nausea; vomiting
Occasional: impaired vision; optic atrophy; fever; exfoliative dermatitis; allergic reactions; tinnitus

Drugs Available from Centers for Disease Control

Agent	Use
Bithionol (Bitin)	Paragonimiasis, Fascioliasis
Dehydroemetine HCl	Amebiasis
Diloxanide Furoate (Furamide)	Amebiasis
Ivermectin (Mectizan)	Onchocerciasis
Melarsoprol (Mel B)	African trypanosomiasis
Nifurtimox (Bayer 2502)	Chagas disease
Quinine dihydrochloride	Plasmodium falciparim malaria
Rifabutin (Ansamycin)	Mycobacterium avium-intracellulare
Sodium stibogluconate (Pentostam)	Leishmaniasis
Suramin sodium (Bayer 205)	African trypanosomiasis (sleeping sickness) Onchocerciasis

Drugs are available without charge under an Investigational New Drug (IND) basis from the FDA. The physician must provide information about the infection, laboratory data and limited patient data (name, age, weight, gender) and must agree to register as a Clinical Investigator by completing FDA form FD-1573.

Product information and the product may be obtained by contacting:

Centers for Disease Control
Drugs and Immunobiologics Service
1600 Clifton Road, Bldg 1, Rm 1259
Atlanta, GA 30333

Telephone:
Business hours: 8:00-4:30 EST
(404) 639-3670
Nights/weekends/holidays:
(404) 639-2888

AIDS

A. Case Definition for Acquired Immunodeficiency Syndrome (Centers for Disease Control, MMWR 36:3S,1987)

For national reporting, a case of AIDS is defined as an illness characterized by one or more of the following "indicator" diseases, depending on the status of laboratory evidence of HIV infection, as shown below.

I. **Without Laboratory Evidence Regarding HIV Infection**

If laboratory tests for HIV were not performed or gave inconclusive results (See Appendix I) and the patient had no other cause of immunodeficiency listed in Section I.A below, then any disease listed in Section I.B indicates AIDS if it was diagnosed by a definitive method (See Appendix II).

A. **Causes of immunodeficiency that disqualify diseases as indicators of AIDS in the absence of laboratory evidence for HIV infection**

1. high-dose or long-term systemic corticosteroid therapy or other immunosuppressive/cytotoxic therapy $\leq$ 3 months before the onset of the indicator disease

2. any of the following diseases diagnosed $\leq$ 3 months after diagnosis of the indicator disease: Hodgkin's disease, non-Hodgkin's lymphoma (other than primary brain lymphoma), lymphocytic leukemia, multiple myeloma, any other cancer of lymphoreticular or histiocytic tissue, or angioimmunoblastic lymphadenopathy

3. a genetic (congenital) immunodeficiency syndrome or an acquired immunodeficiency syndrome atypical of HIV infection, such as one involving hypogammaglobulinemia

B. **Indicator diseases diagnosed definitively (See Appendix II)**

1. candidiasis of the esophagus, trachea, bronchi, or lungs
2. cryptococcosis, extrapulmonary
3. cryptosporidiosis with diarrhea persisting > 1 month
4. cytomegalovirus disease of an organ other than liver, spleen, or lymph nodes in a patient > 1 month of age
5. herpes simplex virus infection causing a mucocutaneous ulcer that persists longer than 1 month; or bronchitis pneumonitis, or esophagitis for any duration affecting a patient > 1 month of age
6. Kaposi's sarcoma affecting a patient < 60 years of age
7. lymphoma of the brain (primary) affecting a patient < 60 years of age
8. lymphoid interstitial pneumonia and/or pulmonary lymphoid hyperplasia (LIP/PLH complex) affecting a child < 13 years of age
9. <u>Mycobacterium</u> <u>avium</u> complex or <u>M</u>. <u>kansasii</u> disease, disseminated (at a site other than or in addition to lungs, skin, or cervical or hilar lymph nodes)
10. <u>Pneumocystis</u> <u>carinii</u> pneumonia
11. progressive multifocal leukoencephalopathy
12. toxoplasmosis of the brain affecting a patient > 1 month of age

II. **With Laboratory Evidence for HIV Infection**

Regardless of the presence of other causes of immunodeficiency (I.A), in the presence of laboratory evidence for HIV infection (See Appendix I), any disease listed above (I.B) or below (II.A or II.B) indicates a diagnosis of AIDS.

A. Indicator diseases diagnosed definitively (See Appendix II)

1. bacterial infections, multiple or recurrent (any combination of at least two within a 2-year period), of the following types affecting a child < 13 years of age:

   septicemia, pneumonia, meningitis, bone or joint infection, or abscess of an internal organ or body cavity (excluding otitis media or superficial skin or mucosal abscesses), caused by Haemophilus, Streptococcus (including pneumococcus), or other pyogenic bacteria

2. coccidioidomycosis, disseminated (at a site other than or in addition to lungs or cervical or hilar lymph nodes)

3. HIV encephalopathy (also called "HIV dementia", "AIDS dementia", or "subacute encephalitis due to HIV") (See Appendix II for description)

4. histoplasmosis, disseminated (at a site other than or in addition to lungs or cervical or hilar lymph nodes)

5. isosporiasis with diarrhea persisting > 1 month

6. Kaposi's sarcoma at any age

7. lymphoma of the brain (primary) at any age

8. other non-Hodgkin's lymphoma of B-cell or unknown immunologic phenotype and the following histologic types:

   a. small noncleaved lymphoma (either Burkitt or non-Burkitt type)

   b. immunoblastic sarcoma (equivalent to any of the following, although not necessarily all in combination: immunoblastic lymphoma, large-cell lymphoma, diffuse histiocytic lymphoma, diffuse undifferentiated lymphoma, or high-grade lymphoma)

   Note: Lymphomas are not included here if they are of T-cell immunologic phenotype or their histologic type is not described or is described as "lymphocytic", "lymphoblastic", "small cleaved", or "plasmacytoid lymphocytic".

9. any mycobacterial disease caused by mycobacteria other than M. tuberculosis, disseminated (at a site other than or in addition to lungs, skin, or cervical or hilar lymph nodes)

10. disease caused by M. tuberculosis, extrapulmonary (involving at least one site outside the lungs, regardless of whether there is concurrent pulmonary involvement)

11. Salmonella (nontyphoid) septicemia, recurrent

12. HIV wasting syndrome (emaciation, "slim disease") (See Appendix II for description)

B. Indicator diseases diagnosed presumptively (by a method other than those in Appendix II)

Note: Given the seriousness of diseases indicative of AIDS, it is generally important to diagnose them definitively, especially when therapy that would be used may have serious side effects or when definitive diagnosis is needed for eligibility for antiretroviral therapy. Nonetheless, in some situations, a patient's condition will not permit the performance of definitive tests. In other situations, accepted clinical practice may be to diagnose presumptively based on the presence of characteristic clinical and laboratory abnormalities. Guidelines for presumptive diagnoses are suggested in Appendix III.

1. candidiasis of the esophagus
2. cytomegalovirus retinitis with loss of vision
3. Kaposi's sarcoma
4. lymphoid interstitial pneumonia and/or pulmonary lymphoid hyperplasia (LIP/PLH complex) affecting a child < 13 years of age
5. mycobacterial disease (acid-fast bacilli with species not identified by culture), disseminated (involving at least one site other than or in addition to lungs, skin, or cervical or hilar lymph nodes)
6. <u>Pneumocystis carinii</u> pneumonia
7. toxoplasmosis of the brain affecting a patient > 1 month of age

III. **With Laboratory Evidence Against HIV Infection**

With laboratory test results negative for HIV infection (See Appendix I), a diagnosis of AIDS for surveillance purposes is ruled out unless:

A. all the other causes of immunodeficiency listed above in Section I.A are excluded; **AND**

B. the patient has had either:

1. <u>Pneumocystis carinii</u> pneumonia diagnosed by a definitive method (See Appendix II); **OR**

2. **a.** any of the other diseases indicative of AIDS listed above in Section I.B diagnosed by a definitive method (See Appendix II); **AND**

   b. a T-helper/inducer (CD4) lymphocyte count < 400/mm^3.

Laboratory Evidence For or Against HIV Infection

1. **For Infection:**
   When a patient has disease consistent with AIDS:
   a. a serum specimen from a patient ≥ 15 months of age, or from a child
       < 15 months of age whose mother is not thought to have had HIV
       infection during the child's perinatal period, that is repeatedly
       reactive for HIV antibody by a screening test (e.g., enzyme-linked
       immunosorbent assay [ELISA]), as long as subsequent HIV-antibody tests
       (e.g., Western blot, immunofluorescence assay), if done, are positive; **OR**
   b. a serum specimen from a child < 15 months of age, whose mother is
       thought to have had HIV infection during the child's perinatal period,
       that is repeatedly reactive for HIV antibody by a screening test (e.g.,
       ELISA), plus increased serum immunoglobulin levels and at least one
       of the following abnormal immunologic test results: reduced absolute
       lymphocyte count, depressed CD4 (T-helper) lymphocyte count, or
       decreased CD4/CD8 (helper/suppressor) ratio, as long as subsequent
       antibody tests (e.g., Western blot, immunofluorescence assay), if done,
       are positive; **OR**
   c. a positive test for HIV serum antigen; **OR**
   d. a positive HIV culture confirmed by both reverse transcriptase
       detection and a specific HIV-antigen test or in situ hybridization
       using a nucleic acid probe; **OR**
   e. a positive result on any other highly specific test for HIV
       (e.g., nucleic acid probe of peripheral blood lymphocytes).

2. **Against Infection:**
   A nonreactive screening test for serum antibody to HIV (e.g., ELISA)
   without a reactive or positive result on any other test for HIV infection
   (e.g., antibody, antigen, culture), if done.

3. **Inconclusive (Neither For Nor Against Infection):**
   a. a repeatedly reactive screening test for serum antibody to HIV (e.g.,
       ELISA) followed by a negative or inconclusive supplemental test (e.g.,
       Western blot, immunofluorescence assay) without a positive HIV
       culture or serum antigen test, if done; **OR**
   b. a serum specimen from a child < 15 months of age, whose mother is
       thought to have had HIV infection during the child's perinatal period,
       that is repeatedly reactive for HIV antibody by a screening test, even
       if positive by a supplemental test, without additional evidence for
       immunodeficiency as described above (in I.b) and without a positive
       HIV culture or serum antigen test, if done.

Definitive Diagnostic Methods for Disease Indicative of AIDS

Diseases	Definitive Diagnostic Methods

cryptosporidiosis
cytomegalovirus
isosporiasis
Kaposi's sarcoma
lymphoma
lymphoid pneumonia
  or hyperplasia
Pneumocystis carinii
  pneumonia
progressive multifocal
  leukoencephalopathy
toxoplasmosis
	microscopy (histology or cytology).

candidiasis	gross inspection by endoscopy or autopsy or by microscopy (histology or cytology) on a specimen obtained directly from the tissues affected (including scrapings from the mucosal surface), not from a culture.
coccidioidomycosis	microscopy (histology or cytology), culture, or detection of antigen in a specimen obtained directly from the tissues affected or a fluid from those tissues.
tuberculosis other mycobacteriosis salmonellosis other bacterial infection	culture.
HIV encephalopathy* (dementia)	clinical findings of disabling congnitive and/or motor dysfunction interfering with occupation or activities of daily living, or loss of behavioral developmental milestones affecting a child, progressing over weeks to months, in the absence of a concurrent illness or condition other than HIV infection that could explain the findings. Methods to rule out such cerebrospinal illnesses and conditions must include cerebrospinal fluid examination and either brain imaging (computed tomography or magnetic resonance) or autopsy.
HIV wasting syndrome*	findings of profound involuntary weight loss <10% of baseline body weight plus either chronic diarrhea (at least two loose stools per day for ≥ 30 days) or chronic weakness and documented fever (for ≥ 30 days, intermittent or constant) in the absence of a concurrent illness or condition other than HIV that could explain the infection findings (e.g., cancer, tuberculosis, cryptosporidiosis, or other specific enteritis).

*For HIV encephalopathy and HIV wasting syndrome, the methods of diagnosis described here are
not truly definitive, but are sufficiently rigorous for surveillance purposes.

APPENDIX III

A. Suggested Guidelines for Presumptive Diagnosis of Diseases Indicative of AIDS

Diseases	Presumptive Diagnostic Criteria
candidiasis of esophagus	a. recent onset of retrosternal pain on swallowing; AND b. oral candidiasis diagnosed by the gross appearance of white patches or plaques on an erythematous base or by the microscopic appearance of fungal mycelial filaments in an uncultured specimen scraped from the oral mucosa.
cytomegalovirus retinitis	a characteristic appearance on serial ophthalmoscopic examinations (e.g., discrete patches of retinal whitening with distinct borders, spreading in a centrifugal manner, following blood vessels, progressing over several months, frequently associated with retinal vasculitis, hemorrhage, and necrosis). Resolution of active disease leaves retinal scarring and atrophy with retinal pigment epithelial mottling.
mycobacteriosis	microscopy of a specimen from stool or normally sterile body fluids or tissue from a site other than lungs, skin, or cervical or hilar lymph nodes, showing acid-fast bacilli of a species not identified by culture.
Kaposi's sarcoma	a characteristic gross appearance of an erythematous or violaceous plaque-like lesion on skin or mucous membrane. (**Note**: Presumptive diagnosis of Kaposi's sarcoma should not be made by clinicians who have seen few cases of it.)
lymphoid interstitial pneumonia	bilateral reticulonodular interstitial pulmonary infiltrates present on chest x-ray for ≥ 2 months with no pathogen identified and no response to antibiotic treatment.
Pneumocystis carinii pneumonia	a. a history of dyspnea on exertion or nonproductive cough of recent onset (within the past 3 months); AND b. chest x-ray evidence of diffuse bilateral interstitial infiltrates or gallium scan evidence of diffuse bilateral pulmonary disease; AND c. arterial blood gas analysis showing an arterial pO_2 of <70 mm Hg or a low respiratory diffusing capacity ($<80\%$ of predicted values) or an increase in the alveolar-arterial oxygen tension gradient; AND d. no evidence of a bacterial pneumonia.
toxoplasmosis of the brain	a. recent onset of a focal neurologic abnormality consistent with intracranial disease or a reduced level of consciousness; AND b. brain imaging evidence of a lesion having a mass effect (on computed tomography or nuclear magnetic resonance) or the radiographic appearance of which is enhanced by injection of contrast medium; AND c. serum antibody to toxoplasmosis or successful response to therapy for toxoplasmosis.

B. Recommendations for HIV Serologic Testing (MMWR 36:509,1987)

"Guidelines are based on public health considerations for HIV testing, including the principles of counseling before and after testing, confidentiality or personal information, and understanding that a person may decline to be tested without being denied health care or other services except where testing is required by law". Specific recommendations:

1. Persons who have sexually transmitted diseases.

2. IV drug abusers.

3. Persons who consider themselves at risk.

4. Women at risk who are of child bearing age or pregnant. Risk categories are: IV drug abuse; prostitution; male sexual partners who are bisexual, IV drug abusers or HIV infected; living in communities or born in countries with high prevalence in women; and blood transfusion between 1978 and 1985.

5. Prostitutes (male and female).

6. Medical evaluation (diagnostic test) for patients with selected clinical findings including generalized lymphadenopathy; unexplained dementia; chronic, unexplained fever or diarrhea; unexplained weight loss; or diseases such as tuberculosis, sexually transmitted diseases, generalized herpes, chronic candidiasis, other opportunistic infections suggesting unexplained defective cell-mediated immunity*, unexplained cytopenias* (anemia, leukopenia, lymphopenia, thrombocytopenia) and unexplained neurologic syndromes* (Guillain-Barre syndrome, aseptic meningitis, peripheral neuropathies).

7. Pregnant women, especially in high incidence areas*.

8. Patients with tuberculosis, especially if severe, extrapulmonary or unusual in presentation, or if patient is in risk category.

9. Recipient and source of blood or body fluid exposures*. Body fluids considered at risk include: semen, vaginal secretions, cerebrospinal fluids, synovial fluid, pleural fluid, peritoneal fluid, pericardial fluid, amniotic fluid and any bloody body fluid. Body fluids not considered at risk are feces, nasal secretions, sputum, saliva, sweat, tears, urine and vomitus unless they contain visible blood (MMWR 37:377,1988).

10. "Consideration categories" depending on seroprevalence, cost-effectiveness, implementation process, etc: persons considering marriage, hospital admissions (age group with high incidence and persons in correctional systems).

---

* Added by author

Management Guidelines for Patients with HIV Infection:
Vaccines and Antimicrobial Agents by Disease Strata
(Adapted from recommendations of FDA, CDC and State-of-Art Conference
sponsored by NIAID, National Institutes of Health, March 3-4, 1990)

Patient population	Tests	Treatment	Comment
All patients	Screening: CBC, T4 count, RPR, PPD[1]	Influenza vaccine[1] Pneumococcal vaccine[1]	Annual, preferably Sept-Nov Once only Positive PPD (induration >5mm) or history of positive PPD, chest x-ray and INH (300 mg/day for ≥ 12 mo.) [1,3]. If no evidence for active disease, prescribe INH monthly.
	HBV serology: HBsAb (HBsAg is optional)	Neg serology: HBV vaccine[1,2] (see comments)	HBV vaccine indications are for active drug users and sexually active gay men.
T4 count > 600/mm³	T4 count q 6 mo.		
T4 count 500-600/mm³	T4 count q 3-4 mo.		T4 counts at 3-4 mo. intervals are also recommended with symptoms of ARC or other significant deterioration.
T4 count 300-500/mm³	T4 count q 6 mo. CBC monthly, then q 3 mo. if stable[3] Baseline CPK	AZT, 500 mg/day[2]	There should be two T4 counts <500/mm³ at least 1 week apart before initiating AZT. Patient should be seen at two weeks after initiating AZT to review side effects, then monthly visits x 3 mo., then q 3 mo. if stable.
T4 count 200-300/mm³	T4 count q 3-4 mo. CBC q 3 mo.[3]	AZT, 500 mg day[2]	
T4 count < 200/mm³	CBC q 3 mo. (while receiving AZT)	PCP prophylaxis: Aerosolized pentamidine, 300 mg q mo.[1,2] or TMP-SMX, 1 DS po bid[1] AZT, 500 mg/day[2]	There should be two T4 counts <200/mm³ at least one week apart before initiating PCP prophylaxis. Patients who can not receive AZT should be considered for alternative retroviral therapy. Monitoring T4 counts is not necessary when <200/mm³. See above regarding monitoring during AZT treatment.
Care providers		Influenza vaccine[1] HBV vaccine[1,2] PPD	Annual Annual

1. Recommendation of the Centers for Disease Control.
2. FDA-approved indication.
3. AZT should be reduced in dose or temporarily discontinued for Hgb < 8 gm or neutrophil count < 750/mm³.

D. Universal Precautions (MMWR 37:377,1988)

1. <u>Blood and body fluid precautions</u> should be used for all patients.
   a. Blood is the single most important source of HIV, HBV and other blood-borne pathogens in the occupational setting. Universal precautions apply to blood and body fluids containing visible blood, semen, vaginal secretions, to tissues and to the following fluids: CSF, synovial fluid and amniotic fluid. The risk of transmission of HIV and HBV from these fluids is unknown.
   b. Universal precautions do not apply to saliva, stool, nasal secretions, sputum, sweat, tears, urine and vomitus (unless bloody).

2. <u>Barrier techniques</u> should be used to prevent skin and mucous membrane exposure when contact with blood and relevant body fluids is anticipated.
   a. Gloves should be worn when touching blood, body fluids, mucous membranes or non-intact skin or when performing venipunctures.
   b. Masks and protective eyeware or face shields should be worn during procedures likely to generate droplets of blood or body fluids to prevent exposure of mucous membranes and eyes.
   c. Gowns or aprons should be worn during procedures likely to generate splashes of blood or body fluids.
   d. Hands and skin should be washed immediately if contaminated with blood or body fluids.
   e. Needles and other sharp instruments should be disposed using a puncture resistant container.
   f. Mouthpieces and resuscitation bags should be available when use is anticipated.
   g. Health care workers with exudative lesions or weeping dermatitis should avoid direct patient contact.

3. <u>Office housekeeping</u>
   a. Surfaces should be cleaned when contaminated.
   b. Scrubbing is as important as the cleaning agent.
   c. Soiled linens should be properly bagged and washed in water at 160°F (71°C) with detergent x 30 min.

4. <u>Sterilization of instruments</u>
   a. Instruments should be thoroughly cleansed prior to sterilization or disinfection.
   b. Common chemical germicides rapidly inactivate HIV.
   c. Sodium hypochlorite (household bleach) at 1:10 concentrations inactivates HIV.

E. Occupational Exposure to HIV (MMWR 39:1,1990)

Definition

<u>Exposure</u>: Needlestick or cut with sharp object, contact with mucous membranes or contact with skin (especially if chapped, abraded or dermatitis, contact is prolonged and/or involves extensive area with blood or tissue).

<u>Body fluid of source</u>: (1) Blood or body fluid, (2) other body fluids to which universal precautions apply: cerebrospinal fluid, synovial fluid, pleural fluid, peritoneal fluid, pericardial fluid and amniotic fluid, or

(3) laboratory specimens containing HIV. (All seroconversions in non-laboratory health care workers have involved blood or bloody fluid.)

Source: Source must be evaluated for hepatitis B virus and HIV. If source has AIDS, is known to be seropositive or refuses testing, the worker is evaluated clinically and serologically for HIV.

Serology: Worker is tested serologically for HIV at 0, 6 weeks (optional), 12 weeks and 6 months post exposure. The worker is advised to report any acute illness, especially if it resembles acute HIV infection (fever, rash, myalgia, lymphadenopathy, dysphagia, hepatosplenomegaly and leuko-penia with atypical lymphocytes). During the follow-up, especially the first 12 weeks, the worker should refrain from donating blood or sperm and should abstain from sexual intercourse or use appropriate measures to prevent HIV transmission.

Prophylactic AZT: Relevant issues

1. The risk of HIV transmission with the usual type of needlestick injury from an HIV infected source is about 0.4% (1/250).

2. Data from animal studies are inadequate to support or refute the potential efficacy of AZT.

3. One anecdotal case of a patient with a large blood exposure showed massive doses of AZT initiated within 45 minutes did not prevent seroconversion (Lange JM et al: NEJM 322:1375,1990).

4. Side effects of AZT in health care workers receiving 1200 mg/day for 6 weeks showed 29% had anemia (Hgb 9.5-12 gm/dL) and 14% discontinued the drug due to reversible subjective complaints (headache, nausea, myalgias). Teratogenic and carcinogenic potentials in man are unknown, although prolonged administration of AZT to rats and mice resulted in vaginal carcinomas in 8% at 22 months. Men and women receiving AZT should avoid conception.

5. Regimens: 100 mg 5x/day x 4-6 weeks; some authorities use 200 mg as the initial dose and some advocate 200 mg 5x/day; recommendations for duration of treatment range from 1-4 mo.

6. Policy of Johns Hopkins Hospital:
   (a) Exposure must satisfy CDC definition.
   (b) Source must have AIDS, known positive HIV serology or be in risk group with >10% incidence rate (gay male, IVDA, hemophiliac or regular sexual partner of person with HIV or at high risk).
   (c) AZT should be started as soon as possible after exposure and no more than 4 hours after exposure. (Some extend to ≤24 hr).
   (d) Recommendations are based on extent of injury:
      Massive (deep injections or transfusions of HIV positive blood) - AZT recommended.
      Serious (deep needlestick, splashes of large amounts of blood into open cuts) - AZT available.
      Less severe (usual needlestick) - AZT available, not encouraged.

Contacts for physicians and occupational health professionals

1. To enroll persons with massive exposure in NIAID study of AZT prophylaxis: 800-537-9978.

2. To enroll exposed worker in CDC prospective surveillance program: (404) 639-1644.

F. Management of Opportunistic Infections in Patients with HIV Infection

	Preferred	Alternative	Comment
PROTOZOA			
Pneumocystis carinii			
Acute infection	Trimethoprim (15-20 mg/kg/day) + sulfamethoxazole (75-100 mg/kg/day) po or IV x 21 days in 3-4 daily doses	Pentamidine (4 mg/kg/day) IV (or IM) x 21 days Aerosolized pentamidine (600 mg/day) x 21 days (mild disease only)	Alternatives for patient with toxicity to primary agents (to complete 21 day course): 1) Dapsone (100 mg po q 24 h)+ trimethoprim (5 mg/kg po or IV q 6 h) 2) Clindamycin (600-900 mg IV q 6 h x 10 days, then 450 mg po q 6 h) + primaquine (30 mg base po/day) 3) Trimetrexate (experimental) (45 mg/m2 + leukovorin (80 mg/m2 po or IV q 6 h) Patients with moderately severe or severe disease (pO2 < 75 mmHg) should receive corticosteroids (prednisone, 40 mg po bid x 5 days, then 40 mg qd x 5 days, then 20 mg/day to completion of treatment)
Prophylaxis	Aerosolized pentamidine (300 mg) q month Trimethoprim (2.5-5 mg/kg + sulfamethoxazole po (1 DS) qd or bid	Dapsone 100 mg po/day Pyrimethamine (25 mg) + sulfadoxine (500 mg) po q wk (1 Fansidar/wk)	Relative merits of these regimens are unknown Prophylaxis is indicated for any HIV infected patient with a history of Pneumocystis pneumonia or a CD4 count < 200/cu mm Serious reactions including death from Stevens-Johnson syndrome have been reported with Fansidar
Toxoplasma encephalitis			
Acute infection	Pyrimethamine (25-75 mg/day) po + folinic acid (5-15 mg/day) po + sulfadiazine or trisulfapyrimidines (4-8 gm/day) po for at least 6 wks	Pyrimethamine + folinic acid (prior doses) + clindamycin (900-1200 mg) IV q6-8h for at least 6 weeks	All patients who respond to primary therapy should receive life-long suppressive therapy (continued)

145

	Preferred	Alternative	Comment
Suppressive therapy	Pyrimethamine (25 mg) po q d plus sulfadiazine or trisulfapyrimidines (2-4 gm/day) po q d or 3-5 x/week	Pyrimethamine (25 mg) po qd plus clindamycin (300-450 mg) po q6-8h	Efficacy of spiramycin and octreotide not established
Cryptosporidia	Spiramycin (experimental) (1 gm) po tid	Octreotide (Sandostatin) 300-500 ug SC	
Isospora			
Acute infection	Trimethoprim (5 mg/kg) + sulfamethoxazole po bid (2 DS po bid) x 1 month	Pyrimethamine, 50-75 mg po/day + folinic acid, 5-10 mg/day x 1 mo.	Duration of high dose therapy is not well defined
Suppressive treatment	Trimethoprim (2.5-5.0 mg/kg) + sulfamethoxazole (1-2 DS/day) po	Pyrimethamine (25 mg) + sulfadoxine (500 mg) po q wk (1 Fansidar/wk) Pyrimethamine, 25 mg + folinic acid 5 mg/day	Duration is not well defined
FUNGI			
Candida			
Thrush			
Initial infection	Ketoconazole (200 mg) po bid; Nystatin (500,000 units qid) orally, Clotrimazole oral troches (10 mg) qid	Amphotericin B (0.3-0.5 mg/kg) IV q day; Fluconazole (100 mg) po qd	Treat until symptoms resolve and then begin maintenance therapy Amphotericin B and fluconazole usually reserved for patients who fail with alternative regimens
Maintenance treatment	Nystatin (above doses), clotrimazole (above doses) or ketoconazole 200 mg q d or bid		Salutary advantage for fluconazole and possibly ketoconazole for maintenance treatment is prevention of cryptococcal infection

(continued)

146

	Preferred	Alternative	Comment
Esophagitis			
Initial infection	Ketoconazole (200 mg) po bid or tid Fluconazole (200 mg) po qd (up to 400 mg/day)	Amphotericin B (0.3-0.5 mg/kg) IV q day ± flucytosine (100 mg/kg/day) x 5-7 days	
Maintenance	Ketoconazole (200 mg) po 1-2 x/day	Fluconazole (100 mg) po q d; nystatin (above doses) or clotrimazole (above doses)	
Cryptococcal meningitis			
Initial treatment	Amphotericin B (0.4-0.6 mg/kg/day) IV with or without 5-flucytosine (75-100 mg/kg/day) po in 6 doses	Fluconazole (200-400 mg/day) po	
Maintenance therapy	Fluconazole (200 mg) po qd (up to 400 mg/day)	Amphotericin B (1 mg/kg/wk)	Maintenance therapy with fluconazole is started when 15 mg/kg Amphotericin B has been given and CSF culture is negative
Histoplasmosis Disseminated			
Initial treatment	Amphotericin B 2-2.5 gm (total dose)		
Maintenance	Amphotericin B (1 mg/kg/wk) or Ketoconazole (200 mg) po bid		
Coccidioidomycosis	Same as histoplasmosis		(continued)

	Preferred	Alternative	Comment
MYCOBACTERIA			
M. tuberculosis	INH (300 mg) po + rifampin (600 mg) po + pyrazinamide (20-30 mg/kg) po/day x 2 months; then INH + rifampin (above doses) for at least 9 months total therapy and 6 months post culture conversion	INH + rifampin + streptomycin (0.75-1.0 mg/kg/day IM) x 2 mo., then INH + rifampin	Ethambutol (15-25 mg/kg/day) should be included in the initial (2 months) of therapy if CNS involvement or INH resistance is suspected. INH prophylaxis for ≥ 1 yr is indicated for all HIV infected patients with positive PPD and no evidence of active disease
M. avium-intracellulare	Clofazimine (50-100 mg/day or 300 mg/day x 1 mo., then 100 mg/day), ethambutol (25 mg/kg/day x 2 mo., then 15 mg/kg/day), rifampin (600 mg/day) ± ciprofloxacin (750 mg po bid) ± amikacin (7.5 mg/kg IM or IV q12h for 4-8 wks)	Other combinations including INH, ethionamide, rifabutin (in place of rifampin), cycloserine, pyrazinamide, imipenem	Efficacy of any treatment regimen is not established; ibuprofen and similar agents may provide symptom relief INH should be included if M. tuberculosis is considered likely, but this drug adds little with M. avium infections Role of in vitro susceptibility tests is controversial
VIRUSES			
Herpes simplex			
Mucocutaneous			
Initial treatment			
Mild	Acyclovir (200 mg) po 5x/day at least 10 days (until lesions crusted)		
Severe	Acyclovir (15 mg/kg/day) IV	Vidarabine (15 mg/kg/day) IV) or foscarnet (90 mg/kg/day IV)	Failure to respond: double oral dose or give IV If it fails to respond to acyclovir give 30 mg/kg/day and test sensitivity of isolates to acyclovir Resistant HSV: high dose IV acyclovir, vidarabine or foscarnet (continued)
Maintenance	Acyclovir (200 mg) po tid		

	Preferred	Alternative	Comment
Visceral	Acyclovir (30 mg/kg/day) IV at least 10 days	Vidarabine (15 mg/kg) IV x 10 days	
Herpes zoster			
Dermatomal	Acyclovir (30 mg/kg/day) IV at least 7 days (until lesions crust)	Acyclovir (800 mg) po 5x/day	Corticosteroids should be avoided Postherpetic neuralgia is unusual No maintenance therapy recommended
Disseminated or visceral	Acyclovir (30 mg/kg/day) IV at least 7 days		
Cytomegalovirus			
Retinitis			
Initial treatment	Ganciclovir (5 mg/kg) IV bid x 14-21 days	Foscarnet (experimental) (90-120 mg/kg) IV q8h x 14 days	Efficacy established for ganciclovir
Maintenance	Ganciclovir (5 mg/kg) IV qd	Foscarnet (experimental) (90 mg/kg) IV qd	Maintenance therapy required life long
Enteritis, colitis, esophagitis, pneumonitis	Ganciclovir (experimental) (5 mg/kg) IV bid x 14-21 days		Efficacy not clearly established Indications for maintenance therapy not established
BACTERIA			
S. pneumoniae	Penicillin	Erythromycin Cephalosporins	Traditional therapy usually adequate
H. influenzae	Cefuroxime/cefamandole Ampicillin/amoxicillin	Trimethoprim-sulfamethoxazole Cephalosporins - 3rd gen	Traditional therapy usually adequate

	Preferred	Alternative	Comment
Salmonella			
Acute	Ampicillin (8-12 gm/day) IV x 1-4 wks; then amoxicillin (500 mg) po tid to complete 2-4 wk course Ciprofloxacin (500-750 mg) po bid x 2-4 wks	Trimethoprim (5-10 mg/kg/day) + sulfamethoxazole IV or po x 4 wks Cephalosporins - 3rd gen	Relapse common
Maintenance	Amoxicillin (250 mg) po bid	Ciprofloxacin (500 mg) po qd or bid Trimethoprim-sulfamethoxazole (2.5 mg/kg trimethoprim or 1 DS) po bid	Indications for maintenance therapy, specific regimens and duration not well defined

PATHOGENS ASSOCIATED WITH IMMUNODEFICIENCY STATUS

Condition	Usual conditions	Pathogens
Neutropenia (<500/ml)	Cancer chemotherapy; Adverse drug reaction; Leukemia	Bacteria: Aerobic GNB (coliforms and pseudomonads) Fungi: Aspergillus, Phycomycetes
Cell-mediated immunity	Organ transplantation: HIV infection; Lymphoma (especially Hodgkin's disease); Cortico-steroid therapy	Bacteria: Listeria, Salmonella, Nocardia, Mycobacteria (M. tuberculosis & M. avium), Legionella Viruses: CMV, H. simplex, Varicella-zoster Parasites: Pneumocystis carinii; Toxoplasma; Strongyloides stercoralis; Cryptosporidia Fungi: Candida, Phycomycetes (Mucor), Cryptococcus
Hypogammaglobulinemia or dysgamma-globulinemia	Multiple myeloma; Congenital or acquired deficiency; Chronic lymphocytic leukemia	Bacteria: S. pneumoniae, H. influenzae (type B) Parasites: Giardia Viruses: Enteroviruses
Complement deficiencies C2, 3	Congenital	Bacteria: S. pneumoniae, H. influenzae
C5		S. pneumoniae, S. aureus Enterobacteriaceae
C6-8		Neisseria meningitidis
Alternative pathway		S. pneumoniae, H. influenzae, Salmonella
Hyposplenism	Splenectomy; Hemolytic anemia	S. pneumoniae, H. influenzae, DF-2

FEVER OF UNKNOWN ORIGIN

A. Definition (Petersdorf RG & Beeson PB, Medicine 40:1,1961)

1) Illness $\geq$ 3 weeks.
2) Documented fever $\geq$ 101°F (38.3°C).
3) Negative diagnostic evaluation with 1 week in hospital.

B. Causes (Adapted from: Larson E et al, Medicine 61:269,1982)*

Infections	32	Neoplastic diseases	33
Abdominal abscesses	11	Lymphoma	6
Mycobacteria	5	Hodgkin's	4
Endocarditis	0	Leukemia	5
HIV infection**	0	Lymphomatoid granulomatosis	2
Cytomegalovirus	4	Malignant histocytosis	4
Miscellaneous***	12	Pre-leukemia	1
Collagen disease	8	Solid tumor****	11
Still's disease	4	Miscellaneous	10
Polyarteritis nodosa	2	Hematoma	3
Rheumatic fever	1	Pulmonary emboli	1
Polymyalgia rheumatica	0	Familial Mediterranean	
Rheumatic fever	1	fever	1
Systemic lupus	0	Myxoma	1
Granulomatous disease	9	Periodic fever	0
Granulomatous hepatitis	4	Factitious fever	3
Sarcoidosis	2	Non-specific pericarditis	1
Giant cell arteritis	1	Undiagnosed	13
Crohn's disease	2		

* This represents an updated version (105 cases; 1970-1980) of the classical report by Petersdorf and Beeson (100 cases, 1952-1957); more recent developments include AIDS and extensive use of scans.
** The Seattle study predated AIDS, but HIV infection would now constitute an important diagnostic consideration.
*** Includes sinusitis, dental infections, osteomyelitis, amebiasis, candidiasis, urinary tract infection.
**** All were solid tumors in the abdomen including hepatoma (2) and hypernephroma (2).

LYME DISEASE

A. Clinical features

Stage clinical feature	Avg time after tick bite (range)	Comment
1 <u>Erythema chronicum migrans</u> (ECM) plus regional adenopathy, fever, arthralgias	7 d (4-30 days)	ECM noted in 50-80%, skin lesions may recur for up to 1 yr; systemic symptoms usually resolve in several days without treatment
2 <u>Cardiac</u>: Usually A-V block with palpitations or syncope; less common: ST & T wave changes	4-5 wks (3-21 wks)	Noted in 8-10%; may progress to complete heart block requiring pacemaker; usually resolves in 3 days to 6 wks with complete recovery
<u>Neurologic</u>: Diverse conditions including aseptic meningitis with fever and stiff neck; cranial nerve palsy (esp Bell's palsy, III, IV & VI); radiculopathy, esp C-5, T8-T12; encephalopathy with poor memory, irritability, dementia, seizures or psychosis	4-5 wks (2-10 wks)	Noted in 10-15%; CSF shows pleocytosis with lymphocytes and increased protein
<u>Musculoskeletal Sx</u>: Migratory pains in joints, muscles and bursae, usually at one or two sites at a time lasting hours to days		
3 <u>Arthritis</u>: Oligoarticular, asymmetrical, large joints (esp knee - > 90%); attacks last average of 1 wk and may recur for yrs; arthritis becomes chronic	6 wks to 2 years	Noted in 50-70% of untreated patients; rheumatoid factor negative; joint fluid shows 2000-100,000 cells/mm^3 with PMN's; x-rays show joint effusions; chronic arthritis with cartilage and bone erosions in 10%
<u>Skin</u>: Acrodermatitis chronica atrophicans		May last for years
<u>Neurologic</u>: Tingling paresthesias, spastic paraparesis, transverse myelitis, dementia		

B. Diagnosis (MMWR 38:668,1989 and Medical Letter 31:57,1989)

Usual test is serologic assay using ELISA or IFA. Current tests are poorly standardized, and false positive or false negative results occur (Barbour AG, Ann Intern Med 110:501,1989). Serologic tests in stage one or two may be falsely negative since 3-6 months may be required for seroconversion. Patients with late stage disease who were treated early with antibiotics have a false negative serology rate estimated at less than 5% (Dattwyler RJ, NEJM 319:1441,1988). Previously untreated patients with late stage disease are unlikely to have false negative serologic tests.

C. Epidemiology: Number of reported cases 1989

New York State	2916	Connecticut	754	Georgia	715
New Jersey	649	Pennsylvania	585	Wisconsin	278
California	253	Rhode Island	183	Massachusetts	129
Maryland	105	Michigan	103	Texas	96
Minnesota	93	Illinois	79	Missouri	39

D. Treatment (Medical Letter 31:57,1989)

Stage	Regimen
Early (ECM)	Doxycycline*, 100 mg po bid x 10-21 days Amoxicillin**, 250-500 mg po tid x 10-21 days Alternative: Erythromycin, 250 mg po qid x 10-21 days
Neurologic disease Mild (Bell's palsy)	Doxycycline*, 100 mg po bid x 4 wks Amoxicillin**, 250-500 mg po qid x 4 wks
More serious	Ceftriaxone, 2 gm/day IV x 14 days Penicillin G, 20-24 mil units IV/day x 10-14 days
Cardiac disease Mild	Doxycycline*, 100 mg po bid x 21 days Amoxicillin**, 250-500 mg po tid x 21 days
More serious	Ceftriaxone, 2 gm/day IV x 10-21 days Penicillin G, 20-24 mil units IV/day x 10-21 days
Arthritis Oral	Doxycycline*, 100 mg po bid x 4 wks Amoxicillin**, 250-500 mg po tid x 4 wks
Parenteral	Ceftriaxone, 2 gm IV x 14-21 days Penicillin g, 20-24 mil units IV/day x 14-21 days

* Or tetracycline, 250-500 mg po qid.
** Some authorities add probenecid.
*** Response may be delayed for several weeks.

INFECTIONS OF THE EPIDERMIS, DERMIS AND SUBCUTANEOUS TISSUE

Condition	Agent	Laboratory diagnosis	Treatment
Superficial erythematous lesions			
Abscess	S. aureus Anaerobes	Culture and gram stain	Drainage
Acne rosacea	?	Appearance	Doxycycline Metronidazole (0.75% topical) Accutane
Acne vulgaris	Propioni- bacterium acnes	Appearance	Tetracycline Topical clindamycin
Cellulitis: Diffuse spreading infection of deep dermis	Gr A strep; S. aureus (Vibrio sp. and Aeromonas sp. with fresh or salt water exposure)	Culture advanced edge of inflammation (rarely positive); 3 mm dermal punch; ulcerated portal of entry; blood Serial DNase titer (gr A strep)	Penicillinase- resistant penicillin, vancomycin, clindamycin, cephalosporin (1st (gen, cefamandole, cephalexin or cefuroxime)
Erysipelas: Superficial infection with raised edge	Gr A strep	Culture: as above Serial DNase titer	Penicillin Clindamycin
Lymphangitis	Gr A strep	As above	As above
Folliculitis: Infected hair follicle	S. aureus P. aeruginosa Proteus sp.	Culture and gram stain (usually unnecessary)	Local compresses or topical antibiotics
Furunculosis carbuncle: Abscess that starts in hair follicle; carbuncle is deeper and more extensive	S. aureus	Culture and gram stain	Drainage Penicillinase- resistant penicillin, clindamycin, vancomycin, cephalosporin (1st gen, cefamandole, cefuroxime) Recurrent furunculosis may be controlled with chronic clindamycin, 150 mg qd

(continued)

Condition	Agent	Laboratory diagnosis	Treatment
Paronychia: Infection of nail fold	S. aureus Candida	Culture and gram stain	
Impetigo: Infection of epidermis	Gr A strep (S. aureus)	Culture and gram stain	Penicillin or erythromycin
Whitlow: Infection of distal phalanx finger	S. aureus H. simplex	Culture and gram stain; viral culture, Tzank prep or FA stain for H. simplex	Penicillinase-resistant penicillin, clindamycin, cephalosporin - 1st gen.
Fungal infections: Keratinized tissue-skin, nails, hair	Candida-red, moist, satellite lesions, esp groin Dermatophytes-Epidermophyton, Trichophyton, "ring worm" Tinea versicolar-Malassezia furfur; red or hypopigmented macules	Scrapings for KOH prep, culture on Sabouraud medium, Wood's light	Topical anti-fungal agent: Lotrimin Ketoconazole
Bites Dog & cat	P. multocida Dysgonic fermenter type 2 (DF2)	Culture and gram stain	Penicillin
Human	Oral flora (strep, anaerobes, etc) S. aureus, Eikenella corrodens	Culture and gram stain	Amoxicillin-clavulanic acid (Augmentin) Clindamycin
Rat	Strepto-bacillus moniliformis Spirillum minus	S. moniliformis: Giemsa stain of blood or pus; culture; serology S. minus: Giemsa stain of blood or exudate	Penicillin Tetracycline Penicillin Tetracycline
Cat scratch disease	GNB (not yet characterized)	Agent cannot be cultivated	Erythromycin (?)

(continued)

Condition	Agent	Laboratory diagnosis	Treatment
Burns	S. aureus, GNB, Candida albicans Aspergillus, Herpes simplex, Gr A strep	Quantitative culture and stain of biopsy	Removal of eschar Topical sulfa; systemic antibiotics based on in vitro sensitivity tests
Sinus tract Osteomyelitis	S. aureus, S. epid., GNB, anaerobes	Culture of sinus tract drainage does not reliably reflect agent(s) of osetomyelitis	Antibiotics optimally based on bone biopsy
Lymph node	S. aureus Mycobacteria (scrofula)	Culture and gram stain AFB smear and culture	Anti-staphylococcal agent TB-Antituberculous drugs M. scrofulaceum- excision
Actinomycosis	A. israelii A. naeslundii A. odentolyticus	FA stain, anaerobic culture	Penicillin G, ampicillin, clindamycin
Madura foot	Nocardia	AFB stain, culture for nocardia	Sulfonamides
	Fungi - Petriellidium boydii, Madurella mycetomatis, Phialophora verrucosa	KOH, culture on Sabouraud medium	
Nodules/ulcers Sporotrichoid (cutaneous inoculation with lymphatic spread)	Sporothrix schenckii (thorns)	Histology (PAS, GMS), culture on Sabouraud medium	Oral KI
	M. marinum (tidal water, swimming pool or tropical fish tank)	Histology, AFB stain & culture (at 30-32°C)	Rifampin + ethambutol Minocycline
	Nocardia	Histology, AFB stain, culture for Nocardia	Sulfonamide (continued)

157

Condition	Agent	Laboratory diagnosis	Treatment
Nodules/ulcers (from hematogenous dissemination)	Blastomycosis– Endemic area	Culture biopsy on Sabouraud medium	Amphotericin B, ketoconazole
	Cryptococcus – Defective cell mediated immunity	Blood for cryptococcal antigen and culture; histopathology and culture of biopsy	Amphotericin B, fluconazole
	Candida - Defective cell mediated immunity	Blood culture; histopathology and culture of biopsy	Amphotericin B
Diabetic foot ulcer and decubitus ulcer	Mixed aerobes- anaerobes S. aureus Gr A strep	Culture and gram stain of wound edge or dermal punch biopsy	Local care - debridement, bed rest Antibiotics-for fever, extensive cellulitis, regional adenopathy or osteomyelitis Agents - parenteral agents as for intra-abdominal sepsis; oral regimen - ciprofloxacin + metronidazole or clindamycin

Deep and Serious Soft Tissue Infections
(from: Bartlett JG, Cecil Textbook of Medicine, W.B. Saunders Co., 1988, pg 1620)

	Gas-Forming Cellulitis	Synergistic Necrotizing Cellulitis	Gas Gangrene	"Streptococcal" Myonecrosis	Necrotizing Fasciitis	Infected Vascular Gangrene	Streptococcal Gangrene
Predisposing conditions	Traumatic	Diabetes, prior local lesion, perirectal lesion	Traumatic or surgical wound	Trauma, surgery	Diabetes, trauma, surgery, perineal infection	Arterial insufficiency	Traumatic or surgical wound
Incubation period	>3 days	3–14 days	1–4 days	3–4 days	1–4 days	>5 days	6 hours—2 days
Etiologic organism(s)	Clostridia, others	Mixed aerobic-anaerobic flora	Clostridia, esp. C. perfringens	Anaerobic streptococci	Mixed aerobic-anaerobic flora	Mixed aerobic-anaerobic flora	S. pyogenes
Systemic toxicity	Minimal	Moderate to severe	Severe	Minimal until late in course	Moderate to severe	Minimal	Severe
Course	Gradual	Acute	Acute	Subacute	Acute or subacute	Subacute	Acute
Wound findings Local pain	Minimal	Moderate to severe	Severe	Late only	Minimal to moderate	Variable	Severe
Skin appearance	Swollen, minimal discoloration	Erythematous or gangrene	Tense and blanched, yellow-bronze, necrosis with hemorrhagic bullae	Erythema or yellow-bronze	Blanched, erythema, necrosis with hemorrhagic bullae	Erythema or necrosis	Erythema, necrosis
Gas	Abundant	Variable	Usually present	Variable	Variable	Variable	No
Muscle involvement	No	Variable	Myonecrosis	Myonecrosis	No	Myonecrosis limited to area of vascular insufficiency	No
Discharge	Thin, dark, sweetish or foul odor	Dark pus or "dishwater," putrid	Serosanguineous, sweet or foul odor	Seropurulent	Seropurulent or "dishwater," putrid	Minimal	None or serosanguineous, no odor
Gram stain	PMNs, gram-positive bacilli	PMNs, mixed flora	Sparse PMNs, gram-positive bacilli	PMNs, gram-positive cocci	PMNs, mixed flora	PMNs, mixed flora	PMNs, gram-positive cocci in chains
Surgical therapy	Debridement	Wide filleting incisions	Extensive excision, amputation	Excision of necrotic muscle	Wide filleting incisions	Amputation	Debridement of necrotic tissue

159

BONE AND JOINT INFECTIONS

I Osteomyelitis

A. Classification

	Hematogenous	Contiguous infection	Vascular insufficiency
Age	1-20 yrs > 50 yrs	> 50 yrs	> 50 yrs
Bones	Long bones Vertebrae	Femur, tibia Skull, mandible	Feet
Associated conditions	Trauma Bacteremia (any source)	Surgery Soft tissue infection	Diabetes Neuropathy Vascualar disease
Bacteriology	S. aureus Gram-neg rods	Mixed S. aureus Gram-neg rods Anaerobes	Mixed S. aureus Streptococci Gram-neg rods

B. Special conditions

	Bones	Bacteriology
Sickle cell disease	Multiple	Salmonella
IV drug abuse	Clavicle	S. aureus
	Vertebrae	Pseudomonas
Penetrating injury	Foot	Pseudomonas
Hemodialysis	Ribs	
	Thoracic vertebrae	S. aureus
Chronic		
Brodie's abscess	Distal tibia	S. aureus
Tuberculosis	Spine (Pott's)	M. tuberculosis
	Hip, knee	
Prosthetic joint	Site of prosthesis	S. aureus S. epidermidis

C. Treatment

Acute: Antibiotics x 4 weeks (S. aureus - nafcillin ± rifampin)
+ draingage of purulent collections.
Chronic: Antibiotics, intravenous x 4-6 weeks, then oral x 2 mo.
(S. aureus - nafcillin IV ± rifampin <u>or</u> cloxacillin, 5 gm/day po
+ probenecid, 2 gm/day) + surgical debridement (Black J et al,
J Infect Dis 155:968,1987).

II   Septic arthritis

A. Acute monarticular arthritis

1. <u>Differential diagnosis</u>: Septic arthritis, rheumatoid arthritis, gout and chondrocalcinosis (pseudogout)

2. <u>Septic arthritis</u> in adults

Agent	Treatment (alternatives)	Comment
S. aureus	Penicillinase resistant penicillin (cephalosporin, vancomycin, clindamycin) x 3 weeks	Accounts for 50-80% of non-gonococcal arthritis cases
N. gonorrhoeae	Ceftriaxone 1 gm IV daily x 24-48 hrs, then oral agent (cefuroxime axetil, ciprofloxacin or amoxicillin + clavulanic acid - all 500 mg bid) to complete $\geq$ 7 day course	Most common cause of monarticular arthritis in young sexually active adults Skin lesions rarely present and blood cultures usually neg with gonococcal monarticular arthritis joint fluid often positive
Streptococci	Penicillin (cephalosporin-1st gen, vancomycin, clindamycin) x 2 wks	Accounts for 10-20% of non-gonococcal septic arthritis cases
Gram-negative bacilli	Based on in vitro sensitivity tests Treat x 3 wks	Accounts for 10-20% of non-gonococcal septic arthritis cases Most commonly in chronically debilitated host Heroin addicts prone to sacroiliac or sterno-clavicular septic arthritis due to Pseudomonas aeruginosa

3. <u>Prosthetic joint</u>:

    a.   Bacteriology: <u>S</u>. <u>aureus</u> (20-30%), <u>S</u>. <u>epidermidis</u> (20-30%), streptococci (15-25%), gram-negative bacilli (15-25%), anaerobes (5-10%).

b. Management
      Surgical drainage, antimicrobials $\geq$ 6 wks, retention of
         prosthesis: 20-30% success
      Removal of prosthesis, bactericidal antibiotics x 6 wks,
         then reimplantation: 90-95% success
      Removal of prosthesis and reimplantation of prosthesis with
         antibiotic impregnated cement plus course of
         bactericidal antibiotics: 70-80% success

B. Chronic Monoarticular Arthritis

1. Bacteria: Brucella, Nocardia

2. Mycobacteria: M. tuberculosis, M. kansasii, M. marinum. M. avium-
   intracellulare, M. fortuitum (See pg 122).

3. Fungi: Sporothrix schenckii, Coccidioides immitis, Blastomyces
   dermatitidis, Pseudallescheria boydii (See pg 99-105).

C. Polyarticular Arthritis

1. Bacteria: Neisseria gonorrhoeae (usually accompanied by skin lesions,
   positive cultures of blood and/or genital tract, negative joint cultures);
   N. meningitidis; Borrelia burgdorferi (Lyme disease, see pg 156-157);
   pyogenic (10% of cases of septic arthritis have two or more joints
   involved).

2. Viral: Hepatitis B (positive serum HBsAg, seen in pre-icteric phase,
   ascribed to immune-complexes, hands most frequently involved); rubella
   (usually small joints of hand, women > men, simultaneous rash, also
   seen with rubella vaccine in up to 40% of susceptible postpubertal
   women); parvovirus B19 (hand/wrists and/or knees; adults > children;
   women > men); mumps (0.5% of mumps cases, large and small joints,
   accompanies parotitis, men > women).

3. Miscellaneous: Acute rheumatic fever (Jones criteria including evidence of
   preceding streptococcal infection); Reiter's syndrome (conjunctivitis
   and urethritis, associated infections - Shigella, Salmonella,
   Campylobacter, Yersinia).

OCULAR AND PERIOCULAR INFECTIONS

Condition	Microbiology	Treatment	Comment
Conjunctivitis	S. pneumoniae	Topical bacitracin, erythromycin	Hyperemia ± discharge photophobia, pain; vision intact
	N. gonorrhoeae	Ceftriaxone, 250 mg x 1	Most are self limited Pharyngoconjunctival fever - Adenovirus 3 & 7
	C. trachomatis	Erythromycin x 3 wks	
	Adenovirus	None	Epidemic keratoconjunctivitis - Adenovirus 8 Lab - conjunctival scraping: bacteria - PMN's, viral -
	Allergic or immune-mediated	Topical prednisone	mononuclear; herpetic - multinucleated cells; chlamydia-mixed; allergic-eosinophils
Keratitis	S. aureus; S. pneumoniae; P. aeruginosa; Moraxella; Serratia	Usually hospitalize for treatment to prevent perforation Antibiotics- systemic, sub- conjunctival and/or topical ± corticosteroids	Pain; no discharge; decreased vision Lab-conjunctival scrapings for stain (Gram, Giemsa, PAS & methenamine silver) + culture for bacteria and fungi Systemic antibiotics for deep corneal ulcers with bacterial infection
	Herpes simplex	trifluridine/ vidarabine and/or corticosteroids	Supportive care with cytoplegics, use of corticosteroids
	Herpes zoster	Acyclovir	controversial
	Fungal-Fusarium solani, Aspergillus, Candida	Topical natamycin, miconazole or flucytosine ± systemic anti- fungal	For topical antibiotics use solutions
	Acanthamoeba	Topical propamadine isethionate, dibromopropamadine isethionate + neomycin; usually requires corneal transplant	

(continued)

Condition	Microbiology	Treatment	Comment
Endophthalmitis	**Bacteria**		
	Post ocular surgery - S. aureus, Pseudomonas, S. epidermidis, P. acnes	IV antibiotics ± intravitreal antibiotics, corticosteroids, vitrectomy	Lab-Aspiration of aqueous and vitreous cavity for stain (Gram, Giemsa, PAS, methenamine silver) and culture for bacteria and fungi
	Penetrating trauma - Bacillus sp.		
	Hematogenous - S. pneumoniae, N. meningitidis (others)		
	Fungal		
	Post ocular surgery- Neurospora, Candida, Scedosporium, Paecilomyces	IV amphotericin + topical natamycin ± corticosteroids vitrectomy	
	Hematogenous - Candida, Aspergillus	IV amphotericin B	
	Histoplasmosis	Systemic cortico-steroids	
	Parasitic		
	Toxoplasmosis	Systemic + local corticosteroids ± pyrimethamine and sulfadiazine	
	Toxocara	Systemic or intra-ocular cortico-steroids	
	Virus: Herpes simplex, H. zoster	Topical atropine + corticosteroids, Acyclovir (?)	Recurrence rate of H. simplex: 30-40%
Periorbital Lid			
Blepharitis	S. aureus - Seborrhea	Topical bacitracin or erythromycin ± topical corticosteroid	
Hordeolum	S. aureus	Topical bacitracin or erythromycin + warm compresses	
Chalazion	Chronic granuloma	Observation or curettage	

(continued)

Condition	Microbiology	Treatment	Comment
Lacrimal apparatus			
Canaliculitis	Anaerobes	Topical penicillin + antibiotic irrigation	
Dacryocystitis	Acute - S. aureus	Systemic antistaphylococcal agent; then digital message + antibiotic drops	
	Chronic - S. pneumoniae S. aureus, Pseudomonas, mixed	Systemic antibiotics; digital message	
Orbital	S. aureus (S. pneumoniae, S. pyogenes)	IV antibiotics- Cephalosporin- Cefuroxime or 3rd gen.	Over 80% have associated sinusitis Treat sinusitis
	Fungi - Phycomycosis, Aspergillus, Bipolaris, Curvularia, Drechslera	Amphotericin B + surgery	

CNS INFECTIONS

I Cerebrospinal Fluid

A. Normal findings

1. Opening pressure: 5-15 mmHg or 65-195 mm H_2O

2. Leukocyte count: <10 mononuclear cells/mm^3 (5-10/ml suspect); 1 PMN (5%)

   > Bloody tap: Usually 1 WBC/700 RBC with normal peripheral RBC and WBC counts; if abnormal: true CSF WBC = WBC (CSF) - WBC (blood) x RBC (CSF)/RBC (blood)
   > Note: WBC's begin to disintegrate after 90 minutes

3. Protein: 15-45 mg/dl (higher in elderly)
   Formula: 23.8 x 0.39 x age $\pm$ 15 mg/100 ml or (more simply) less than patient's age (above 35 yrs)
   Traumatic tap: 1 mg/1000 RBC's

4. Glucose: 40-80 mg% or CSF/blood glucose ratio > 0.6
   (with high serum glucose usual ratio is 0.3)

B. Abnormal CSF with non-infectious causes

1. Traumatic tap: Increased protein; RBC's; WBC count and differential proportionate to RBC's in peripheral blood; clear and colorless supernatant of centrifuged CSF.

2. Chemical meningitis (injection of anesthetics, chemotherapeutic agents, air, radiographic dyes): Increased protein, lymphocytes (occasionally PMN's).

3. Cerebral contusion, subarachnoid hemorrhage, intracerebral bleed: RBC's, increased protein (1 mg/1000 RBC's), disproportionately increased PMN's (peak at 72-96 hrs); decreased glucose in 15-20%).

4. Vasculitis (SLE, etc): Increased protein (50-100 mg/dl), increased WBC's (usually mononuclear cells, occasionally PMN's); normal glucose.

5. Postictal (repeated generalized seizures): RBC's (0-500/mm^3), WBC's (10-100/mm^3 with variable % PMN's with peak at 1 day), protein normal or slight increase.

6. Tumors (esp. glioblastomas, leukemia, lymphoma, breast cancer, pancreatic cancer): Low glucose, increased protein, moderate PMN's.

7. Neurosurgery: Blood; increased protein; WBC's (disproportionate to RBC's with predominance of mononuclear cells) up to 2 weeks post-op.

8. Sarcoidosis: Increased protein; WBC's (up to 100/mm^3 predominately mononuclear cells); low glucose in 10%.

(continued)

C. CNS infections

	Cell count (/mm³)	Predominant cell type	Glucose (mg/dl)	Protein (mg/dl)	Microscopic exam	Culture
Meningitis						
Viral	10–2,000	Monos	40–80	10–45	Neg	Neg
Bacterial						
Untreated	10–100,000	PMN's	Low	Normal to 600	85–90% pos	90% pos
Partially treated	10–100,000	PMN's	Low or normal	Increased	Variable	Neg, esp with meningococcus or pneumococcus
Tuberculosis	10–1,000	30–100% mono's	Low	Increased 100–500	Rarely pos	Usually positive
Fungal	5–1,000	Mono's	Low or normal	Normal to 500	Rarely pos except India ink prep for Cryptococcus	Usually positive
Encephalitis	0–2,000	Early-PMN's Late-Mono's	Normal	Normal to 120	Neg	Neg
Brain abscess	5–500	Mixed	Normal	Normal to 500	Neg	Neg
AIDS encephalitis/ dementia complex	0–200	Mono's	Normal	Normal to 120	Neg	Often yields HIV

II. Meningitis

A. Likely pathogens and treatment

| Setting | Likely agent | Empiric treatment* | | Comment |
		Preferred	Alternative	
Adult, immunocompetent community-acquired**	S. pneumoniae N. meningitidis	Penicillin G	Chloramphenicol Cefotaxime Ceftriaxone Ceftizoxime Ceftazidime Ampicillin	Increased frequency of Enterobacteriaceae in alcoholics, debilitated and elderly patients; consider third generation cephalosporins for initial treatment
Immunosuppressed Defective humoral immunity, asplenia, complement defect	S. pneumoniae N. meningitidis	As above	As above	
Defective cell-mediated immunity	Listeria Cryptococcus	Ampicillin ± aminoglycoside	Trimethoprim-sulfamethoxazole	Cephalosporins not active vs. Listeria
Post-neurosurgical procedure	Enterobacteriaceae Pseudomonas sp. Staph aureus	Aminoglycoside + antipseudomonad penicillin (or ceftazidime) + antistaph penicillin (or vancomycin)		In vitro sensitivity tests required, bactericidal activity preferred Infections that are refractory or involve resistant GNB may require intrathecal or intra-ventricular aminoglycosides

(continued)

168

Setting	Likely agent	Empiric treatment*		Comment
		Preferred	Alternative	
Cranial or spinal trauma Early (0-3 days)	S. pneumoniae	Penicillin or ampicillin	Chloramphenicol	Occasional cases with H. influenzae or Strep pyogenes
Late (over 3 days)	Enterobacteraceae Pseudomonas S. aureus S. pneumoniae	Treat as recommended for postsurgical complication		
Ventricular shunt	S. epidermidis	Vancomycin	Anti-staphylococcal penicillin	In vitro sensitivity tests required Necessity to remove shunt is highly variable; most advocate antibiotics via shunt

*Antibiotic recommendations assuming clinical (± initial CSF analysis) evidence supporting this diagnosis with no direct clues to the etiologic agent.

**Consider dexamethasone as adjunctive therapy (0.6 mg/kg/day x 4 days) (See Tuomanen E, Ann Intern Med 109:690,1988).

B.   Treatment by organism (See Tunkel A et al. Ann Intern Med 112:610,1990)

Organism	Preferred drug	Alternative	Comment
Strep pneumoniae	Penicillin G or ampicillin	Chloramphenicol Cefuroxime Cefotaxime Ceftizoxime Ceftriaxone	Test susceptibility to penicillin Resistant strains: chloramphenicol or vancomycin Treat $\geq$ 10 days
Neisseria meningitidis	Penicillin G or ampicillin	(As above)	Intimate contacts should receive rifampin Treat $\geq$ 7 days
Haemophilus influenzae Ampicillin sensitive	Ampicillin	Chloramphenicol Cefotaxime Cefuroxime (see comment) Ceftizoxime Ceftriaxone Ceftazidime	If children < 4 yrs in household, contacts should receive rifampin prophylaxis (type B only) Type $\geq$ 10 days Cefuroxime found inferior to ceftriaxone (NEJM 322:141,1990)
Ampicillin resistant	Cephalosporins - 3rd gen	Chloramphenicol	
Listeria monocytogenes	Ampicillin + aminoglycosides or penicillin + aminoglycoside	Trimethoprim-sulfamethoxazole	Cephalosporins are not effective Treat 14-21 days (continued)

170

Organism	Preferred drug	Alternative	Comment
E. coli and other coliforms	Cefotaxime Ceftizoxime Ceftriaxone Ceftazidime	Aminoglycoside ± antipseudomonad penicillin Aztreonam* Quinolone*	In vitro sensitivity tests required; MBC data preferred Chloramphenicol lacks bactericidal activity vs GNB Aminoglycosides are given systemically ± intrathecally Treat ≥ 21 days Ceftazidime should be reserved for suspected or established P. aeruginosa
Pseudomonas aeruginosa	Aminoglycoside + ceftazidime	Antipseudomonad penicillin (carbenicillin, ticarcillin, mezlocillin, piperacillin, azlocillin) + aminoglycoside Aztreonam* Imipenem* Quinolones*	Aminoglycoside is given systemically and intrathecally
Staph aureus	Antistaphylococcal penicillin ± rifampin	Vancomycin	Vancomycin for methicillin-resistant S. aureus
Staph epidermidis	Vancomycin + rifampin		
Emperic treatment			
3 mo - 18 yrs	Cephalosporin (3rd generation) ampicillin or chloramphenicol		
18-50 yrs	Penicillin G or ampicillin		
> 50 yrs	Ampicillin + cephalosporin (3rd generation)		

* Effectiveness in meningitis is not known

171

C. **Doses of Drugs for CNS Infections***

1. Aminoglycosides

Agent	Systemic	Intrathecal/intraventricular
Gentamicin	1.7-2.0 mg/kg (see pg 33,34)	4-5 mg q 12-24 h
Tobramycin	1.7-2.0 mg/kg (see pg 33,34)	4-5 mg q 12-24 h
Amikacin	5.0-7.5 mg/kg (see pg 33,34)	10-12 mg q 12-24 h

2. Cephalosporins
   Cefuroxime: 9 gm/day in 3 doses
   Cefotaxime: 12 gm/day in 6 doses**
   Ceftizoxime: 9 gm/day in 3 doses**
   Ceftriaxone: 4-6 gm/day in 2 doses**
   Ceftazidime: 6-12 gm/day in 3 doses**

3. Chloramphenicol: 4-6 gm/day in 4 doses**

4. Penicillins

   Ampicillin: 12 gm/day in 6 doses**

   Antipseudomonad penicillins
   Ticarcillin: 18-24 gm/day in 6 doses (40-60 mg/kg q 4 h)
   Mezlocillin: 18-24 gm/day in 6 doses (40-60 mg/kg q 4 h)
   Azlocillin: 18-24 gm/day in 6 doses (40-60 mg/kg q 4 h)
   Pipericillin: 18-24 gm/day in 6 doses (40-60 mg/kg q 4 h)

   Antistaphylococcal penicillins
   Nafcillin: 9-12 gm/day in 6 doses
   Oxacillin: 9-12 gm/day in 6 doses

   Penicillin G: 20-24 million units/day in 6 doses**

5. Trimethoprim-sulfamethoxazole: 15-20 mg/kg/day (trimethoprim) in 4 doses
   Metronidazole: 2 gm/day in 2-4 doses
   Vancomycin: 2 gm/day in 2 doses**

---

* Assume adult patient with normal renal function.
** Recommendation of Tunkel AR et al. Ann Intern Med 112:610,1990.

D. **Aseptic Meningitis:** Infectious and Non-infectious Causes* (from American Academy of Pediatrics, Pediatrics 78 (Supplement):970,1986)

Infectious Agents and Diseases
    Bacteria: Partially treated meningitis, <u>Mycobacterium</u>
        <u>tuberculosis</u>, parameningeal focus (brain abscess,
        epidural abscess), acute or subacute bacterial
        endocarditis
    Viruses: Enteroviruses, mumps, lymphocytic choriomeningitis, Epstein-
        Barr, arboviruses (Eastern equine, Western equine,
        St. Louis), cytomegalovirus, varicella-zoster, herpes
        simplex, human immunodeficiency virus
    Rickettsiae: Rocky Mountain spotted fever
    Spirochetes: Syphilis, leptospirosis, Lyme disease
    Mycoplasma: <u>M</u>. pneumoniae, <u>M</u>. hominis (neonates)
    Fungi: <u>Candida</u> <u>albicans</u>, <u>Coccidioides</u> <u>immitis</u>, <u>Cryptococcus</u>
        <u>neoformans</u>
    Protozoa: <u>Toxoplasma</u> <u>gondii</u>, malaria, amebas, visceral larval migrans
        (<u>Taenia</u> <u>canis</u>)
    Nematode: Rat lung worm larvae (eosinophilic meningitis)
    Cestodes: Cysticercosis
Non-infectious Diseases
    Malignancy: Primary medulloblastoma, metastatic leukemia, Hodgkin's
        disease
    Collagen-vascular disease: Lupus erythematosus
    Trauma: Subarachnoid bleed, traumatic lumbar puncture, neurosurgery
    Granulomatous disease: Sarcoidosis
    Direct toxin: Intrathecal injections of contrast medium, spinal anesthesia
    Poison: Lead, mercury
    Autoimmune disease: Guillain-Barre syndrome
    Unknown: Multiple sclerosis, Mollaret's meningitis, Behcet's syndrome,
        Vogt-Koyanagi syndrome, Harada's syndrome, Kawasaki disease

---

* Aseptic meningitis is defined as meningitis in the absence of evidence of a bacterial pathogen detectable in CSF by usual laboratory techniques.

UPPER RESPIRATORY TRACT INFECTIONS

Condition	Usual pathogens	Preferred treatment	Alternatives	Comment
Ear & Mastoids				
Acute otitis media	S. pneumoniae H. influenzae	Ampicillin or amoxicillin	Trimethoprim- sulfamethoxazole Cefaclor Amoxicillin + clavulinate Erythromycin + sulfoxazole Cefuroxime axetil Cefixime Parenteral: Cephalo- sporin-3rd gen	Tympanocentesis rarely indicated Less frequent pathogens: S. aureus, Strep. pyogenes, Moraxella catarrhalis Oral or nasal decongestants $\pm$ antihistamine
Chronic suppurative otitis media	Pseudomonas Staph. aureus	Neomycin/polymyxin/ hydrocortisone otic drops	Chloramphenicol otic drops	Persistent effusion: myringotomy
Malignant otitis externa	P. aeruginosa	Tobramycin or amikacin + ticarcillin, mezlocillin or piperacillin	Tobramycin or amikacin + cefoperazone, ceftazidine, imipenem or ciprofloxacin	Surgical drainage and/or debridement sometimes required
Acute diffuse otitis externa ("swimmer's ear")	P. aeruginosa Coliforms Staph. aureus	Neomycin/polymyxin Hydrocortisone otic drops	Boric or acetic acid (2%) drops	Initially cleanse with 3% saline or 70-95% alcohol + acetic acid Systemic antibiotics for significant tissue infection (continued)

174

Condition	Usual pathogens	Preferred treatment	Alternatives	Comment
Otomycosis	Aspergillus niger	Boric or acetic acid drops	M-cresyl acetic otic drops	
Acute mastoiditis	S. pneumoniae H. influenzae	Cefuroxime, trimethoprim-sulfamethoxazole, cephalosporin-3rd gen	Amoxicillin or ampicillin Amoxicillin + clavulinate	Surgery required for abscess in mastoid bone S. aureus is occasional pathogen, esp. in subacute cases
Chronic mastoiditis	Anaerobes Pseudomonas sp. Coliforms Staph. aureus	None		Surgery often required Pre-op: Tobramycin + ticarcillin or piperacillin
Sinusitis				
Acute sinusitis	H. influenzae S. pneumoniae M. catarrhalis	Amoxicillin or ampicillin Trimethoprim-sulfamethoxazole Cefaclor, cefuroxime axetil Amoxicillin + clavulinate	Erythromycin	Nasal decongestant Sinus lavage for refractory cases
Chronic sinusitis	Anaerobes S. aureus	Penicillin or ampicillin	Amoxicillin + clavulinate Clindamycin	Usually reserve antibiotic treatment for acute flares Surgery may be required
Nosocomial sinusitis	Pseudomonas Coliforms	Aminoglycoside + anti-pseudomonad penicillin or aminoglycoside + cephalosporin-3rd gen (ceftazidime)	Imipenem, cephalosporin-3rd gen	Complication of nasal intubation

(continued)

Condition	Usual pathogens	Preferred treatment	Alternatives	Comment
Pharynx				
Pharyngitis	Strep. pyogenes Corynebacterium hemolyticum (mycoplasma, viruses including EBV)	Penicillin (strep only)	Erythromycin	If compliance questionable use benzathine pen G x 1 IM; treatment with oral pen V or erythromycin for 10 days
Gonococcal pharyngitis	N. gonorrhoeae	Ceftriaxone (250 mg x 1)	Ciprofloxacin (500 mg x 1)	Most cases are as asymptomatic
Peritonsillar or tonsillar abscess	Strep. pyogenes Peptostreptococci	Penicillin G	Clindamycin	Drainage necessary
Membranous pharyngitis	C. diphtheriae Epstein-Barr virus Vincent's angina (anaerobes)	Penicillin or erythromycin (diphtheria) Penicillin/clindamycin (anaerobes)		Diphtheria: Antitoxin
Epiglottitis	H. influenzae	Chloramphenicol ± ampicillin Cefuroxime, cefamandole, cefotaxime, ceftizoxime, ceftriaxone, ceftazidime		Ensure patent airway (usually with endotracheal tube) Rifampin prophylaxis for household contacts < 4 yrs (x 4 days)
Laryngitis	Viruses (M. catarrhalis)			For M. catarrhalis: trimethoprim-sulfa, erythromycin, amoxicillin-clavulinate or cefaclor (continued)

176

Condition	Usual pathogens	Preferred treatment	Alternatives	Comment
Perimandibular				
Actinomycosis	A. israelii	Penicillin G or V	Clindamycin, tetracycline, erythromycin	Treat for 3-6 months
Parotitis	S. aureus (anaerobes)	Penicillinase-resistant penicillin	Cephalosporin-1st gen Clindamycin, vancomycin	Surgical drainage usually required
Space infections	Anaerobes	Penicillin Clindamycin	Cefoxitin, penicillin + metronidazole	Surgical drainage required
Cervical				
Cervical adenitis				
Acute	S. aureus Strep. pyogenes Anaerobes Viral Toxoplasmosis	Penicillin (S. pyogenes, anaerobes) Penicillinase-resistant penicillin (S. aureus)	Erythromycin Clindamycin Amoxicillin + clavulinate (Bacterial infections)	
Chronic	Mycobacteria, cat scratch disease, HIV infection	TB: INH, rifampin + pyrazinamide M. scrofulaceum: excision		Non-infectious causes include tumors, lymphoma, sarcoid
Dental				
Periapical abscess Gum boil Gingivitis Pyorrhoea	Anaerobes Streptococci	Penicillin Clindamycin	Metronidazole + penicillin	Metronidazole often preferred for periodontal disease, i.e. gingivitis, periodontitis
Stomatitis				
Thrush	C. albicans	Oral nystatin (swish and swallow) or clotrimazole troches	Ketoconazole po Fluconazole po	
				(continued)

Condition	Usual pathogens	Preferred treatment	Alternatives	Comment
Vincent's angina	Anaerobes	Penicillin Clindamycin	Metronidazole, tetracycline	
Aphthous stomatitis	No pathogen identified	Topical corticosteroid (Topicort <u>gel</u>)	Systemic corticosteroids (Prednisone, 40 mg/day, then rapid taper) Silver nitrate	
Herpetiform ulcers	H. simplex	Acyclovir		Usually reserved for immunocompromised hosts

Cost of Oral Drugs Commonly Used for Upper Respiratory Infections

	Wholesale price for 10 day supply*
Penicillins	
Penicillin G: 400,000 units po qid	$ 2.40** ($5.00)
Penicillin V: 500 mg po qid	$ 3.20** ($9.20)
Ampicillin: 500 mg po qid	$ 6.00** ($13.00)
Amoxicillin: 250 mg po tid	$ 5.00** ($6.30)
Amoxicillin + clavulinate 250 mg po tid	$31.00 -
Dicloxacillin: 500 mg po qid	$23.00** ($70.00)
Cephalosporins	
Cefaclor: 250 mg po qid	$48.00 -
Cephalexin: 250 mg po qid	$14.00** ($30.00)
Cephradine: 250 mg po qid	$18.00** ($30.00)
Cefuroxime axetil: 250 mg po bid	$36.00 -
Clindamycin: 300 mg po tid	$55.00 -
Trimethoprim-sulfamethoxazole: 1 DS bid	$ 3.80** ($12.80)
Metronidazole: 500 mg po bid	$ 2.80** ($28.00)
Erythromycin: 500 mg po qid	$10.00** ($17.60)
Tetracycline: 500 mg po qid	$ 2.40** ($5.20)
Doxycycline: 100 mg po bid	$ 4.00** ($41.00)

* Approximate wholesale prices according to "American Druggist Blue Book 1988-1989". (Prices to patient will be higher.)

** Price provided is for generic product; price in parentheses is for a representative brand product.

A. **Specimens and Tests for Detection of Lower Respiratory Pathogens (Reprinted with permission from: Bartlett JG et al: Cumitech 7A, Sept 1987, pg 3)**

Organism	Specimen	Test			
		Microscopy	Culture	Serology	Other
Bacteria					
Aerobic and facultatively anaerobic	Expectorated sputum, blood, TTA, empyema fluid, lung biopsy	Gram stain	X		
Anaerobic	TTA, empyema fluid, tissue, abscess	Gram stain	X		
Legionella sp.	Sputum, lung biopsy, pleural fluid, TTA, serum	FA	X	FA	
Nocardia sp.	Expectorated sputum, TTA, bronchial washings, BAL fluid, tissue, abscess	Gram and/or modified carbol fuchsin stain	X		
Chlamydia sp.	Nasopharyngeal swab, lung aspirate or biopsy, serum		X	FA for *C. trachomatis* and CF for *C. psittaci*	
Mycoplasma sp.	Expectorated sputum, nasopharyngeal swab, serum		X	CF, FA, or MI; cold agglutinins	
Mycobacteria	Expectorated or induced sputum, bronchial washings, BAL fluid, tissue, gastric washings	Fluorochrome stain or carbol fuchsin	X		PPD
Fungi					
Deep-seated					
Blastomyces sp.	Expectorated or induced sputum, TTA, bronchial washing or biopsy, BAL fluid, tissue, serum	KOH with phase contrast; GMS stain	X	CF, ID	
Coccidioides sp.				CF, ID, LA	
Histoplasma sp.				CF, ID	
Opportunistic					
Aspergillus sp.	Lung biopsy, serum	H & E, GMS stain	X	ID	
Candida sp.	Lung biopsy, serum	H & E, GMS stain	X	ID, CIE, LA	
Cryptococcus sp.	Expectorated sputum, serum	H & E, GMS stain, Calcofluor white	X	LA	
Zygomycetes	Expectorated sputum, tissue	H & E, GMS stain	X		
Viruses	Nasal washings, nasopharyngeal aspirate or swab, BAL fluid, lung biopsy, serum	FA	X	CF, EIA, LA, FA	
Pneumocystis sp.	Lung biopsy, TTA, bronchial brushings or washings, BAL fluid	Toluidine blue, Giemsa, or GMS stain			

a Abbreviations: CF, complement fixation; MI, metabolic inhibition; PPD, purified protein derivative; ID, immunodiffusion; LA, latex agglutination; H & E, hematoxylin and eosin; CIE, counterimmunoelectrophoresis; EIA, enzyme immunoassay.

B. Preferred Antibiotics for Pulmonary Infections

Agent	Preferred antimicrobial	Alternatives	Comment
Bacteria			
<u>S. pneumoniae</u>	Penicillin G or V	Ampicillin/amoxicillin Cephalosporins Erythromycin Clindamycin Tetracycline Chloramphenicol	Aminoglycosides are inactive <u>in vitro</u>; quinolones (ciprofloxacin) and some 3rd generation cephalosporins (ceftriaxone) are relatively inactive
Enterobacteriaceae (coliforms)	Cephalosporin, Antipseudomonad penicillin, Imipenem or Beta-lactam- betalactamase inhibitor Ciprofloxacin	Aminoglycoside	In vitro sensitivity tests required Aminoglycoside + second agent may be required for multiply resistant GNB
<u>Pseudomonas aeruginosa</u>	Aminoglycoside + anti- pseudomonad penicillin, ceftazidime or imipenem	Ciprofloxacin ± aminoglycoside	In vitro sensitivity tests required Antimicrobial combinations required for serious infections
<u>Moraxella catarrhalis</u> (Branhamella catarrhalis)	Trimethoprim-sulfa Erythromycin	Tetracycline Amoxicillin + clavulanic acid Cephalosporins	70-80% of strains produce betalactamase
<u>S. aureus</u> Methicillin-sensitive	Penicillinase resistant penicillin (nafcillin, oxacillin)	Cephalosporin - 1st generation or cefamandole/cefuroxime Vancomycin Clindamycin	May add aminoglycoside or rifampin for serious or refractory infections (continued)

181

Agent	Preferred antimicrobial	Alternatives	Comment
Methicillin-resistant	Vancomycin	Ciprofloxacin Sulfa-trimethoprim	
H. influenzae	Ampicillin/amoxicillin (susceptible strains) Cefamandole/cefuroxime Sulfa-trimethoprim	Cephalosporins - 3rd generation Tetracycline Chloramphenicol Betalactam-betalactamase inhibitor Ciprofloxacin	15-30% of strains are ampicillin resistant
Anaerobes	Clindamycin	Penicillin Metronidazole + penicillin	Penicillins other than anti- staphylococcal agents are equally effective compared to penicillin G Cephalosporins (esp cefoxitin) are probably effective, but published experience is limited Metronidazole should not be used alone
Mycoplasma pneumoniae	Tetracycline Erythromycin		Treat for 1-2 weeks
Chlamydia pneumoniae (TWAR agent)	Tetracycline or erythromycin		Treat for 10-14 days
Legionella	Erythromycin	Erythromycin + rifampin Sulfa-trimethoprim + rifampin	Treat for 3 weeks; moderate-
Nocardia	Sulfonamide	Doxycycline Sulfa-trimethoprim	Usual sulfa is sulfadiazine Treat 3-6 months (continued)

Agent	Preferred antimicrobial	Alternatives	Comment
Mycobacteria			
M. <u>tuberculosis</u>	INH plus rifampin ± pyrazinamide		See pg 116-119
M. <u>avium</u>	INH, ethambutol, rifampin and streptomycin	Additional agents: Ethionamide, rifabutin, cycloserine, ciprofloxacin, kanamycin, amikacin, clofazimine, viomycin, erythromycin, pyrazinamide	Recommended regimen is for moderately advanced pulmonary disease; 5-6 drugs advocated for far advanced disease or progression during treatment; no regimen has established efficacy in patients with AIDS Treat for 2 years
M. <u>kansasii</u>	INH, rifampin and ethambutol	Same 3 agents + streptomycin x 3 mo.	Treat for 18 months; regimen with streptomycin is 12 mo.
Fungi			
Aspergillus	Amphotericin B		Corticosteroids for PIE syndrome; see pg 99
Blastomyces	Ketoconazole	Amphotericin B	See pg 99
Coccidioides	Ketoconazole	Amphotericin B	See pg 102
Cryptococcus	Amphotericin B ± fluconazole	Ketoconazole	See pg 103
Histoplasma	Ketoconazole	Amphotericin B	See pg 104
Phycomycetes (mucor)	Amphotericin B		See pg 105 (continued)

183

Agent	Preferred antimicrobial	Alternatives	Comment
Viruses			
Influenza A	Amantadine	Rimantadine	See pg 113
Herpes simplex	Acyclovir	Vidarabine; Foscarnet	See pg 111
Varicella-zoster	Acyclovir	Vidarabine	See pg 112
Cytomegalovirus	Ganciclovir	Ganciclovir plus IV gamma globulin	Efficacy in CMV pneumonitis is not clearly established; see pg 112
Parasites			
Pneumocystis carinii	Sulfa-trimethoprim	Pentamidine Dapsone + Trimethoprim Clindamycin + primaquin	See pg 148

TREATMENT OF ENDOCARDITIS

A. **Medical Management**
   (Committee on Rheumatic Fever, Endocarditis and Kawasaki Disease of
   the American Heart Association's Council on Cardiovascular Disease in
   the Young: Antimicrobial Treatment of Infective Endocarditis due to Viridans
   Streptococci, Enterococci and Staphylococci. JAMA 261:1471,1989)

I.   Streptococci

A. Penicillin-sensitive streptococci (minimum inhibitory concentration $< 0.1\ \mu g/mL$)

1. <u>Penicillin only</u>: Aqueous penicillin G, 10-20 million units/day IV x 4
   weeks. (Preferred regimen for patients with a relative contraindication
   to streptomycin including age > 65 years, renal impairment or prior
   8th cranial nerve damage.)

2. <u>Penicillin + streptomycin x 4 weeks</u>: Procaine penicillin G, 1.2 million
   units IM q 6 h <u>or</u> aqueous penicillin G, 10-20 million units/day x 4 weeks
   <u>plus</u> streptomycin, 7.5 mg/kg IM (up to 500 mg) q 12 h or gentamicin, 1
   mg/kg IM or IV (up to 80 mg) q 8 h for first 2 weeks. (The disadvantage
   of the procaine penicillin + streptomycin is the necessity of 140 IM
   injections.)

3. <u>Two week course</u>: Procaine penicillin G, 1.2 million units q 6 h IM <u>or</u>
   aqueous penicillin G, 10-20 million units <u>plus</u> streptomycin, 7.5 mg/kg
   IM (up to 500 mg) q 12 h. (Advocated as most cost-effective regimen by
   Mayo Clinic group for uncomplicated cases with relapse rates of < 1%.)

4. <u>Penicillin allergy</u>: Vancomycin, 30 mg/kg/day IV x 4 weeks in 2-4 doses
   not to exceed 2 gm/day unless serum levels are monitored.

5. <u>Penicillin allergy, cephalosporins</u>: Cephalothin, 2 gm q 4 h x 4 wks or
   cefazolin, 1 gm IM or IV q 8 h x 4 wks. (Avoid in patients with
   immediate hypersensitivity to penicillin.)

<u>Note</u> ·

1. Aqueous penicillin G should be given in 6 equally divided daily doses or
   by continuous infusion; disadvantage of procaine penicillin is the large
   number of IM injections.

2. Streptococcus bovis and tolerant streptococci with MIC $< 0.1\ \mu g/mL$ may
   receive any of these regimens.

3. Nutritionally deficient streptococci with MIC $< 0.1\ \mu g/mL$ should receive
   regimen #2 with IV penicillin; if susceptibility cannot be reliably
   determined treat for MIC > 0.1 mg/mL and $< 0.5\ \mu g/mL$.

4. Prosthetic valve endocarditis: Regimen #2 with IV penicillin for 6 weeks
   and aminoglycoside (streptomycin or gentamicin) for at least two weeks.

5. Streptococci with MIC's > 1000 mg/mL to streptomycin should be treated
   with gentamicin in aminoglycoside containing regimens. Gentamicin and
   streptomycin are considered equally effective for strains sensitive to both.
   An advantage of gentamicin is the ability to administer IV as well as IM.

6. Cephalosporin regimens: Other cephalosporins may be effective, but clinical experience for agents other than cephalothin and cefazolin is limited.

7. Two week treatment regimen is <u>not</u> recommended for complicated cases, e.g. shock, extracardiac foci of infection or intracardiac abscess.

8. Desired peak serum levels if obtained: Streptomycin - 20 μg/mL, gentamicin - 3 μg/mL, vancomycin - 20-35 μg/mL (qid), or 30-45 μg/mL (bid).

B. Viridans streptococci and <u>Streptococcus bovis</u> relatively resistant to penicillin G (minimum inhibitory concentration > 0.1 μg/mL and < 0.5 μg/mL).

1. Aqueous penicillin G, 20 million units/day IV x 4 weeks <u>plus</u> streptomycin, 7.5 mg/kg IM (up to 500 mg) q 12 h or gentamicin, 1.0 mg/kg (up to 80 mg) q 8 h x 2 wks.

2. <u>Penicillin allergy</u>: Vancomycin, 30 mg/kg/day x 4 wks in 2-4 daily doses.

3. <u>Penicillin allergy, cephalosporins</u>: Cephalothin, 2 gm IV q 4 h or cefazolin, 1 gm IM or IV q 8 h x 4 wks.

C. Penicillin-resistant streptococci including enterococci and strains with minimum inhibitory concentrations of > 0.5 μg/ml.

1. <u>Penicillin + aminoglycoside</u>:
   Aqueous penicillin G   Streptomycin, 7.5 mg/kg IM q 12 h ⎱
   20-30 million units/day IV <u>plus</u>   <u>or</u>   ⎰ 4-6
   <u>or</u>   Gentamicin, 1 mg/kg IM or IV q 8 h ⎰ wks
   Ampicillin, 12 mg/day IV

2. <u>Penicillin allergy</u>: <u>Vancomycin + aminoglycoside</u>
   Vancomycin, 30 mg/kg/day <u>plus</u> Streptomycin, 7.5 mg/kg IM q 12 h ⎱
   IV in 2-4 doses   <u>or</u>   ⎰ 4-6
                             Gentamicin 1 mg/kg IM or IV q 8 h ⎰ wks

Note
1. Choice of aminoglycoside is usually determined by <u>in vitro</u> sensitivity testing. Gentamicin and streptomycin are considered equally effective for treatment of strains susceptible at 2000 μg/mL; high level resistance is more likely with streptomycin so that gentamicin is preferred when <u>in vitro</u> testing cannot be done. Other aminoglycosides should not be used.

2. Occasional strains produce beta-lactamase and should be treated with vancomycin.

3. Patients with symptoms for over 3 months prior to treatment and those with prosthetic valve endocarditis should receive combined treatment for 6 wks.

4. Serum levels of aminoglycosides should be monitored. Desirable peak levels are: Streptomycin - 20 μg/mL and gentamicin - 3 μg/mL.

II. Staphylococcus aureus or S. epidermidis

A. No prosthetic device - methicillin-sensitive

1. Nafcillin or oxacillin, 2 gm IV q 4 h x 4-6 wks ± gentamicin, 1 mg/kg IV or IM q 8 h x 3-5 days.

2. **Penicillin allergy, cephalosporin**: Cephalothin, 2 gm IV q 4 h or cefazolin, 2 gm IV q 8 h x 4-6 wks ± gentamicin, 1 mg/kg IV or IM q 8 h x 3-5 days (should not be used with immediate type penicillin hypersensitivity).

3. **Penicillin allergy**: Vancomycin, 30 mg/kg/day in 2-4 doses (not to exceed 2 gm/day unless serum levels monitored) x 4-6 wks.

4. **Methicillin-resistant strain**: Vancomycin, 30 mg/kg/day in 2-4 doses (not to exceed 2 gm/day unless serum levels monitored) x 4-6 wks.

B. Prosthetic valve or prosthetic material

1. Methicillin-sensitive strains: Nafcillin, 2 gm IV q 4 h x ≥ 6 wks plus rifampin, 300 mg po q 8 h x ≥ 6 wks plus gentamicin, 1 mg/kg IV or IM (not to exceed 80 mg) x 2 wks.

2. Methicillin-resistant strains: Vancomycin, 30 mg/kg/day in 2-4 doses (not to exceed 2 gm/day unless serum levels monitored) x ≥ 6 wks plus rifampin, 300 mg po q 8 h x ≥ 6 wks plus gentamicin, 1 mg/kg IV or IM (not to exceed 80 mg) x 2 wks.

Note

1. Methicillin-resistant staphylococci should be considered resistant to cephalosporins.

2. Tolerance has no important effect on antibiotic selection.

3. The occasional strains of staphylococci that are sensitive to penicillin G at ≤ 0.1 μg/mL may be treated with regimens advocated for penicillin-sensitive streptococci.

4. For native valve endocarditis, the addition of gentamicin to nafcillin or oxacillin causes a more rapid clearing of bacteremia, but has no impact on cure rates; use of gentamicin (or rifampin) with either methicillin-sensitive or methicillin-resistant strains is arbitrary. With vancomycin regimens, there is evidence for synergistic nephrotoxic effects and no enhanced efficacy; addition of aminoglycosides should be restricted to cases involving aminoglycoside-sensitive strains and duration limited to 3-5 days.

5. Coagulase-negative strains infecting prosthetic valves should be considered methicillin-resistant unless sensitivity is conclusively demonstrated.

6. Aminoglycoside selection for coagulase- negative strains should be selected on the basis of in vitro sensitivity tests; if not active, these agents should be omitted.

B. **Indications for Cardiac Surgery in Patients with Endocarditis (Alsip SG, et al: Amer J Med 78(suppl 6B):138,1985)**

I. Indications for urgent cardiac surgery

> Hemodynamic compromise
> > Severe heart failure (esp with aortic insufficiency)
> > Vascular obstruction
> Uncontrolled infection
> > Fungal endocarditis
> > Persistent bacteremia (or persistent signs of sepsis)
> > Lack of effective antimicrobial agents
> Unstable prosthetic valve

II. Relative indications for cardiac surgery

> **1.** Native valve
> > Bacterial agent other than susceptible streptococci
> > (such as S. aureus or gram-neg bacilli)
> > Relapse (esp if non-streptococcal agent)
> > Evidence of intracardiac extension
> > > Rupture of sinus of Valsalva or ventricular septum
> > > Ruptured chordae tendineae or papillary muscle
> > > Heart block (new conduction disturbance)
> > > Abscess shown by echo or catheterization
> > Two or more emboli
> > Vegetations demonstrated by echo (especially large
> > vegetation or aortic valve vegetations)
> > Mitral valve preclosure by echo (correlates with severe acute
> > aortic insufficiency)

> **2.** Prosthetic valve
> > Early post-operative endocarditis (< 8 wks)
> > Nonstreptococcal late endocarditis
> > Periprosthetic leak
> > Two or more emboli
> > Relapse
> > Evidence of intracardiac extension (see above)
> > Miscellaneous: Heart failure, aortic valve involvement, new
> > or increased regurgitant murmur or mechanical valve
> > versus bioprosthesis

III. Point system: Urgent surgery should be strongly considered with 5
accumulated points (Cobbs CG and Gnann JW: Indications for surgery
in infective endocarditis. In Sande MA, Kaye D (Eds) Contemporary
Issues in Infectious Disease. Churchill Livingstone, New York, 1984,
pp 201-212).

	Native valve	Prosthetic valve
Heart failure		
Severe	5	5
Moderate	3	5
Mild	1	2
Fungal etiology	5	5
Persistent bacteremia	5	5
Organism other than susceptible strep	1	2
Relapse	2	3
One major embolus	2	2
Two or more systemic emboli	4	4
Vegetations by echocardiography	1	1
Ruptured chordae tendinae or papillary mm.	3	-
Ruptured sinus of Valsalva	4	4
Ruptured ventricular septum	4	4
Heart block	3	3
Early mitral valve closure by echo	2	-
Unstable prosthesis	-	5
Early prosthetic valve endocarditis	-	2
Periprosthetic leak	-	2

INTRA-ABDOMINAL SEPSIS: ANTIBIOTIC SELECTION

I. Peritonitis

A. Polymicrobial infection

1. Combination treatment*

   An aminoglycoside vs. coliforms

   a. Gentamicin, 2.0 mg/kg, then 1.7 mg/kg IV q 8 h (usually preferred) or
   b. Tobramycin, 2.0 mg/kg, then 1.7 mg/kg IV q 8 h or
   c. Amikacin, 7.5 mg/kg, then 5.0 mg/kg IV q 8 h

   Plus an agent vs. anaerobes

   a. Clindamycin, 600 mg IV q 8 h or
   b. Cefoxitin, 2 gm IV q 6 h or
   c. Metronidazole, 500 mg IV q 8 h

   ---
   * Some authorities add an agent for the enterococcus: Ampicillin, 1-2 gm IV q 6 h.

2. Single drug treatment

   a. Cefoxitin, 2 gm IV q 6 h (not advocated as single agent if infection was acquired during hospitalization or if there has been antibiotic administration during prior two weeks). Alternatives to cefoxitin are: cefotetan, 1 gm IV q 12 h or cefmetazole, 2 gm q6-12h.

   b. Imipenem, 500 mg IV q 6-8 h

   c. Ticarcillin, 3 gm + clavulanic acid, 100 mg (Timentin) IV q 4-6 h

   d. Ampicillin, 2 gm + sulbactam, 1 gm (Unasyn) IV q 6 h

B. Monomicrobial infections

1. Spontaneous peritonitis or "primary peritonitis"

   a. Gentamicin or tobramycin, 2 mg/kg IV, then 1.7 mg/kg q 8 h plus a betalactam: Cefoxitin, 2 gm IV q 6 h; cefotaxime, 1.5-2 gm IV q 6 h; ampicillin, 2 gm IV q 6 h; or piperacillin, 4-5 gm IV q 6 h

   b. Cefotaxime, 1.5-2 gm IV q 6 h ± ampicillin, 2 gm IV q 6 h

2. Peritonitis associated with peritoneal dialysis

   a. Vancomycin, 1 gm IV (single dose)

    b. Antibiotics added to dialysate based on <u>in</u> <u>vitro</u> sensitivity:
Nafcillin, 10 mg/L; ampicillin, 20 mg/L; ticarcillin,
100 mg/L; penicillin G, 1,000-2,000 units/L; cephalothin,
20 mg/L; gentamicin or tobramycin, 5 mg/L; amikacin,
25 mg/L; clindamycin, 10 mg/L

  3. Candida peritonitis

    a. Amphotericin B, 200-1000 mg (total dose) 1 mg IV over 6 hrs,
then increase by 5-10 mg/day to maintenance dose of 20-30
mg/day

    b. Peritoneal dialysis: Systemic amphotericin B (above regimen)
plus addition to dialysate, 2-5 μg/ml

  4. Tuberculous
INH, 300 mg/day po, <u>plus</u> rifampin, 600 mg/day po, <u>plus</u>
pyrazinamide, 15-30 mg/kg/day po x 2 months, then INH <u>plus</u>
rifampin x 7-22 months

II. Localized Infections

A. <u>Intra-abdominal abscess(es)</u> (not further defined): Use regimens
recommended for polymicrobial infections with peritonitis.

B. <u>Liver abscess</u>

  1. Amebic

    a. Preferred: Metronidazole, 750 mg po or IV tid x 10 days plus
diloxanide furate, 500 mg po tid x 10 day or paromomycin, 500 mg
po bid x 7 days.

    b. Alternative: Emetine, 1 mg/kg/day IM x 5 days (or dehydro-
emetine, 1-1.5 mg/kg day x 5 days) <u>followed by</u> chloroquine,
500 mg po bid x 2 days, then 250 mg po bid x 3 weeks <u>plus</u>
iodoquinol, 650 mg po tid x 20 days

  2. Pyogenic

    a. Gentamicin <u>or</u> tobramycin, 2.0 mg/kg IV, then 1.7 mg/kg IV
q 8 h <u>plus</u> metronidazole, 500 mg IV q 8 h; clindamycin,
600 mg IV q 8 h, or cefoxitin, 2 gm IV q 6 h <u>plus</u> ampicillin,
2 gm IV q 6 h or penicillin G, 2 million units IV q 6 h

    b. Gentamicin or tobramycin (above doses) <u>plus</u> clindamycin (above
doses), cefoxitin (above doses) <u>or</u> piperacillin 4-5 gm IV q 6 h

C. <u>Biliary tract infections</u>

  1. Cholecystitis

a. Combination treatment: Gentamicin or tobramycin, 2.0 mg/kg IV, then 1.7 mg/kg IV q 8 h <u>plus</u> ampicillin, 2 gm IV q 6 h, piperacillin, 2-5 gm IV q 6 h, or cefoperazone, 1-2 gm IV q 12 h*

b. Single agent: Cefoperazone, 1-2 gm IV q 12 h*

---

* Other cephalosporins (2nd and 3rd generation) are probably equally effective. Some authorities add ampicillin (1-2 gm IV q 6 h) to cephalosporin containing regimens.

2. Ascending cholangitis, empyema of the gallbladder, or emphasematous cholecystitis: Treat with regimens advocated for peritonitis or intra-abdominal abscess.

D. <u>Appendicitis</u> (adult doses) (Role of antibiotics in nonperforative appendicitis is unclear.)

1. Combination treatment: Gentamicin <u>or</u> tobramycin, 2.0 mg/kg IV, then 1.7 mg/kg q 8 h <u>plus</u> clindamycin, 600 mg IV q 8 h, cefoxitin, 2 gm IV q 6 h <u>or</u> metronidazole, 500 mg IV q 6 h

2. Single agent: Cefoxitin, 2 gm IV q 6 h

E. <u>Diverticulitis</u> (Role of antibiotics in uncomplicated diverticulitis is unclear.)

1. Ambulatory patient

  a. Ampicillin, 500 mg po qid
  b. Tetracycline, 500 mg po qid
  c. Amoxicillin plus clavulanic acid (Augmentin), 500 mg po qid
  d. Cephalexin, 500 mg po qid <u>plus</u> metronidazole, 500 mg po qid

2. Hospitalized patients: Use regimens advocated for peritonitis or intra-abdominal abscess.

HEPATITIS

A. Types, clinical features and prognosis (MMWR 34:313,1985; MMWR 37:341,1988 and MMWR 39:1, 1990)

Type	Source	Incubation period	Diagnosis of acute viral hepatitis*	Prognosis
A (HAV)	Person-to-person fecal-oral Contaminated food & water (epidemic) Seroprevalence: Anti-HAV in adults U.S.: 40-50%	15-50 days Avg: 28 days	IgM anti-HAV	Self limited: > 99% Fulminant & fatal: 0.6% No carrier state or chronic infection Severity increases with age
B (HBV)	Sexual contact or contaminated needles from HBsAg carrier source (transmission via blood transfusions is rare due to HBsAg screening) Efficacy of transmission increased if source is HBeAg positive Seroprevalence (any marker, U.S.) (see pg 83) General population: 3-14% blacks: 14%; whites: 3% IV drug abuse: 60-80% Gay men: 35-80% Hemodialysis patients: 20-80% Health care workers (unvaccinated, frequent blood exp): 15-30% (unvaccinated, no frequent blood exp): 3-10%	45-160 days Avg: 120 days	HBsAg and/or IgM anti-HBc	Fulminant & fatal: 1.4% Carrier state (defined as HBsAg-pos, twice separated by 6 months or HBsAg pos and IgM anti-HBc neg): 6-10% of adults; 25-50% of children < 5 yrs (this means 6-10% of adults with any marker will be HBsAg pos) Chronic carriers: 25% develop chronic active hepatitis which progresses to cirrhosis in 15-30%, fatal cirrhosis in 1%/yr and/or fatal hepatocellular carcinoma in 0.25%/yr Perinatal with HBsAg-pos and HBeAg-pos mother: 70-90% acquire perinatal HBV infection and 85-90% of these will become chronic carriers; > 25% of these carriers will develop cirrhosis or hepatocellular carcinoma Risk of transmission with needlestick from HBsAg-pos source: 6-30% (continued)

Type	Source	Incubation period	Diagnosis of acute viral hepatitis*	Prognosis
C (HCV) (parenterally transmitted non-A,non-B) also causes sporadic NANB hepatitis	Contaminated transfused blood: 10%; IVDA-0%; heterosexual contact-10%; unknown-40% Seroprevalence rates (U.S.) Blood donors: 0.5-0.6% General population: 2% Hemophiliacs: 2% IV drug abuse: 60-90% Dialysis patients: 15-20% Gay men: 4%	14-84 days	Neg IgM anti-HAV, neg HBsAg and/or IgM anti-HBc; anti-HCV now available, but requires mean of 6 months to seroconvert with acute hepatitis; only about 30% of positive serologic tests in blood donors are true positives	Fulminant & fatal: rare Chronic hepatitis: 50%; cirrhosis: 10% (20% of those with chronic hepatitis); relationship to hepatocellular carcinoma is probable
ENANB (enterally transmitted non-A,non-B or epidemic NANB)	Epidemic fecal-oral (Southeast Asia, North Africa, India, Soviet Union, Mexico)	20-60 days (mean 40 days)	As above but neg anti-HCV at 1 yr No chronic infection	Mortality in pregnant women is 10-20% Usually mild disease in young, non-pregnant adults
Delta	Defective virus that requires presence of active HBV, e.g. co-infection with HBV or superinfection in HBsAg carrier; main source is blood (IV drug abuse, hemophilia) Seroprevalence in HBsAg carriers: IV drug abusers: 10-40%	Superinfection: 30-60 days Co-infection: same as HBV	HBsAg + anti-HDV, but in acute delta hepatitis anti-HDV appears late and is short lived Co-infection: IgM anti-HBc + anti-HDV Superinfection: persistent HBs + anti-HDV in high titer (> 1:100)	Acute co-infection with HBV: 1-10% acute fatality; < 5% chronic hepatitis Acute superinfection: 5-20% acute fatality; > 75% develop chronic hepatitis with 70-80% developing cirrhosis Epidemics in underdeveloped countries: fulminant fatal hepatitis in 10-20% of children Chronic delta hepatitis: Worsens prognosis of chronic HBV infection

(continued)

194

Type	Source	Incubation period	Diagnosis of acute viral hepatitis*	Prognosis
	Hemophiliacs: 50-80%			
	Hemodialysis patients: 20%			
	Endemic areas (Mediterranean			
	Basin, Middle East, Amazon			
	Basin): 20-40%			
	Medical care workers and			
	gay men: low			

* Symptoms or signs of viral hepatitis, serum aminotransferase > 2.5 x upper limit of normal, and absence of other causes of liver injury.

<u>Centers for Disease Control Hepatitis Hotline</u>: Automated telephone information system concerning modes of transmission, prevention, serologic diagnosis, statistics and infection control (404) 332-4555.

B. Hepatitis nomenclature (MMWR 39:6,1990)

	Abbreviation	Term	Definition/Comments
A. Hepatitis A	HAV	Hepatitis A virus	Etiologic agent of "infectious" hepatitis; a picornavirus; single serotype.
	Anti-HAV	Antibody to HAV	Detectable at onset of symptoms; lifetime persistence.
	IgM anti-HAV	IgM class antibody to HAV	Indicates recent infection with hepatitis A; detectable for 4-6 months after infection.
B. Hepatitis B	HBV	Hepatitis B virus	Etiologic agent of "serum" hepatitis; also known as Dane particle.
	HBsAg	Hepatitis B surface antigen	Surface antigen(s) of HBV detectable in large quantity in serum; several subtypes identified.
	HBeAg	Hepatitis B e antigen	Soluble antigen; correlates with HBV replication, high titer HBV in serum, and infectivity of serum.
	HBcAg	Hepatitis B core antigen	No commercial test available.
	Anti-HBs	Antibody to HBsAg	Indicates past infection with and immunity to HBV, passive antibody from HBIG, or immune response from HB vaccine.
	Anti-HBe	Antibody to HBeAg	Presence in serum of HBsAg carrier indicates lower titer of HBV.
	Anti-HBc	Antibody to HBcAg	Indicates prior infection with HBV at some undefined time.
	IgM anti-HBc	IgM class antibody to HBcAg	Indicates recent infection with HBV; detectable for 4-6 months after infection.
C. Delta hepatitis	HDV	Hepatitis D virus	Etiologic agent of delta hepatitis; can cause infection only in presence of HBV.
	HDAg	Delta antigen	Detectable in early acute delta infection.
	Anti-HDV	Antibody to delta antigen	Indicates present or past infection with delta virus.
D. Non-A, non-B hepatitis	PT-NANB	Parenterally transmitted	Diagnosis by exclusion. At least two candidate viruses, one of which has been proposed as hepatitis C virus; shares epidemiologic features with hepatitis B.
	ET-NANB	Enterically transmitted	Diagnosis by exclusion. Causes large epidemics in Asia, Africa, and Mexico; fecal-oral or waterborne.
E. Immune globulins	IG	Immune globulin (previously ISG, immune serum globulin, or gamma globulin)	Contains antibodies to HAV, low-titer antibodies to HBV.
	HBIG	Hepatitis B immune globulin	Contains high-titer antibodies to HBV.

INFECTIOUS DIARRHEA

A. Antimicrobial Treatment

Microbial Agent	Preferred	Alternative	Comment
Bacteria			
<u>Aeromonas hydrophilia</u>	Sulfa-trimethoprim 1 DS bid x 5 days Ciprofloxacin, 500 mg po bid x 5 days	Tetracycline, 500 mg po qid x 5 days	Efficacy of treatment not established and should be reserved for patients with severe disease, immunosuppression, extraintestinal infection or prolonged diarrhea.
<u>Campylobacter jejuni</u>	Erythromycin, 250-500 mg po qid x 7 days	Ciprofloxacin, 500 mg po bid x 7 days Doxycycline, 100 mg po bid x 7 days Furazolidone, 100 mg po qid x 7 days	May not alter course unless given early or for severe Sx. Indications include: acutely ill, persistent fever, bloody diarrhea, > 8 stools/day, dehydration or symptoms persisting for > 1 week. Resistance to erythromycin has been described.
<u>Chlamydia trachomatis</u>	Tetracycline, 500 mg po qid x 7 days Doxycycline, 100 mg po bid x 7 days	Erythromycin, 500 mg po qid x 7 days	Prolonged course (3-4 wks) for LGV serovars.
<u>Clostridium difficile</u>	Vancomycin, 125 mg po q6h x 7-10 days Metronidazole, 500 mg po tid x 7-10 days	Bacitracin, 25,000 units po qid x 7-10 days Cholestyramine, 3 gm packet qid x 7-10 days	Vancomycin is preferred for severe disease. Discontinuation of implicated antibiotic is often adequate. Relapses: Vancomycin or metronidazole x 7-10 days, <u>then</u> cholestyramine (3 gm po qid), vancomycin (125 mg qod) <u>or</u> lactobacilli (1 gm qid) x 21 days <u>or</u> vancomycin + rifampin (600 mg/day). (continued)

197

Microbial Agent	Preferred	Alternative	Comment
E. coli			
Enterotoxigenic E. coli (ETEC) Enteroadherent E. coli (EAEC)	Bismuth subsalicylate 60 ml qid x 5 days Sulfa-trimethoprim 1 DS po bid x 5 days	Trimethoprim, 200 mg po bid x 5 days Doxycycline, 100 mg po bid x 5 days Ciprofloxacin, 500 mg po bid x 5 days	Efficacy not established except for enterotoxin producing strains, e.g. ETEC (traveler's diarrhea).
Enterohemorrhagic E. coli (EHEC)	Ciprofloxacin, 500-750 mg po bid x 5-7 days		Efficacy not established. Sulfa-trimethoprim may increase toxin production.
Enteroinvasive E. coli (EIEC)	Ampicillin, 500 mg po or 1 gm IV qid x 5 days Sulfa-trimethoprim 1 DS po bid x 5 days		
Enteropathogenic E. coli (EPEC)	Sulfa-trimethoprim 1 DS po bid x 3-5 days	Neomycin, 100 mg/kg/day po x 3-5 days Furazolidone, 100 mg po qid x 3-5 days	
Food poisoning **Clostridium perfringens, Staph. aureus, Bacillus cereus, Listeria**	None		Self-limited and toxin mediated: antimicrobial treatment is not indicated.
Plesiomonas shigelloides	Sulfa-trimethoprim, 1 DS po bid x 5 days Ciprofloxacin, 500 mg po bid x 5 days	Tetracycline, 500 mg po qid x 5 days	Efficacy of treatment is not established and should be reserved for patients with extraintestinal infection, prolonged diarrhea or immunosuppression. (continued)

Microbial Agent	Preferred	Alternative	Comment
Mild disease	Metronidazole, 500 mg po tid x 5-10 days, then diloxanide furoate (as above)	Paromomycin, 500 mg po tid x 7 days Metronidazole, 2.4 gm/day x 2-3 days, then diloxanide furoate Metronidazole, 50 mg/kg x 1, then diloxanide furoate	
Cyst passer	Diloxanide furoate, 500 mg po tid x 10 days Paromomycin, 500 mg po tid x 7 days	Metronidazole, 500-750 mg po tid x 10 days Iodoquinol, 650 mg po tid x 21 days	Need to treat is arbitrary, but luminal amebicides (diloxanide furoate, paromomycin or iodoquinol) are preferred.
Giardia lamblia	Quinacrine, 100 mg po tid x 5-7 days	Metronidazole, 250 mg po tid x 7 days Furazolidone, 8 mg/kg/day po x 10 days Tinidazole, 2 gm single dose	Metronidazole is less effective then quinacrine, but better tolerated. Pregnancy: Consider paromomycin, 25-30 mg/kg/day x 5-10 days.
Isospora belli	Sulfa-trimethoprim 2 DS po bid x 2 wks	Anecdotal reports of response to pyrimethamine, metronidazole, quinacrine or nitrofurantoin	Patients with AIDS and other immuno-suppressive disorders usually require prolonged maintenance treatment.
Viruses			
H. simplex	Acyclovir, 200 mg po 5x/day		Refers to treatment of herpes proctitis; recurrent disease may require maintenance with acyclovir, 200 mg po 2-5 x daily.
Cytomegalovirus	Ganciclovir, 5 mg/kg IV bid x 14-21 days		Response is variable.

B. Fecal Leukocyte Exam

Often present	Variable	Not present
Campylobacter jejuni	Salmonella	Vibrio cholerae
Shigella	Yersinia	Enteroadherent
Enteroinvasive E. coli	Vibrio parahaemolyticus	E. coli
Exacerbations of	C. difficile	Enterotoxigenic
inflammatory bowel	Aeromonas	E. coli
disease	Plesiomonas	Food poisoning
	Enterohemorrhagic	S. aureus
	E. coli	B. cereus
		C. perfringens
		Viral gastroenteritis
		Adenovirus
		Rotavirus
		Norwalk agent
		Calicivirus
		Parasitic infection
		Giardia
		E. histolytica*
		Cryptosporidia
		Isospora
		Small bowel overgrowth
		"AIDS enteropathy"

* Frequency associated with blood.

C. Empiric treatment: Patients with acute, severe diarrhea (adults with ≥ 4 watery stools/day, ≤ 7 days) may be treated empirically with ciprofloxacin (500 mg po bid x 5 days). (See L. Goodman et al: Arch Intern Med 150:541,1990.)

Helicobacter pylori (formerly **Campylobacter pyloris**)
(Adapted from: Ormand J et al, Mayo Clin Proc 65:414,1990)

A.   **Diagnostic studies to detect H. pyloris**

	Sensitivity	Specificity
Histology (gastric biopsy x $\geq$ 2)	85-100%	85-100%
Culture (gastric biopsy)	50-100%	100%
Urease test	65-95%	60-100%
^{13}C and ^{14}C breath tests	90-100%	95-100%
Serology	80-100%	75-100%

B.   **Pathologic and clinical associations with H. pylori**

Chronic non-specific gastritis (pathologic diagnosis): 70-100%
Duodenal ulcer disease: 90-95%
   Recurrent duodenal ulcer at 1 year following eradication
      of H. pylori: 20-25%; without eradication of H. pylori: 80%
Gastric ulcer disease: 70%
Non-ulcer dyspepsia: 50%
Healthy persons (US)
   Age < 30 yrs: 0-10%
   Age 40-50 yrs: 30-40%
   Age 50-70 yrs: 50-70%

C.   **Treatment recommendations**

1.   Indications:

   a.   H. pylori per se: None.

   b.   Reasonable: Relapsing H. pylori-associated duodenal ulcer disease
        (after healing with traditional therapy).

   c.   Equivocal (treatment preferably limited to research protocols
        only): Gastric ulcer, non-ulcer dyspepsia and chronic non-specific
        gastritis.

2.   Regimens:

   1.   Bismuth subsalicylate (Pepto-Bismol), 2 tablets or 30 ml (524 mg)
        qid, plus metronidazole (or tinidazole), 500 mg po bid plus
        amoxicillin, 250-500 mg po tid or doxycycline, 100 mg po bid.
        Duration of regimen is arbitrary, but must continue 2-4 wks or
        use antibiotics 2-4 wks and continue bismuth up to 4-6 weeks.

   2.   Alternative is bismuth subsalicylate plus metronidazole (above doses).

URINARY TRACT INFECTIONS

1. **Management recommendations** (Reproduced with permission from: Kunin CM, Amer J Med 71:851,1981)

Group	Ease of Management	Type of Patient	Clinical Characteristics	Organism	Probability of Tissue Invasion	Therapy
I	Excellent	Female, child or adult	Few previous episodes; reliable, with good follow-up available; less than 2 days between onset of symptoms and treatment	Usually E. coli sensitive to most agents	Low	One dose amoxicillin, sulfonamide, TMP/SMZ, kanamycin
II	Good	Female, child or adult	Few previous episodes; follow-up poor	Usually E. coli sensitive to most agents	High or low	3–10 days. Prophylaxis for closely spaced recurrences
III	Fair	Female, child or adult	Many previous episodes; history of early recurrence, or diabetic, or renal transplantation	Variable, tends to have more resistant bacteria, susceptibility tests essential	High	4–6 weeks. Prophylaxis for closely spaced recurrences
IV	Fair	Male, adult	Recurrent infections, some underlying anatomic abnormality	Variable, susceptibility tests needed	High, often prostatic colonization	4–12 weeks. Prophylaxis for closely spaced recurrences
V	Poor	Male or female	Neurogenic bladder, large volume residual urine	Variable, susceptibility tests needed	High	Intermittent catheterization (treatment for symptomatic infections only)
VI	Very poor	Male or female	Continuous drainage required	Variable, susceptibility tests needed	Very high	Indwelling catheter closed drainage (treatment for sepsis only)

Note: TMP/SMZ = trimethoprim with sulfamethoxazole.

204

II. **Management recommendations of Medical Letter consultants** (Medical Letter 23:69,1981)

A. **Asymptomatic infection**: Treat only pregnant women and children.

B. **Single dose regimens**: Advocated for uncomplicated infections in non-pregnant females with dysuria-frequency syndrome who are likely to return for follow-up urine cultures in 48-72 hours.
   1. Amoxicillin (3 gm)
   2. Sulfisoxazole (2 gm)
   3. Trimethoprim (160 mg) - sulfamethoxazole (800 mg) (1 DS tab)

C. **Pyelonephritis**: Treat 10-14 days, usually with an aminoglycoside, betalactam or trimethoprim-sulfamethoxazole selected by in vitro sensitivity tests.

D. **Relapses**: Patients with recurrent infections involving the same bacterial strain according to speciation, serotyping and/or in vitro sensitivity tests should: 1) be investigated for anatomical abnormality, calculus, prostatitis, etc; 2) be treated two additional weeks if no abnormality is found.

E. **Prophylaxis**

   1. **Regimens: a)** Trimethoprim 40 mg - sulfamethoxazole 200 mg (1/2 tab) every other day.

      b) Nitrofurantoin, 50 mg daily (risk for serious reactions, especially pulmonary fibrosis).

      c) Infections clearly related to intercourse: may be prevented with single dose of an antimicrobial taken after intercourse.

   2. **Duration**: Usually 6 months; if symptoms recur frequently when prophylaxis is discontinued, it may be reinstituted for 2 years or more.

F. **Radiologic investigation**: Intravenous pyelogram is advocated for:
   1) Girls < 6 years; 2) girls or women with recurrent infections;
   3) males regardless of age; 4) pyelonephritis; 5) failure to respond to antibiotics.

G. **Catheterized patient**: Treat only for symptomatic infections; antimicrobial prophylaxis has no established merit.

III. Definitions of bacteriuric syndromes (Reprinted with permission from: Wilhelm MP and Edson RS, Mayo Clin Proc 62:1027,1987)*

Syndrome	Definition
Lower urinary tract infection	Lower urinary tract symptoms† + urine culture with ≥10^2 bacteria/ml
Acute cystitis	Lower urinary tract symptoms + urine culture with ≥10^5 bacteria/ml
Acute urethral syndrome	Lower urinary tract symptoms + 10^2 to 10^5 bacteria/ml or venereally transmitted agent (for example, *Neisseria gonorrhoeae*, *Chlamydia trachomatis*, *Herpes simplex*) or no identifiable pathogen
Acute pyelonephritis	Upper urinary tract symptoms‡ + urine with ≥10^5 bacteria/ml
Asymptomatic bacteriuria	No symptoms + urine culture with ≥10^5 bacteria/ml
Recurrent bacteriuria	Recurrent lower urinary tract symptoms§ + urine culture with ≥10^2 bacteria/ml
Relapse	Recurrent infection with same bacterial strain
Reinfection	Recurrent infection with different bacterial strain
Complicated bacteriuria	Urine culture with ≥10^5 bacteria/ml with associated structural abnormality of the urinary tract§ (for example, involvement with stones or catheter)

*All syndromes usually associated with pyuria (≥8 leukocytes/mm³ unspun urine).
†Dysuria, urgency, frequency, suprapubic pain.
‡Fever, rigors, flank pain, nausea, prostration.
§May be asymptomatic.

IV. Outpatient management of urinary tract infections (Adapted from Wilhelm MP & Edson RS: Mayo Clin Proc 62:1025,1987)

Prophylaxis
Preferred
    Trimethoprim-sulfamethoxazole, 1/2 tab q d or q o d
    Macrodantin, 50 mg tabs, 1 tab q d
    Trimethoprim, 100 mg tabs, 1/2 tab q d

Alternatives
    Cephalexin, 250 mg tabs, 1 tab q d
    Methenamine mandelate, 1 gm tabs, 1 tab q 6 h
    Methenamine hippurate, 1 gm tabs, 1 tab q 12 h

Treatment
    Trimethoprim-sulfamethoxazole, 2 DS tabs ⎫
    Amoxicillin, 500 mg caps, 6 caps (3 gm) ⎬ single dose
    Sulfisoxazole, 500 mg tabs, 4 tabs (2 gm) ⎭
    Trimethoprim-sulfamethoxazole, 1 DS tab q 12 h x 3 days or 7-10 days
    Amoxicillin, 250 mg caps, 1 cap q 8 h x 7-10 days
    Trimethoprim, 100 mg tabs, 1 tab q 12 h x 7-10 days
    Nitrofurantoin macrocrystals, 100 mg caps, 1 cap q 6 h x 7-10 days
    Nalidixic acid, 1 gm caps, 1 cap q 6 h x 7-10 days
    Norfloxacin, 400 mg tabs, 1 tab q 12 h x 7-10 days
    Tetracycline, 250 mg cap, 1 cap q 6 h x 7-10 days
    Ciprofloxacin, 250 mg tab, 1 tab bid x 7-10 days

Recommendations of J. Johnson and W.E. Stamm (Urinary Tract Infections in Women: Diagnosis and Treatment. Ann Intern Med 111:906,1989)

Cystitis: Single dose (only for uncomplicated cases)

    Trimethoprim, 400 mg*
    Sulfa-trimethoprim, 320/1600 mg (2 DS)*
    Nitrofurantoin, 200 mg*
    Amoxicillin, 3 gm
    Amoxicillin plus clavulanate, 500 mg
    Ampicillin, 3.5 gm
    Cephalexin, 2 gm
    Sulfisoxazole, 2 gm
    Ciprofloxacin, 250 mg
    Norfloxacin, 400 mg

Cystitis: Multidose regimens (3-7 days)

    Trimethoprim, 100 mg q 12 h*
    Sulfa-trimethoprim, 160/800 mg q 12 h*
    Nitrofurantoin, 100 mg q 6 h*
    Amoxicillin, 500 mg q 8 h
    Amoxicillin plus clavulanate, 500 mg q 8 h
    Cephalexin, 500 mg q 6 h
    Ciprofloxacin, 250 mg q 12 h
    Norfloxacin, 400 mg q 12 h
    Sulfisoxazole, 500 mg q 6 h
    Tetracycline, 500 mg q 6 h

Pyelonephritis, oral therapy for mild pyelonephritis (treat ≥ 14 days)

    Trimethoprim, 100 mg q 12 h*
    Sulfa-trimethoprim, 160/800 q 12 h*
    Cephalexin, 500 mg q 6 h
    Amoxicillin, 500 mg q 8 h
    Amoxicillin plus clavulanate, 500 mg q 8 h
    Ciprofloxacin, 250 mg q 12 h
    Norfloxacin, 400 q 12 h

Pyelonephritis, parenteral therapy (Intravenous administration until afebrile and improved, then oral therapy to complete total of 14 days)

    Gentamicin, 1.5 mg/kg q 8 h*
    Ceftriaxone, 1 gm q 12 h*
    Trimethoprim-sulfamethoxazole, 160/800 mg q 12 h*
    Ampicillin, 1 gm (or higher) q 8 h
    Ampicillin plus gentamicin (above doses) q 8 h
    Cefazolin, 1 gm (or higher) q 8 h
    Mezlocillin, 1 gm (or higher) q 6 h

    * Preferred regimens

V. Cost of oral drugs commonly used for urinary tract infections

Antimicrobial agent and regimen	Wholesale price for 10 day supply*
Ampicillin: 500 mg po qid	$ 6.00** ($13.00)
Amoxicillin: 250 mg po tid	$ 5.00** ($6.30)
Amoxicillin + clavulanate (Augmentin): 250 mg po tid	$31.00
Carbenicillin (Geocillin): 380 mg po qid	$42.00
Cephradine (Anspor, Velosef): 250 mg po qid	$18.00** ($30.00)
Cephalexin (Keflex): 250 mg po qid	$14.00** ($30.00)
Ciprofloxacin (Cipro): 500 mg po bid	$37.00
Doxycycline (Vibramycin): 100 mg po bid	$ 4.00** ($41.00)
Methenamine mandelate: 1 gm po qid	$ 2.00
Methenamine hippurate (Hiprex): 1 gm po bid	$10.00
Nalidixic acid (NegGram): 1 gm caplet po qid	$31.00
Nitrofurantoin (Furadantin, Macrodantin): 50 mg cap po qid	$ 4.80
Norfloxacin (Noroxin): 400 mg po bid	$42.00
Sulfisoxazole (Gantrisin): 1 gm po qid	$ 4.40** ($10.40)
Tetracycline: 500 mg po qid	$ 2.40** ($5.20)
Trimethoprim: 100 mg po bid	$ 3.60
Trimethoprim-sulfamethoxazole (Bactrim,Septra): 1 DS po bid	$ 3.80** ($12.80)

* Approximate wholesale prices according to "American Druggist Blue Book" 1988-1989 (prices to patient will be higher).

**Price is provided for generic product if available; price in parentheses is for representative brand product.

SEXUALLY TRANSMITTED DISEASES
(CDC recommendations adapted from MMWR 38:S8, pp 1-43, 1989)

I <u>Gonococcal infections</u>

A. Treatment recommendations are influenced by:

1) Spread of infections due to antibiotic-resistant <u>N</u>. <u>gonorrhoeae</u> including penicillinase-producing strains (PPNG), tetracycline-resistant strains (TRNG) and strains with chromosomally-mediated resistance to multiple antibiotics.
2) High frequency of chlamydial infections in patients with gonorrhea.
3) Recognition of serious complications of chlamydial and gonococcal infection.
4) Absence of a rapid, inexpensive and highly accurate test for chlamydial infection.

B. All cases of gonorrhea should be diagnosed or confirmed by culture to enable antimicrobial susceptibility testing.

C. Treatment of uncomplicated urethral, endocervical and rectal infections

1. <u>Recommended</u>: Ceftriaxone, 250 mg IM x 1 <u>plus</u> doxycycline*, 100 mg po bid x 7 days.
2. <u>Alternative</u>: Spectinomycin**, 2 gm IM x 1 <u>plus</u> doxycycline*, 100 mg po bid x 7 days.
3. <u>Other alternatives</u>
   a. Ciprofloxacin, 500 mg po x 1 * **
   b. Norfloxacin, 800 mg po x 1 * **
   c. Cefuroxime axetil, 1 gm po x 1 + probenecid, 1 gm *
   d. Cefotaxime, 1 gm IM x 1 *
   e. Ceftizoxime, 500 mg IM x 1 *
   f. Penicillin sensitive strain *: Amoxicillin, 3 gm po plus probenecid, 1 gm x 1

   * All regimens should include a 7 day course of doxycycline (100 mg po bid x 7 days) or tetracycline (500 mg po qid x 7 days) for presumed concurrent infection with <u>Chlamydia</u> <u>trachomatis</u>. Alternative to tetracyclines for <u>C</u>. <u>trachomatis</u> is erythromycin base or stearate (500 mg po qid x 7 days) or erythromycin ethylsuccinate (800 mg po qid x 7 days).

   ** Quinolones are contraindicated in pregnant females and children < 16 yrs; activity of quinolones or spectinomycin in incubating syphilis is unknown so serology for syphilis should be obtained in 1 month.

4. <u>Special considerations</u>
   a. <u>Incubating syphilis</u>: All patients with gonorrhea should have syphilis serology; patients treated with quinolones or spectinomycin should have repeat serology in 1 month to exclude incubating syphilis.

209   (continued)

    b.   <u>Sex partners</u>: All persons exposed during preceding 30 days should be examined, cultured and treated (for gonorrhea and chlamydial infection).

    c.   <u>Follow-up</u>: Treatment failure with ceftriaxone-doxycycline regimen is rare so that "test-of-cure" is probably not essential; re-exam at 1-2 months ("re-screening") may be more cost effective. Patients treated with alternative regimens should have follow-up cultures ("test-of-cure") at 4-7 days after treatment is concluded.

    d.   <u>Treatment failures</u>: Culture for <u>N</u>. <u>gonorrhoeae</u> and test for antibiotic sensitivity. Many "treatment failures" are due to chlamydial infection, reinfection or non-compliance. Treat recurrent gonococcal infection with ceftriaxone, 250 mg IM x 1 plus doxycycline, 100 mg po bid x 7 days.

    e.   <u>Pharyngeal gonococcal infection</u>: Ceftriaxone, 250 mg IM x 1; alternative: Ciprofloxacin, 500 mg po x 1 and repeat culture 4-7 days later.

    f.   <u>Pregnancy</u>: Ceftriaxone, 250 mg IM x 1 <u>plus</u> erythromycin base or stearate, 500 mg po qid x 7 days. (Quinolones and tetracyclines are contraindicated.)

D. Gonococcal infection at other anatomical sites

    1.   <u>Pharyngeal infection</u>: Ceftriaxone, 250 mg IM x 1; alternative: Ciprofloxacin, 500 mg po x 1 and repeat culture 4-7 days later.

    2.   <u>Salpingitis</u>: See Pelvic inflammatory disease.

    3.   <u>Disseminated gonococcal infection (DGI)</u>
        Hospitalize and treat with
            Ceftriaxone*, 1 gm IV or IM q24h <u>or</u>
            Ceftizoxime*, 1 gm IV q8h <u>or</u>
            Ceftazidime*, 1 gm IV q8h
            Alternative to betalactams: Spectinomycin*, 2 gm IM q12h
            Alternative for penicillin-sensitive strains: Ampicillin*,
                1 gm IV q6h
            * Test for genital chlamydia or treat empirically; reliable patients with uncomplicated DGI may be discharged at 24-48 hrs after symptoms resolve and should complete 1 wk of treatment with cefuroxime axetil, 500 mg bid, amoxicillin with clavulanic acid (Augmentin), 500 mg bid or ciprofloxacin, 500 mg bid.

    4.   <u>Gonococcal endocarditis or meningitis</u>
        IV therapy with effective agent such as ceftriaxone 1-2 gm q12h for 10-14 days (meningitis) or 4 weeks (endocarditis).

    5.   <u>Gonococcal ophthalmia</u>
        Treatment of adult: Ceftriaxone, 1 gm IM x 1 <u>plus</u> ophthalmologic assessment.

        Prevention in newborn infants (required by law in most states, must be done within 1 hr after delivery, efficacy in preventing chlamydial infections of eye is unknown):
        Erythromycin 0.5% ophthalmic ointment x 1 <u>or</u>
        Tetracycline 1% ophthalmic ointment x 1 <u>or</u>
        Silver nitrate 1% aqueous solution

II   <u>Syphilis</u>

A.   Treatment (adult, non-pregnant)

1. Exposed: Evaluate clinically and serologically; if exposure < 90 days treat presumptively (regimen for early syphilis).

2. <u>Early syphilis</u> including primary, secondary or latent of less than one year duration.

   - Benzathine penicillin G, 2.4 million units IM x 1.

   - Penicillin allergy: Doxycycline, 100 mg po bid x 14 days or tetracycline, 500 mg po qid x 14 days.

   - Penicillin allergy and tetracycline contraindication or intolerance: **a)** erythromycin, 500 mg po qid x 15 days (this is acceptable only if compliance plus follow-up serology is assured); **b)** skin testing for penicillin allergy and desensitization if necessary; **c)** ceftriaxone, 250 mg IM x 1/day x 10 days with caution for sensitivity reaction.

3. Syphilis over 1 year (except neurosyphilis) including latent syphilis, cardiovascular syphilis or gummas.

   - Benzathine penicillin G, 2.4 million units q week x 3 successive weeks.

   - Penicillin allergy (efficacy of alternative regimens for neurosyphilis not established and CSF exam mandatory to exclude this complication): Doxycycline, 100 mg po bid or tetracycline, 500 mg po qid x 4 weeks.

4. Neurosyphilis

   - Aqueous penicillin G, 12-24 million units IV/day x 10-14 days, then benzathine penicillin G, 2.4 million units IM weekly x 3.

   - Procaine penicillin G, 2-4 million units IM daily plus probenecid, 500 mg po qid x 10-14 days; some recommend adding benzathine penicillin G, 2.4 million units IM weekly x 3.

   - Benzathine penicillin G, 2.4 million units IM weekly x 3 doses.

   - Penicillin allergy: Confirm allergy and "consult expert".

5. Pregnancy

   - Penicillin regimens as noted above.

   - Tetracyclines are contraindicated in pregnancy and erythromycins have a high failure rate in fetal infection. Patients with convincing histories of penicillin allergy should have skin testing and desensitization.

6. HIV infection

   a. All patients with syphilis should be counseled concerning risks of HIV and encouraged to have HIV serology.

   b. CSF from patients with HIV infection often shows mononuclear cells and increased protein. With a negative CSF VDRL there is no practical method to confirm or exclude neurosyphilis.

B. CSF exam: Should be performed in patients with clinical symptoms or signs consistent with neurosyphilis and is desired in all persons with syphilis > 1 yr, although this decision should be individualized. Tests in CSF should include leukocyte count, protein and VDRL. A positive VDRL is diagnostic of neurosyphilis; negative VDRL doesn't exclude it.

C. Follow up

Form	Follow-up quantitative non-treponemal test*	Expectation	Additional comments
Early syphilis	3 & 6 months post treatment	4-fold decrease by 3 mo. or by 6 mo. with early latent syphilis	If titer not decreased should do CSF exam and re-treat
Early syphilis + HIV infected	1,2,3,6,9 and 12 mo.		If titer does not decrease (4-fold) by 3 mo. for primary or by 6 mo. for secondary, or if titer increases (4-fold): reevaluate for treatment failure versus reinfection, and examine CSF
Syphilis > 1 yr	6 and 12 months post treatment	Titer declines more gradually	CSF exam if there are neurological signs or symptoms; treatment failure (titer increases 4-fold or initially high titer of $\geq$ 1:32 fails to decrease); non-penicillin therapy; HIV seropositive

212

Form	Follow-up quantitative non-treponemal test*	Expectation	Additional comments
Neurosyphilis	Six month intervals at least 2 yrs (see comments)		Clinical evaluation and CSF analysis at 6 month intervals until cell count normal; if titer not decreased at 6 mo. or normal at 2 yrs consider retreatment

* Nontreponemal tests = VDRL and RPR; treponemal tests = FTA-ABS, MHA-TP and HATTS

III   Chlamydia trachomatis

A.   Treatment (urethral, endocervical and rectal infection)

- Tetracycline, 500 mg po qid x 7 days.

- Doxycycline, 100 mg po bid x 7 days.

- Tetracycline contraindication: Erythromycin base or stearate, 500 mg po qid x 7 days or erythromycin ethylsuccinate, 800 mg po qid x 7 days.

- Pregnancy: Treat as described for tetracycline contraindication with erythromycin. Women who cannot tolerate this regimen should receive half the suggested daily dose qid for at least 14 days. Alternative to erythromycin is ampicillin, 500 mg po tid x 7 days.

B.   Sex partners: Examine for STD and treat using above regimen if contact was within 30 days.

C.   Follow-up: Post treatment test-of-cure cultures are not advocated because treatment failures with recommended regimens have not been observed.

IV   Genital herpes simplex

A.   Treatment

1.   First episode (genital or rectal infection)

Genital: Acyclovir, 200 mg po 5 x daily for 7-10 days or until clinical resolution occurs.

Rectal: 400 mg po 5 x daily for 10 days or until clinical resolution occurs.

213

Hospitalized patients: 5 mg/kg IV q8h for 5-7 days or until clinical resolution occurs.

2. Recurrent episodes (most do not benefit from treatment unless recurrences are severe and acyclovir is started at the beginning of the prodrome or within 2 days of onset of lesions).

   - Acyclovir, 200 mg po 5 times daily x 5 days or acyclovir, 800 mg po bid x 5 days.

3. Prophylaxis for recurrences (for patients with > 6 recurrences/yr): 200 mg po 2-5 x/day or 400 mg po bid. HSV resistant to acyclovir have been noted during suppressive treatment, but their clinical significance is not known. This suppressive regimen is contraindicated in women who become pregnant during treatment.

B. HIV disease: The need for higher therapeutic or suppressive doses is suspected, but not established.

C. Pregnancy: Safety of acyclovir is not established and it should not be used except for life-threatening maternal HSV disease.

V   Chancroid (Haemophilus ducreyi) infection: Recommended treatment varies by susceptibility of strains in different geographic areas.

Recommended: Ceftriaxone, 250 mg IM x 1 or
Erythromycin, 500 mg po qid x 7 days.

Alternative regimens: Trimethoprim-sulfamethoxazole, 1 double strength tablet (160/800 mg) po bid x at least 7 days; amoxicillin, 500 mg plus clavulanic acid 125 mg po tid x 7 days or ciprofloxacin, 500 mg po bid x 3 days (ciprofloxacin is contraindicated in pregnancy and children < 16 yrs).

VI   Lymphogranuloma venereum treatment (genital, inguinal and anorectal)

Recommended: Doxycycline, 100 mg po bid x 21 days.

Alternatives: Tetracycline, 500 mg po qid x 21 days or
     Erythromycin, 500 mg po qid x 21 days or
     Sulfasoxazole, 500 mg qid x 21 days

VII   Pediculosis pubis

A. Treatment

   Permethrin (1%) cream rinse applied to affected area and washed after 10 minutes or

   Lindane (1%) shampoo applied 4 minutes and then thoroughly washed off (not recommened for pregnant or lactating women) or

   Pyrethrins and piperonyl butoxide (non-prescription) applied to affected areas and washed off after 10 minutes.

Adjunctive: Retreat after 7 days if lice or eggs are detected at hair-skin junction. Clothes and bed linen of past 2 days should be washed and dried by machine (hot cycle each) or dry cleaned.

C.   **Sex partners**: Treat as above.

VIII Scabies

Recommended: Lindane (1%) 1 oz lotion or 30 gm cream applied thinly to all areas of body below neck and washed thoroughly at 8 hr. (Not recommended for pregnant or lactating women.)

Alternatives: Crotamiton (10%) applied to body below neck nightly for 2 nights and washed thoroughly 24 hr after second application.

Note: Permethrin (5% cream, 30 gm) massaged and left 8-14 hrs considered preferable drug for scabies by Medical Letter consultants (32:21-22,1990).

Sex partners and close household contacts: Treat as above.

Adjunctive: Clothing or bed linen contaminated by patient should be washed and dried by machine (hot cycle) or dry cleaned.

IX   Warts (Condylomata acuminata)

Location	Treatment	Comment
External genital and perianal	Cryotherapy, e.g. liquid nitrogen or cryoprobe Podophyllin, 10% applied carefully to each wart, wash at 1-4 hr, and reapply weekly Trichloroacetic acid (TCA) applied locally and repeat weekly; powder with talc or baking soda to remove unreacted acid Alternatives: Surgical removal, electrocautery, laser therapy	All treatments show high rate of recurrence Podophyllin is contra-indicated in pregnancy Women with anogenital warts should have Pap smear annually Cryotherapy is preferred because it is non-toxic, does not require anesthesia and does not cause scarring Interferon is not recommended because of low efficacy, frequent toxicity and high cost
Vaginal	Cryotherapy with liquid nitrogen Alternatives: TCA (80-90%) or podophyllin (10-25%) as above	Podophyllin is contraindicated in pregnancy

Location	Treatment	Comment
Cervical	(See comment)	Must rule out dysphagia so that an expert consultant is required
Urethral and meatal	Cryotherapy with liquid nitrogen Alternative: Podophyllin (10-25% as above)	Podophyllin is contraindicated in pregnancy
Anal	Cryotherapy with liquid nitrogen Alternative: TCA, electrocautery, or surgical excision	Podophyllin is contraindicated

Syndromes - Female

I   Pelvic inflammatory disease

A. Agents

1. Gonococcal PID: N. gonorrhoeae.

2. Non-gonococcal PID: Chlamydia trachomatis, anaerobic bacteria ± facultative gram-negative bacilli, Actinomyces israelii, streptococci and mycoplasmas.

B. Indications for hospitalization: 1) diagnosis uncertain, 2) surgical emergencies cannot be excluded (such as appendicitis or ectopic pregnancy), 3) pelvic abscess suspected, 4) severe illness prevents outpatient management, 5) pregnancy, 6) patient unable to follow or tolerate outpatient treatment, 7) failure to respond within 72 hours to outpatient treatment, 8) clinical follow-up at 72 hours not possible, 9) patient is an adolescent (less reliable and greater long-term sequelae).

C. Treatment

1.   Antibiotics: Outpatient regimen.

Recommended: Ceftriaxone, 250 mg IM x 1 dose or cefoxitin, 2 gm IM plus probenecid, 1 gm concurrently plus doxycycline, 100 mg po bid or tetracycline, 500 mg po qid for 10-14 days.

Alternative to tetracyclines: Erythromycin, 500 mg po qid x 10-14 days.

2.   Antibiotics: Inpatient regimen.

Initial*	Oral follow-up**
Doxycycline, 100 mg IV bid + cefoxitin, 2 gm IV qid or cefotetan, 2 gm IV q12h	Doxycycline, 100 mg po bid
Clindamycin, 900 mg IV qid + gentamicin, 2.0 mg/kg IV, then 1.5 mg/kg tid	Clindamycin, 450 mg po 5x/day or doxycycline, 100 mg po bid (doxycycline preferred if C. trachomatis is suspected or confirmed)

* Parenteral treatment to continue at least 48 hrs after patient clinically improves.
** Oral regimen to be continued to complete 10-14 days of treatment.

3. Male sex partners: Examine and treat with regimen for uncomplicated gonococcal and chlamydial infection.

4. Follow-up: Outpatients should be re-evaluated within 72 hrs and patients not responding should be hospitalized.

5. Intra-uterine device: Removal is recommended soon after antimicrobial treatment is started.

Mucopurulent cervicitis

A. Diagnosis: (1) Mucopurulent endocervical exudate that may appear yellow or green on white cotton-tipped swab (positive swab test); (2) gram-stained smear of endocervical secretions shows over 10 PMN/oil immersion field; or (3) cervicitis documented by cervical friability (bleeding when the first swab is taken) and/or erythema or edema within a zone of cervical ectopy.

B. Laboratory evaluation: Gram stain, culture for N. gonorrhoeae, test for Chlamydia trachomatis and wet mount for Trichomonas.

C. Treatment

1. Gonococcal: N. gonorrhoeae found on gram stain or culture - treat for uncomplicated gonococcal infection and presumed chlamydial infection.

2. Non-gonococcal: N. gonorrhoeae not found on gram stain or culture - treat for C. trachomatis (pg 216).

Vaginitis/vaginosis

A. Trichomoniasis (almost always a STD)

1. Diagnosis: Wet mount or culture.

2. Usual treatment: Metronidazole, 2 gm po as single dose
   Alternative: Metronidazole, 500 mg po bid x 7 days.

3. Asymptomatic women: Treat as above.

4. Pregnant women: Metronidazole is contraindicated in first
   trimester and should be avoided throughout pregnancy. For
   severe, symptomatic disease after first trimester give
   metronidazole, 2 gm x 1.

5. Lactating women: Treat with 2 gm dose of metronidazole and
   suspend breast feeding x 24 hours.

6. Sex partners: Treat with 2 gm dose of metronidazole or 500 mg
   po bid x 7 days.

7. Treatment failures: Retreat with metronidazole, 500 mg po bid
   x 7 days. Persistent failures: 2 gm dose daily x 3-5 days.

B. Bacterial vaginosis (non-specific vaginitis)

   1. Diagnosis: Non-irritating, malodorous, thin, white vaginal
      disharge with pH over 4.5, elaboration of fishy odor after 10%
      KOH, microscopic exam showing sparse lactobacilli and numerous
      coccobacillary forms on epithelial cells ("clue cells"). Cultures for
      Gardnerella vaginalis are not recommended. Asymptomatic
      infections are common; necessity to treat asymptomatic infections
      is controversial.

   2. Treatment
      - Metronidazole, 500 mg po bid x 7 days.
      - Alternative: Clindamycin, 300 mg po bid x 7 days.

   3. Sex partners: Treatment not indicated

   4. Pregnancy: Metronidazole is contraindicated; use clindamycin
      regimen.

C. Vulvovaginal candidiasis (not considered an STD)

   1. Treatment

      Recommended: Miconazole nitrate suppository or clotrimazole
      (tablet, 200 mg) intravaginally at bedtime x 3 days; betaconazole
      (2% cream, 5 g) intravaginally at bedtime x 3 days; tetaconazole
      (80 mg suppository or 0.4% cream) intravaginally at bedtime x 3
      days.

      Alternatives: Miconazole nitrate vaginal suppository (100 mg or
      2% cream, 5 g) intravaginally at bedtime x 7 days or clotrimazole
      (vaginal tabs, 100 mg or 1% cream, 5 gm) intravaginally at
      bedtime x 7 days).

2. Sex partners: Treat only for <u>Candida</u> <u>balanitis</u>.

3. Pregnancy: As for non-pregnant patients.

Syndromes - Male

I Urethritis

A. Categories

1. Gonococcal

2. Non-gonococcal: Usually caused by <u>C</u>. <u>trachomatis</u> (40-50%), other organisms (10-15%) (<u>Ureaplasma</u> <u>urealyticum</u>, <u>T</u>. <u>vaginalis</u>, herpes simplex virus); unknown cause (35-50%).

B. Diagnosis: Gram stain and culture of urethral discharge or urethral swab obtained with calcium amalgamate swab.

1. Gram negative intracellular diplococci or positive culture for <u>N</u>. <u>gonorrhoeae</u>: Treat for uncomplicated gonococci infection (pg 212-213).

2. Gram stain shows > 5 PMN/low power field plus no intracellular gram-negative intracellular diplococci: Treat for <u>Chlamydia</u> <u>trachomatis</u> (pg 216).

3. Stain shows < 5 PMN: Patient should return for repeat test next morning prior to voiding.

C. Persistent or recurrent NGU: Consider

1. Failure to treat sexual partner.

2. Alternative causes of discharge.

II Epididymitis

A. <u>STD form</u>: Usually occurs in adults < 35 yrs in association with urethritis without urinary tract infection or underlying GU pathology.

1. Usual agents: <u>C</u>. <u>trachomatis</u> and/or <u>N</u>. <u>gonorrhoeae</u>.

2. Evaluation: Urethral smear for gram stain, culture for <u>N</u>. <u>gonorrhoeae</u> and <u>Chlamydia</u> <u>trachomatis</u> and urine culture.

3. Treatment: Use regimens for uncomplicated <u>N</u>. <u>gonorrhoeae</u> infection.

4. Adjuncts: Bed rest and scrotal elevation recommended until fever and local inflammation have resolved.

B. <u>Non-STD form</u> (usually older men in association with GU pathology and/or UTI verified by positive urine gram stain and culture).

1. Agents: Coliforms and pseudomonads (usual agents of urinary tract infections).

2. Treatment: Based on severity of disease and urine culture results.

3. Adjunctive treatment as above.

DURATION OF ANTIBIOTIC TREATMENT

Location	Diagnosis	Duration (days)
Bone	Osteomyelitis, acute	4 wks IV
	chronic	4 wks IV, then po x 2 mo
Central nervous system	Cerebral abscess	4-6 wks, then oral
	Meningitis: H. influenzae	10 days
	Listeria	14-21 days
	N. meningitidis	7 days
	S. pneumoniae	10 days
	Bacteremia: GNB	10-14 days
Ear	Otitis media, acute	10 days
Endovascular	S. aureus, portal of entry known	2 wks
	S. aureus, no portal of entry	4 wks
	Line sepsis: Bacteria	3-5 days (post removal)
	Candida	10 days (post removal)
	Vascular graft	4 wks (post removal)
Gastrointestinal	Diarrhea: C. difficile	10-14 days
	C. jejuni	7 days
	E. histolytica	5-10 days
	Giardia	5-7 days
	Salmonella	14 days
	Shigella	3-5 days
	Traveler's	3-5 days
	Gastritis, H. pylori	$\geq$ 4 wks
	Sprue	6 mo
	Whipple's disease	1 yr
Heart	Endocarditis: Pen-sensitive strep	14-28 days
	Pen-resistant strep	4-6 wks
	Staph. aureus	4 wks
	Microbes, other	4 wks
	Prosthetic valve	$\geq$ 6 wks
Intra-abdominal	Cholecystitis	3-7 days post cholecystectomy
	Primary peritonitis	10-14 days
	Peritonitis/intra-abdominal abscess	7-10 days after drainage
Joint	Septic arthritis, gonococcal	7 days
	Pyogenic, non-gonococcal	3 wks
	Prosthetic joint	6 wks

(continued)

Location	Diagnosis	Duration (days)
Liver	Pyogenic liver abscess	4-16 wks
	Amebic	10 days
Lung	Pneumonia: Chlamydia pneumoniae	10-14 days
	Legionella	21 days
	Mycoplasma	2-3 wks
	Nocardia	6-12 wks (or longer)
	Pneumococcal	Until febrile 3-5 days
	Pneumocystis	21 days
	Staphylococcal	$\geq$ 21 days
	Tuberculosis	6-9 mo
	Lung abscess	Until x-ray clear or until small stable residual lesion
Pharynx	Pharyngitis - Gr A strep	10 days
	Pharyngitis, gonococcal	1 dose
	Diphtheria	14 days
Prostate	Prostatitis, acute	2 wks
	chronic	3-4 mo
Sinus	Sinusitis, acute	10 days
Sexually transmitted disease	Cervicitis, gonococcal	1 dose
	Chancroid	7 days
	Chlamydia	7 days
	Disseminated gonococcal infection	7 days
	H. simplex	7-10 days
	Lymphogranuloma venereum	21 days
	Pelvic inflammatory disease	10-14 days
	Syphilis	10-21 days
	Urethritis, gonococcal	1 dose
Systemic	Brucellosis	6 wks
	Listeria: Immunosuppressed host	3-6 wks
	Lyme disease	14-21 days
	Meningococcemia	7-10 days
	Rocky Mountain spotted fever	7 days
	Salmonellosis	
	Bacteremia	10-14 days
	AIDS patients	$\geq$ 3-4 wks
	Localized infection	4-6 wks
	Carrier state	6 wks
	Tuberculosis, pulmonary	6-9 mo
	extrapulmonary	9 mo
	Tularemia	7-14 days
Vaginitis	Bacterial vaginosis	7 days
	Candida albicans	3 days
	Trichomoniasis	7 days

227

KEYS TO DISCIPLINING YOUR YOUNG CHILD

Eleanor Siegel, M.A., and
Linda Siegel, M.D.

BARRON'S

All inquiries should be addressed to:
Barron's Educational Series, Inc.
250 Wireless Boulevard
Hauppauge, NY 11788

Library of Congress Catalog Card No. 92-11348

International Standard Book No. 0-8120-4938-1

Library of Congress Cataloging-in-Publication Data

Siegel, Eleanor.
Keys to disciplining your child : from infant to toddler /
by Eleanor Siegel and Linda Siegel.
p. cm. — (Barron's parenting keys)
Includes index.
ISBN 0-8120-4938-1
1. Discipline of children—United States. I. Siegel, Linda.
II. Title.   III. Series.
HQ770.4.S53   1993
649′.64–dc20   92-11348
                                                          CIP
PRINTED IN THE UNITED STATES OF AMERICA
3456 5500 987654321